Campfire Tales from Hell

Musings on Martial Arts, Survival, Bouncing, and General Thug Stuff

D1456970

Edited by Rory Miller

Campfire Tales from Hell: Musings on Martial Arts, Survival, Bouncing, and General Thug Stuff
Published by Marc MacYoung.
All articles copyright 2012 by their respective authors.
Cover design by Kamila Zeman Miller.
Layout by Frederick J. Ross.

ISBN: 9781477681275

Contents

Introduction

There is an old saying in my family about the ten greatest stories in western literature. They have all been lost, because they were told in Irish pubs, no one remembered them the next morning, and nobody wrote them down.

Once a year, in the mountains of Colorado, there is a gathering. Men and women meet under tiki torches. Old friends and new brawl and teach and learn during the days. At night, they barbecue and drink and tell stories. People come from as far as Singapore, Spain and Japan to be there.

Some are old warriors, and among them they have seen action from Vietnam to Panama to Iraq and the Hindu Kush... and other places that can't be named. The guy who likes to do dishes is also a lieutenant with the New York State Police. Paramedics and pediatric surgeons argue, talk and even sometimes sing with street kids and bouncers and professors of, among other things, logic and psychology. Best selling authors rub shoulders with (former) criminals.

First and foremost, they are people. Some are effective and some are profoundly damaged and many are both. That's the way life is, in a group like this. I watch, from my table by the narghila, and see a tribe, a clan, some of whom feel accepted only here.

It is an event with its own rituals and own language. A glass is filled for the people the group has lost – Arkaidy, Rabbi Stan, Mark and Tim. "Have a hamburger" is code for, "The individual you are lecturing has thirty years of martial training and over five hundred actual encounters and you are making a fool of yourself." The elevation is over a mile and there is a special t-shirt for the person who collapses during play... and a stuffed baby seal for the newbie who gets his mind most thoroughly blown.

A lot of information passes through that group. How a federal air marshal looks at close range combat. How you can make a functional shank from a Styrofoam cup. Designing and implementing scenarios. How to kick in high heels. How mob enforcers set up, and why axe handles are preferable to baseball bats. The difference between Level 2 and Level 3 weapon retention. The psychology of a kill. On and on...

This is our attempt to make sure the information isn't lost. Our attempt, as a group, to remember that we are, in fact, literate tool-users.

It won't be the same as being at the gathering, I'll tell you that. You won't hear the voices or smell the coals, or taste the creations of the cooking tent... but maybe you'll learn something.

—Rory Miller, 2012

Editor's Note

As much as possible, I tried to preserve the unique voices in these stories. A handful of the authors are professional writers, and it shows, but some of the best articles came from amateur writers who shared unique experiences, and did so with heart. A few were written in a second language. Some are clearly more accustomed to writing reports. And for a few, writing is a painful chore.

But the voices, like the people, are unique and special.

Authors listed in quotation marks, e.g. "M.G. FAM" are, of course, pseudonyms. Whether for professional, legal or personal reasons I honored all requests for anonymity.

Opinions expressed in the articles are those of the writers, not necessarily the editor or anyone else involved with this project. That should be obvious, and it is a good thing. There are three kinds of people that I learn the most from—intelligent people I disagree with, especially if they are brilliant like Denton or introspective like Eddie; people who have experienced parts of the world I have not (and most of those stories have anonymous authors in this volume); and people who have seen what I have seen, better. I'm good at reading a bad guy. Terry is better.

Special thanks to Jocelyne Thomas, who did the heavy lifting with the final proofreading.

Section 1: Technical

Seven stories that you might need to know. Specialized stories ranging from a Federal Air Marshal's (and former Border Patrol agent) take on adrenaline effects, to what an ER nurse thinks you need to know about trauma, to an expert in both stage combat and street violence talking about the difference between the two. And other cool stuff.

All Fighting Is On Drugs

by MG, FAM

"We don't rise to the level of our expectations – we fall to the level of our training"

—Archilochus, Greek soldier

I'm a specialist. I'm trained to operate under extremely specialized environments, under special jurisdictions, and, to use specialized skill sets and tools. Most of what I do today is completely useless to someone who doesn't operate under similar conditions. Correction: Worse than useless. Suicidal. Our tactical doctrine flies in the face of basic tenets of control and defense due to our unique environment. My problem-solving tactics would get most people killed.

Most, however, doesn't mean all. While the tactics I utilize are irrelevant outside those environs, the underlying training principles are extremely sound in all walks of physical altercations, be they armed or unarmed.

Anyone who studies in order to have to physically intercede with another, resisting human being has had a teacher. I've had some of the best in the world.

Unfortunately I've also had some of the worst. Generations of police officers have been "taught" by television and movies, which do certain things for dramatic purposes. I know, I was one of those officers. And I sucked. Undoing the damage the entertainment industry did to my tactics was a laborious process.

Other times, the instructor believes that what he's teaching will work, but he's only passing down information he learned from his instructor. Have they ever taken it for a test drive? How do they know it will work under the situation you might be called to use it in? Can you make what will work under sterile, calm conditions work when you're scared out of your mind? On a cold day, when your opponent is wearing heavy clothing? On ice? At the swimming pool? While drunk in a bar?

And, to really top it off, can you justify what you did later to some forceful fellows with badges who will be asking you difficult questions? I've scrapped a whole lot of "departmentally approved and taught" training because it simply didn't work. Or I couldn't make it work, which is not the same thing but might as well be.

The main thing my teachers didn't teach me until more than midway through my career (after I had already learned it myself through experience) is that, almost without exception, I would have to perform while high. As in chemically altered. Stoned, whacked out of my gourd, flying high, fucked up, whatever you want to call it.

This one seems a little odd when you read it, but bear with me. All those cool moves you've learned in a nice, safe, structured environment? All those moves you refined while shadow boxing or rolling or sparring or at the range with your friends and fellow students? They'll most likely not be available to you. Or unavailable to you until you make some adjustments and retool your training. Because you'll be stoned.

When you get into a fight outside your normally accustomed routine, adrenaline will be present. And in amounts that you've probably never felt before. Adrenaline is released when a part of your brain called the amygdala detects danger. And make no mistake, adrenaline is a drug. It physiologically alters your body. And it's done automatically. You have no control over it. The effects are varied, and change from person to person. So you may experience some effects and not experience others.

A list of the effects includes:

- Blood will flow to your core
- Pain resistance
- The world may narrow down to the immediate threat, the so-called tunnel vision
- Excluding what the amygdala perceives as extraneous and irrelevant information,
- Instinctive thought and reactions
- Auditory exclusion…

and other effects.

These can be good things. Pain resistance is a sweet thing when you're in the middle of being hurt. Blood pooling to the core protects vital organs and ensures you don't bleed out if you take hits to your limbs, which will be in action and are likely to receive damage. Tunnel vision eliminates distractions.

They can also be detrimental. Your tunnel vision may blind you to other threats closing in. That blood pooling to your core will lessen your manual dexterity, which means your fine motor skills may be inaccessible. Fancy won't be available to you. It's entirely possible you'll revert back to trying to club someone on the head instead of that epic take down you envisioned.

All of this is obvious when you think about it. How well could you do your martial art while drunk? How about on cocaine? How about a mixture? Because that's what's going to happen. Parts of you are going to be slow and clumsy, like when you're intoxicated, and other parts are going to be racing out of control. Not the best scenario to do your whiz-bang stuff, is it? And that doesn't even go into what happens if you've already added other, manmade intoxicants to your system. There's a reason, after all, that lots of fights happen in bars.

So, if you're convinced you're going to be high when you fight, the questions then become

1. How does this drug affect our bodies' ability to act and react?

2. What can we do about it?

Glad you asked.

What Adrenaline Does to Your Body:

Your IQ will plummet

In a critical incident you probably won't be able to think clearly, because what we know as 'thinking' is incredibly slow. Critical incidents happen fast. A second is an eternity. Ever seen a dog attack a cat? It's completely over in a second or two if not sooner, yet there's a lot going on. If either of those animals had to think about what they did, cats would be extinct, or dogs wouldn't be able to kill them. They both operate on instinct. You will operate on instinct, should it come to it, unless you've trained enough to instill a skill set that your body can execute with the speed and fluidity of instinct. But instinct is your body's default. Training certain moves and responses may override those defaults, or they may not. Many factors will decide this, including the quality and number of your repetitions in those moves, the training of those moves in less than optimal environments and conditions, and training them while under the effects of adrenaline, to name a few.

That's hard to do, and very, very few put in the time to make it happen.

What we normally do when we practice our art—and especially as we are learning it, be it martial arts, guns, whatever—is mostly done at an intellectual level. We think about what's next. "Okay, I block the punch then counter with..."

Eventual mastery of technique will get us past this, if we do enough rote drilling. Yet this thinking happens again when we move out of simple drills (punching the bag, shadow boxing, shooting at the range, etc.) to more challenging venues (sparring, rolling, shooting a course for time). You probably experienced this the first time you sparred, or ran a new drill on the range. Things were coming at you too fast to recognize what was happening and select the best response to it. You probably went back to a tried-and-true strategy, something you had confidence in until you could figure out what was going on and adapt. A couple of standby punches or kicks, for instance. The rest of your moves from kata or what have you? Might as well never have learned them, until you could start thinking enough to remember to use them.

But in a critical incident that kind of thought is a luxury. It's like a leisurely stroll down the lane, when what your body needs is the mental equivalent of a sprint. So what may happen is your amygdala will simply bypass your higher consciousness and make the decision for you and pick the strategy it deems most effective. It sprints, leaving your higher consciousness in the dust, and picks the best response for its survival.

While there are a number of actual responses, only three are relevant for movement (or lack thereof): staying put, moving toward or moving away.

Be advised that freezing in place and doing absolutely nothing is a viable survival strategy. Deer do it all the time. Most predators in the world operate off of some combination of color, contrast and/or movement. If you eliminate movement, your chances of survival just went way up, by at least a third. Freeze in place and maybe the predator won't see you. This is a brilliant survival strategy—unless you happen to freeze in front of a speeding truck. Then you're road pizza (hmmm, pizza). And, of course, that survival doesn't have to work in every individual case, only most of them, to be effective for the species in question. This is, I'm sure, a warm comfort for those that are turned into pizza.

Another option is to just lay into the threat, swinging wildly and without precision. Attack. This is the fight mechanism of the flight or flight dichotomy we've all heard about. Uncontrolled and unfocused adrenaline increases strength but can really negatively affect precision. This strength is great if you're fighting a smaller, weaker person, or catch someone with a lucky blow. But what if they've got a knife? How much good is your thrashing going to do? We're probably back to pizza.

Or you may just run, haul ass. This is also a great species survival strategy. One of the group may be caught and eaten, but it's the slow one, which culls the weak and strengthens the group. But what if there is no group? What if it's only you? What if it's you and your family? Running may be your best tactic, or not. The situation will dictate that. But I've yet to see anyone outrun a bullet. Can you say "pizza?" Knew you could.

So just blindly trusting the brain to come up with the best movement alternative (freeze, attack, run) is essentially gambling. And there's a reason casinos give away free booze while you're gambling – because you don't make good decisions. Instinct can work against you when you're bombed out of your skull on adrenaline.

Your technique is going to suck

When the adrenaline hits your body, blood flows away from extremities and into your core. As I noted above, this is great for surviving defensive wounds to the arms and legs. You can get cut up a lot more and bleed a lot less in those areas. Humans instinctively defend their core with their arms and hands. They can take more damage to the extremities and survive. So it makes sense to remove life-giving blood from that region while boosting pain tolerance.

On the other hand, this also means your fine motor skills deteriorate to a great degree. You will probably be clumsy. Your fingers won't work well. Specific targeting will be off. Footwork will disappear, as will the concept of stance. So the more complicated and intricate the movement is, the more likely it will be to fail. Reloads on a pistol using the slide release become problematic, to say the least, because your fingers can't find the little button. Grabbing the threat may be impossible, as your fingers can't seem to close at the right time. Fancy knife work? Not a smart bet.

You can't see or hear shit

This is not to say you'll be deaf and blind, exactly. What this means is that the brain will exclude those things it denotes as extraneous and focus on the threat it views as dangerous to its survival. It's a laser focus, and it exists for a reason. You don't want to be listening to the birdies chirp or admiring the view when a predator is about to pounce and have you for lunch. So excluding sounds and tunnel vision on the threat makes sense.

Again, though, there is a down side. You won't hear or see other threats closing on you because you're focusing on just the one. This is one of the successful strategies of pack predators. Get the prey focused on one, then spring the ambush. Works a treat. Human predators take advantage of the same mechanism. How about so being so focused on the yelling he's doing you lose sight of his hands? Happens all the time.

Those are some of the things that can happen to an adrenally-stimulated person. So how do we avoid becoming a thin crust, extra pepperoni with oregano? How do we establish the control and effectiveness of our responses? Keep the benefits of adrenaline while lessening and mitigating the detrimental aspects?

There are three options.

1. Develop your skill set to the point that it becomes automatic.

Train your responses to such a level that they just happen on their own under certain parameters. In essence you're overwriting your instinctual responses with trained, automatic ones. This is a matter of putting in the reps.

And at what point does that occur? No one really knows. I know, I know. But the truth is each person is different. Trained and battle-hardened soldiers have frozen in their hundredth firefight. They'd been there before, were trained for it, yet something happened outside normal experience and the body just said, "Stay put, you jack wagon, and maybe we'll live." The best studies have shown the average for this, however, is three hundred to five hundred reps to begin approaching what's often called muscle memory. It's worse if you have to unlearn something already established in the neural pathways. It'll take three thousand to five thousand reps of a new technique to overwrite the old one. Which gives more impetus to learning things right the first time, I guess.

This is how the military and law enforcement do it. Drilling. Martial arts as well, for the most part. You receive a stimulus (punch to your head, pop-up target, etc) and you just react (block or deflect punch, pull gun and shoot target, etc.) Its efficiency is speed, where, as I said, a second is a long, long time. With your brain not having to make a choice, only react, the only speed limitation is a purely physical one. It boils down to your individual reflexes, which should be pretty decent, with all that training under your belt.

The downside to this option comes when one encounters a situation that's outside your normal list of responses. It's easy if you train to fight someone who starts on his side of the cage and you on yours then close to the middle and get it on. You know generally what to do. Then it's just a matter of countering his moves and enforcing yours. Action, reaction. Or just shooting pop-up targets – it pops up and you shoot it. No judgment is necessary. But what happens when it's not so clearly delineated? If the guy is threatening to "fuck you up" while his hands are in his pockets? If he's screaming in your face because you just backed up into his car? If he says he's going back to his car to get his gun and shoot you? Now you have to utilize judgment, and at the absolute worst time, because, as we've noted, you might not be able to think so very clearly.

What would you do, for instance, to pick an example out of thin air, if you've been sent to investigate an area and a naked, mentally ill man with a dick the size of the Graf Zeppelin sees you and sprints right at you, stops just outside your reach and begins to masturbate? While looking directly into your eyes and smiling? Do you think they cover this kind of event in police academies? In security training? Because I assure you they don't. What I can also assure you is that your brain will most likely vapor lock, and you'll stand there like an idiot, wondering what the fuck is going on. And wondering how this mentally ill guy is so gifted in the dick department and you're making do with standard issue. Although that part comes later.

Or, to pick another random example, if a couple of solid citizens are trying to brain you with rocks the size of your fist, while you're trapped at the bottom of a small cliff. You whip out your pistol. That should scare them off, right? Or frighten them into compliance. But it doesn't. They laugh at your gun. Plan A is a failure. What's Plan B? Do you shoot them? I mean, the papers next day will say it was just rocks, after all. Why did the jack booted thug have to shoot them? Why not shoot them in the hand? Pepper spray them? Taser?

You come around the corner and a guy with a machete runs at you, hollering like a madman, waving the blade over his head? If you're saying right now "how far away is he, so I can decide whether I can draw and shoot in time, per the Tueller Drill, or do I need to offline first or seek cover" you're not paying attention. Those are extremely logical and necessary questions, but not relevant until you learn to control the adrenal response. Your brain simply won't register them. It'll just act.

All of this could go through your mind in the middle of a critical incident. It's easy to say, while reading this in a safe and cozy environment, what you would do. But that's only what you *think* you would do. It's like yelling at the TV screen at the quarterback what he should have done on that last play. You didn't see what he saw, feel the pressure he felt. You're simply judging it from a technical standpoint, minus the impact of how emotion affects judgment and performance. You can't know what it feels like until you've lived it. Until it's rushed right at you, dick in hand, at the speed of life.

2. Gain a tolerance

Another option is to develop a tolerance to adrenaline. Like any other drug, you can become resistant to its effects given enough exposure. It takes a metric ton of caffeine to affect me anymore. Some people can get drunk off of one or two drinks, whereas regular drinkers need a lot more.

So repeated exposure to adrenaline can help you not be stunned when it hits your body during a critical incident. Essentially, you've felt it before, know what's happening and can think about what to do next. So if you, say, see the guy stroking his meat at you, you can tell him to cut that out and put his hands behind his back. Because while this is a novel incident (to say the least), feeling adrenaline is not novel. Been there, done that. And since it's not your first boat ride, you know what to do, how to steer in these waters. Handy stuff, experience.

The downside is, of course, as we noted earlier, that thought is a slow process where milliseconds matter. Sometimes you need to be beyond thought. Sometimes you need to be able to simply react. Threat/ response. It doesn't always do a whole lot of good to be able to think if thought is an irrelevant option.

3. Combo

This is what we should be striving for – automatic responses when needed and the ability to think and plan when time permits. This is the best of both worlds. In those instances where rote responses are called for, your body performs as it needs to. If a cop turns the corner and there's a guy with a gun pointed at him, he doesn't need to think, he needs to act—draw and engage. On the other hand, if he turns the corner and there's a guy holding a knife to a woman's neck, ready to cut, he needs to be able to think and figure out what to do. Pulling the pistol and blasting won't get it done.

To wrap up this section, I'll point out a parallel – the terrifying world of public speaking. It consistently ranks as number one when people are polled about their greatest fear. Why is that, do you think? It's not an issue of proficiency or technique. They remain as fluent in their language when they speak publicly as they do when they speak in their everyday life. Yet people are terrified of getting up in front of a crowd of people, all eyes on them, waiting for the speech. So what's the prescription for that, do you think? Well, what do you know – it's a combination of drilling technique (the composition and nuance (cadence, intonation, etc.) of speech giving) and actual practice of getting up in front of people to become used to that stress and fear (read: adrenaline).

Both reinforce the other. Smoothness of technique in speaking gives confidence in ability, which mitigates fear. At the same time, being accustomed to that fear and adrenaline allows for a smoother delivery, which enhances technique, which enhances confidence even more, and so on and so on. And if you do hit a rough patch, you will be better equipped to recover and press on.

The methodology is the same. Only the stakes are different.

Ways To Control the Adrenal Response

Technique and tactics are beyond the scope of this little article. Besides, I'm really not qualified or interested in talking about tactics. Tactics are fluid and change from situation to situation. Which moves you use are your business and what you've probably been training for. What I may be able to do, though, is give you some help in performing more optimally when you leap into your remarkable action.

There are really only three ways of interest to us to stimulate the adrenal response to a level that positively impacts performance in the physical realm: exertion, woofing and scenarios. They all have their pros and cons. And I've utilized them all at one point or the other.

Exertion

Exertion is just that – physical effort to a degree that takes the heart rate high enough to simulate what happens in a critical incident. When adrenaline hits your system, your heart rate speeds up. And if it hits too high a level, performance degrades. A little bit is a good thing, it speeds up and strengthens the body. Too much, though, and you risk a shut-down, or severely degraded performance. So if we get our bodies used to performing our moves and techniques with a seriously elevated heart rate, this can help us perform.

As in most of what we've been talking about there are advantages and disadvantages to exertion.

The biggest advantage is the ability to train alone. You can do this anywhere you normally do your training. You need no other equipment. Simply exhaust yourself before you do your normal drills. Let's say you train in a martial art. So before you do your kata or whatever, push yourself hard. And I mean hard. What to do is entirely up to you and your fitness level (obviously it's detrimental to performance if you keel over from a heart attack because you pushed yourself beyond your limits). Shooters and knife people, same thing. Push your body hard, then shoot or do sinawali or whatever. Watch your performance suffer. It will, if you push hard enough.

Find that level where the wheels fall off the bus, then back off. Once you find where you're out of control, just back from there is where you want to train exertion. But once you get comfortable being uncomfortable, you'll notice that, even as you're winded you're able to bring your body back under control and perform. Your point of 'out of control' will get higher and higher. You'll probably get a bit more fit as well, which is a nice fringe benefit.

As soon as you're done with whatever exertion exercise(s) you chose, *Do not rest. Go.* Practice bringing your body under control while drilling, not before. You won't have the option of rest and recovery in a real incident.

My version of this is to work the heavy bag or shadowboxing hard and fast for several minutes prior to working on drills. At the range we've done sprints and pull ups and pushups for time before shooting courses for time or in competition. I've done fifty burpees for time and then shot a course. That sound I heard was the sound of my soul dying. And my performance was sub-optimal, I can promise you. But it gets better, and the more you do it the better it gets.

The main thing you can do to help yourself, in either of the three methods of adrenal training is, when given a chance, *breath*. This is profoundly simple in theory and explanation and profoundly difficult in implementation. Slow down your breathing. Three seconds in, three seconds out. This will help slow your heart rate and get your physical abilities back under control. Performance will go way up. Being more physically fit will also help with this.

The disadvantage of exertion as training methodology is the lack of judgment. It's really only another version of drilling. It covers part of the problem of adrenal response – 'degradation of technique' – but not the whole enchilada, as it misses the 'difficulty thinking' part. You can't train problem-solving and adaptation if there's no one to give you a problem while you're adrenalized.

Woofing

Woofing is having someone in your face, yelling and saying things which stimulate an adrenal response, then attacking. This is more along the lines of a bar fight, where someone is talking shit, trying to get you to freeze up before attacking. Many street fighters use this tactic – woof on you, get you to freeze up, then sucker punch. Usually that's all it takes – fight's over.

Woofing stimulates adrenaline, then makes you perform while stimulated. It also helps inure you to its effects next time. Done correctly it can help you work on personal triggers, which will numb you some to things someone might say to you to get you riled up and not thinking straight. An example would be woofing on police officers in training by calling them things like "fucking pigs." Or calling a black person a "nigger." Everyone has a button, you just have to find it and press it under the right circumstances. So the goal is to find the buttons and push them in this type training, in a safe environment. Not to hurt feelings, but to identify a button someone might use against the student in the real world and take that button away from the bad guys. Make it a non-issue.

You don't need many people in woofing. Three will do – one doing the training, one as the woofer and one as a safety officer. I can't stress the safety officer enough. It's like a referee in a fight – you need someone to pull the guy off if he gets too locked in and doesn't hear or understand when to quit. And that could be either the student or the woofer. Emotions can run really high in this kind of training, and you need someone emotionally detached to make sure things go well.

All that said, the disadvantages are obvious. You need a lot of safety equipment, particularly if you're doing hand-to-hand training. You really need to be able to go hard. If there's no fear of pain, the effect is lessened. Shooters need something like Simunitions™ or Airsoft™. A Shocknife™ can be a nice tool with non-stab oriented arts. I guarantee the pucker factor will rise with that bad boy in play. You also need people to play along, and that don't mind being hit. Finding these people is surprisingly difficult, when it comes to it. Everyone thinks they want to train hard in a martial art, until it comes to get a little bloody. Then bodies can get scarce. You will, sooner or later, get hurt. And there's not a lot of judgment involved, so again the problem-solving portion is still underdeveloped.

Scenarios

Scenario training is where is all comes together. Scenarios, if done right, train it all. They give you an adrenal response, affecting you physically, as well as give you problems to solve and decisions to make, which affect the outcome of the scenario. The scenario may go an entirely different direction depending on the trainee's actions. What started off as a potential bar fight could end up as a homicide if the wrong decisions are made. Just. Like. In. Real. Life.

In scenario training you have to deal with the physiological responses that adrenaline is giving you and you also must make decisions, and those decisions have repercussions. This is wonderful shit, for a given value of wonderful. The overwhelming majority of training and drilling focuses on technique and not on applying judgment to situations, which is completely bass-ackward. Technique is really the least important attribute. Accurately recognizing what is happening and making sound judgment is far, far more important. Drilling scenarios gives you that ability.

The down sides of scenario training are many. It requires many people to really do right. It's my experience that it's the presence of a lot of people that most acutely causes the adrenal response. No one likes to look like a tool in front of their peers. The role players cannot suck. Role players make or break the scenario. The same training equipment noted in woofing is required here as well. You will be hurt at some point in scenario training if you do it long and hard enough.

And you will have to. How did you get good at blocking/slipping punches? Punching hard? Hitting what you're shooting at? Deflecting and countering bladed strikes? Practice. Same goes for scenarios. Drill them. You weren't that good when you started your art of choice. Why do you think it'll be any different with scenarios? You will most likely suck when you start out, and it will likely be very deflating. You most likely won't perform up to your expectations.

But with continued exposures you will not only perform better, but I bet you that you will find yourself using more and more of the tools you've trained, and at a higher level. Which is not to say you won't have bad runs. We train scenarios around every other month, and I've been doing this over a decade. I've run hundreds of full speed force on force scenarios, both armed (Simunitions) and unarmed (hand to hand). I've done incredibly well and fucked them up as badly as they could be fucked. Sometimes both in the same day. There are no guarantees in the fight game. All you can do is try and stack the odds as much as possible in your favor. But you can do everything exactly right and still lose. And in this game, lose can mean die. Never forget the stakes.

Finally, and most importantly, you need someone who can devise realistic and practical scenarios and be a good safety officer. A good scenario trainer is invaluable. They keep everyone safe while also pushing them to the razor edge of their limits. They know the student in question, what buttons to push, what scenarios most accurately train them for what they will most likely face. They have to be a student of both civilian and criminal behavior. They have to be able to develop scenarios, and pull them off safely, from bar brawls to carjackings to rapes. And, when it's all over, they have to make sure everyone is friends. Because harsh things will most likely have been said. Feelings may be hurt. They have to critique performance of the student while at the same time not Monday Morning Quarterback it. They need to be able to teach and incorporate into scenarios the fact that the overwhelming majority of physical altercations can be walked away from, unless you're in an occupation with a duty to act. It's a tough, thankless gig.

You may have noticed a lack of detail of the "how to" of woofing and scenario training. I'm not going to go into those specifics. Not because I'm selling you something, because I have nothing to sell. It's simply a matter of my belief that you really need to search out qualified and trained people to teach this kind of thing. There are a number of places that give excellent instruction in woofing and scenario training, available to anyone. The two I have the most experience with are FAST Defense and RMCAT. I can recommend both without hesitation. I disagree with a few of their tactics, personally, but that's minor stuff. Tactics aren't really the point anyway. You and only you will decide what tactics to use. If you like their way of doing business, great. Whatever makes your peanut butter brown. If your art teaches something different that you like to do better, go with that. What this training excels at is giving you the best chance of putting whatever plan you have into action. It won't win you the fight. What it will do is help make sure you're in it.

I'm sorry I couldn't go into the how to of woofing and scenario training, because I honestly believe it's the missing piece of most people's training methodologies who train for self-defense. But the stakes are just too high. Inadequate equipment cost my dear friend an eye while doing Simunitions training, and that was while doing departmentally authorized and required training. He will never see out of his eye again. It cost him his eye and his career. And that was with cutting edge training and equipment, not some thrown together training done in the backyard. New equipment came out and was implemented because of this accident. This kind of stuff is serious business. I believe you need it, if you train, because you may believe you may have to do it for real, but it's not to be taken lightly or done in a slipshod manner. Don't fuck around with it.

Historical European Martial Arts

by Bert Bruijnen

Jungk Ritter Lere – Young Knight Learn

This is the first line in a poem written by Johannes Liechtenauer, who was a 14th century sword-fighting master whose pupils both recorded his teachings and continued a martial tradition that only died out in the 1600's with the decline of the longsword as a weapon. The fact that this tradition spanned a range of two hundred to three hundred years tells us that this must have been an influential and leading style. Because of that and because of these recorded teachings there is a treasure of manuscripts left for research and revival of the once widely-practiced martial arts of Europe.

The features of this longsword made it suitable to wield with two hands. The fact that it had a pommel meant that the rotation of the blade was also controlled and it was, all in all, a very easy to handle and very agile weapon to use

The theoretical basis of the longsword fighting style of Johannes Liechtenauer

Now follows a small overview of the core basis of the system as it was being taught in and around the 14th century in Europe. They always considered two sorts of fighting: fighting in harness, and fighting without harness. The techniques described here are for unprotected fighting.

Apart from standard and very general concepts like timing, balance, distance etc. I will focus on style-specific concepts, because they give a better insight on how the weapon was used.

Draw first blood

The first and main tenet is the so-called: "Vorschlag" (first strike). It means that you hit the opponent first—you draw first blood. It also means initiative. You want to be and remain in the active, attacking and initiating role. That also means that your opponent is in the defensive role. As long as you have the initiative you are in the so called: "Vor" (before), your opponent is in the "nach" – this means he reacts, he is pressed into a defensive role.

Three main attack categories

The techniques used to attack always fall under one of the three categories of: strike, slice and thrust. These three are called the "Drey Wunder" (three ways to wound your opponent).

Four targets

These attacks are, in terms of target, aimed at the so-called "four openings" or "4 Blössen". If you would draw a line along the vertical axis of the human body, from head to toe, and if you would draw a line along the horizontal axis from left to right, the body is now divided into four quarters. Each of these quarters is a target area. A solid attack anywhere in each area will do damage with sharp steel.

The fact that this is an easy and simple division in target areas also means that it is applicable under very high pressure situations.

Two covering and protecting guards

Each of these areas is covered and defended by two main guards: "Ochs" and "Pflug" (Ox and Plough). The Ox guard for the higher two openings (above right and left) and the Plough for the two lower openings (below, left and right). Remember that the guards are either starting or ending positions of strikes, thrusts and slices. These are not passive positions, they develop and emerge during the attacks. So in essence a counterattack ends in a protective guard and simultaneously it will also attack the opponent and protect you from harm. The attack line of the opponent is closed by the simultaneous counter. This concept of simultaneous attack and defense is called "Indes," and it stands for reacting 'in that moment' or simultaneously.

Other main guards

Further main guards that are used are called: "Vom tag" (above head, or above shoulder); and "Alber" (fools guard, point low and in front).

Countering attacks and closing attack lines

Each attack that either is made from or develops into each of these guards is countered by the "vier Versetzen" (four ways to set the attacks from or into these guards aside). The second function of these is to close the attack line—from, through and into that guard.

The very core

So in the very core the system revolves around initiative—keeping it, maintaining it, and regaining it. The attack categories are three sorts, all three aimed at the four targets that are emerging with the covering or uncovering of these four openings. The openings are in turn protected by the two guards of Ox and Plough. And these are broken by the "vier versetzen"

Different situations

Further, there are the situations of "Zufechten" and "Krieg." "Zufechten," or fighting from a longer range, also means that you have to take at least one or more steps to be able to hit the opponent. "Krieg" is fighting from a distance where you can directly hit the opponent without taking a step.

When the blades happen to come into contact with each other it is called a bind. Fighting from the bind comes down to dealing with pressure applied to your blade and the direction in which the pressure is applied.

Fighting with this longsword involves the wrestling at the sword and 'half swording'. The wrestling at the sword is done by using parts of the sword to apply leverage in combination with wrestling. The 'half swording' is done by grabbing the blade (with an armoured glove it is possible) and thrusting the sword like a short spear. That is mainly done against a knight in full plate harness.

The above is a description in a nutshell and it contains an absolutely very basic overview of the concepts, techniques and theoretical basis of these fighting arts, it is not a conclusive overview because that would make the article perhaps very long.

Stage Fighting is not Real Fighting

by Michael Johnson

Two opponents face off against each other. The animosity they have toward each other is so palpable that those watching the two men know that a physical confrontation will happen at any second. Suddenly, one man throws a wide right hook punch at the other man's head. The other man bobs and weaves, avoiding the punch, and retaliates with his own wide hook punch. The first man also avoids the punch with a bob and weave.

They stand looking at each other, realizing how close they came to taking each other's heads off and having the same thing done to them. This will not be as easy as they thought. Another tactic must be employed.

The first man launches an explosive hook (roundhouse) kick to the second man's stomach. The second man blocks the kick with his forearms stopping the kick. He then sends a right back fist to the first man's nose, followed by a left cross to the chin and a right pile driver to the man's left cheek. This rocks the first man and he nearly falls on his knees. The second man sees this and raises his fists high, preparing to slam the sides of them onto the first man's spine. Before he can even start his downward motion, the first man grabs the second man's groin with his left hand and squeezes, hard. The second man bends over from the excruciating pain. The first man grabs the back of the second man's neck and, pushing down with that hand as he pushes up with his left hand, flips the man onto his back.

Capitalizing on his advantage, the first man stands over the second man's head. He bends over and grabs the second man by the throat with his right hand and raises his left fist, preparing to send a pile driver to the second man's nose. The second man grabs the hand around his throat and with his other hand throws a straight punch into the first man's groin. The first man bends over in pain, releases his grip on the second man's throat and covers his groin with both of his hands. The second man kicks the first man square in the face, sending the first man back and into a nearby wall.

The first man sides down the wall onto the floor writhing in pain. The second man is also writhing in pain on the floor. They both have done significant damage to each other, but not so much that they can't continue. And they want to continue. So they slowly rise to one knee while maintaining a wary eye on each other. This fight is far from over.

Cut! Back to one!

The two men help each other up, giving each other a hug, before going back to the spot where they started the fight.

Quiet on the set.

Rolling.

Speed.

And...action!

And the "fight" begins again

Welcome to stage combat (aka stage fighting or stage violence); an art form that is just as physically strenuous, as mentally tasking, and as intricate as dance, gymnastics, mime and yes, the martial arts. In fact, stage combat is a form of martial arts that exponents (both performers and fight directors) must train as diligently in as other martial artists, in order to perform and choreograph well. Exponents of stage combat must be experts at selling to the audience that they are seeing a "fight" that is not a fight. Or, to put a twist to Bruce Lee's words from *Enter the Dragon*, stage combat is "the art of fighting without fighting."

But first, let me state the obvious: Staged fighting is not real fighting.

Yes, that is a "Duh, Johnson" statement, but there are enough people who have a difficult time discerning that "Duh, Johnson" statement that I felt the need to make it. Now allow me to elaborate.

Every fight you've seen on TV or in the movies or on stage has been choreographed, hopefully by a professional who knows the differences between a real fight and a staged fight. And there are differences.

- A staged fight is choreographed, like a dance. The actors know how it starts and how it ends.

- Not only is there no choreography in a real fight, no one knows how it will start nor how it will end until it happens.

- A staged fight can take hours to perfect by the fight director and the actors. Then that fight must be performed over and over again either in front of a camera or every night on stage.

- Unless it's a sport fight that has a certain amount of rounds to determine the winner, a real fight usually lasts only seconds.

- In a staged fight, the fight director can highlight the different styles of the characters for the audience to see. In fact, to be able to see the different styles, the audience needs to see the techniques being used. Which means the actors must exaggerate the techniques so the audience can see them.

- You'd be lucky to see any techniques in the flurry of most real fights. As for discerning a specific style, the planets will have to be in the correct alignment before that happens.

- In a staged fight, the actors rarely get severely hurt. They may have a few bumps and bruises, but that's par for the course. The blood you see is stage blood that can be made of food coloring, syrup, water, peanut butter and, if it gets on the costumes, soap powder.

- The blood you see in a real fight is real, possibly from both fighters. So are the swollen bruises, the disfigured bones and the broken hands from punching the face with a fist. Someone may be going to the hospital, and if someone is extreme unlucky, s/he'll be going to the morgue.

- The consequences of a staged fight are the good feelings the actors have of doing a great job, the applause from the audience of a live performance for doing a good job, and a weekly paycheck.

- The consequences of a real fight can be jail, the hospital and/or the morgue. However, the most excruciating consequence of a real fight is the cost to your soul.

There is one main similarity between staged fights and real fights —consequences. Or as one old friend says, "The cost of it." If you have good playwrights, or script writers who understand violence on a visceral level, they can convey the consequences of violence in their writings. To this day, the best playwright who has ever done that, in my opinion, is William Shakespeare. One of his best plays that convey his understanding of the consequences is Romeo and Juliet.

At the beginning of Romeo and Juliet we find out that two noble households of Verona – the Capulets and Montagues – have been feuding with each other for generations, to the point that even their respective servants freely participate in the feud. A servant from the Montague household instigates a brawl by the subtly insulting act of biting his thumb at servants from the Capulet household, which would be a disgrace to the Capulet servants if they ignore it. They don't, of course. And what commences is an elegant woof between the two sets of servants, as only Shakespeare can write.

> *ABRAM – Do you bite your thumb at us, sir?*
>
> *SAMPSON – I do bite my thumb, sir.*
>
> *ABRAM – Do you bite your thumb at us, sir?*
>
> *SAMPSON – [Aside to Gregory] Is the law of our side if I say ay?*
>
> *GREGORY – [Aside to Sampson] No.*
>
> *SAMPSON – No, sir, I do not bite my thumb at you, sir; but I bite my thumb, sir.*
>
> *GREGORY – Do you quarrel, sir?*
>
> *ABRAM – Quarrel, sir? No, sir.*
>
> *SAMPSON – But if you do, sir, I am for you. I serve as good a man as you.*
>
> *ABRAM – No better?*
>
> *SAMPSON – Well, sir.*
>
> *GREGORY [Aside to Sampson] Say "better." Here comes one of my master's kinsmen.*
>
> *SAMPSON – Yes, better, sir.*
>
> *ABRAM – You lie.*
>
> *SAMPSON – Draw if you be men.*

And the brawl ensues, drawing in Benvolio Montague (whom Gregory spotted coming) and Tybalt Capulet. Eventually, the Lords Capulet and Montagues show up wanting to enter the fray, but the Ladies Capulet and Montague restrain them.

Then the Prince of Verona enters with his men. The brawl is quickly squelched and Lords Capulet and Montague are kneeling before the

Prince as he admonishes them. Within that admonishment, the Prince proclaims to the Lords:

"If ever you disturb our streets again,
You lives shall pay the forfeit of the peace."

The Prince is forced to modify his threat when, later on in the play, Tybalt kills one of the Prince's kinsmen, Mercutio, during their impromptu duel on the street. Romeo, who inadvertently contributed to Mercutio's death when he tried to break up the duel, wants Tybalt's blood. In the middle of Tybalt's woofing and charge at Romeo, Romeo intercepts Tybalt's charge, fatally stabbing him. Benvolio, who has witnessed all of this, tells Romeo to run before the Prince arrives. Romeo does, calling himself "fortune's fool."

When the Prince, the Capulets and the Montagues arrive to see the carnage, Benvolio tells them what happens. The Capulets demand that the Prince sentence Romeo to death according to his decree. The Prince, having lost Mercutio to Tybalt's blade, and knowing that Romeo avenged Mercutio's death, decides to exile Romeo from Verona forever. He thereby sentences Romeo to a fate worse than death; for no one, except Friar Lawrence and Juliet's Nurse, knows that Romeo and Juliet were secretly married just hours before the tragic deaths.

Butt has met ugly…and then it gets worse.

By the end of the play, Romeo and Juliet have killed themselves for love. Paris, another kinsman of the Prince, is also killed in the process. The Friar, in his own grief, confesses his part in the secret marriage and his failed plan to bring the young lovers together away from Verona. The consequences of everyone's actions weigh, heavily, on their souls, and because of that "All are punished," the Prince says.

That leaves the Capulets and Montagues, who have continued the feud, and the Prince, who turned a blind eye to the feud and in doing so lost "A brace of kinsman," to pick-up the pieces of their losses and finally end the generational violence that has wracked these families.

Consequences, or "the cost of it" – the one main aspect that is shared by both real violence and staged violence. A good writer will add that into their script to tell a complete story. A good fight director will find a way to incorporate some part of it into his or her choreography. Good actors will use the choreography to help them convey the consequences of their "fight" through their characterizations. A good director will use the consequences of the "fights" to shape the overall story of the show.

An astute audience will use the lessons of the story they've seen to understand the violence that happens in the real world much better.

But no matter how good the violence in a show is written, choreographed and performed, and the consequences are conveyed, it is not real violence. It is only "A dance of implied violence," to paraphrase a quote from the late Brandon Lee said. Or, as my old friend and colleague, Lewis Shaw once called it "Ugly ballet with dangerous props."

We must always keep that in mind.

Let's Talk Trauma

by Eric Gaden

I am an ER travel nurse and I have worked in emergency rooms all over the country. I have seen more trauma cases than I can or care to remember. I am also a brown belt in Kajukembo, so I have an idea of what is taught in martial arts classes and seminars. Today I want to talk to you about trauma, the martial arts, and what your instructor might not have told you.

First things first. I have been to seminars and in various classes have heard a lot of claims about how effective some moves are. When shown to the class, these killer moves are usually accompanied by a phrase such as, "You can bet this will put him down" or "He won't bother you after that". This is said with a knowing look and everything short of a wink. Groin strikes, knee strikes, throat strikes, base of the skull, etc. While much damage can be done by these moves, and we will be visiting that later, there are no guarantees. I personally have seen a man shot in the face with a good caliber handgun walk into the emergency room. I have seen a man shot in the chest in a drive-by walk out of the emergency department two hours after coming in. The bullet channeled around his ribs and didn't touch anything vital. There are few if any guarantees when it comes to trauma.

Now that we know that those surefire, killer-commando moves don't always work, let's talk about what happens if they do. I want to start with throat strikes because a throat strike thrown with harmful intent can kill someone. A throat strike thrown in training can do the same. There are multiple ways this can happen. There is a bone located at the upper end of the windpipe called the hyoid bone that, if impacted, can tear through the tissue and cartilage causing what is known as subcutaneous emphysema, which is when the air is no longer going into the lungs, but into the space below the skin. It doesn't do any good there by the way. Also, with the accompanying swelling, it can close off the airway entirely.

Now, if there is someone on scene with the proper training, they can save your life. Does anyone in your class have that training? Do you think that there will be anyone in the bar parking lot where the fight took place capable of doing it? If it happens to you, or your opponent, that's a bad night.

Another fun possibility from throat strikes and even from chokes is a ruptured esophageal varices or a ruptured esophagus. Many chronic drinkers suffer from esophageal varices, which are enlarged blood vessels in the esophagus. Like any enlarged blood vessel, they are at a greatly increased risk of rupture. Kind of like an overfilled water balloon. Alcoholics often rupture them while vomiting. A choke or strike could certainly do the trick. They can then bleed to death or even choke to death on their own blood. Not that alcoholics and heavy drinkers ever fight.

Did you know that one of the original ways to reboot the heart in the event of a lethal arrhythmia was called a precardial thump? That was when someone balled up a fist and hammered it onto the center of the chest of the patient. The number I heard was the equivalent of a fifty joule shock from a defibrillator. Not only can that restart a heart, but if there is an underlying problem, it can stop one as well.

With a few years practice under my belt, I can't figure out yet how to tell who has a heart condition just by looking at them. Can you?

How about that knockout punch you just landed perfectly on their jaw? That likely isn't going to kill them, but there are multiple recorded cases of the person dying from the head injury that resulted from the fall immediately after. Most violent encounters don't take place in a ring and an unprotected fall, where you don't even try to break your momentum, can be deadly.

You hear a lot of talk in the sports world about concussions these days. There is a good reason for that as information comes in and more research is done on the short- and long-term effects of Traumatic Brain Injury. Concussions are so common from fighting that one of the long-term syndromes related to concussions is called *dementia pugilistica*. 'Pugilistic' as in fighting or boxing. At least in professional boxing they have the courtesy of putting padded gloves on before punching each other.

Traumatic brain injury is usually rated on a scale. The light end of the scale is concussion. The effects can range from prolonged unconsciousness, which incidentally isn't a good fight strategy, to personality changes, persistent headaches and post-concussion syndrome, which can cause irritability, headache, memory loss and fatigue for months or years. That is the low end of the scale.

Higher up you get into diffuse axonal injury which can cause speech impediments, other physical impairments, and other syndromes with symptoms that can mimic paranoid schizophrenia, right on up to swelling of the brain. I had a patient recently diagnosed with a diffuse axonal injury from a moderate motor vehicle accident. It took two years to get that diagnosis and the appropriate treatment. Prior to that he had been diagnosed with PTSD and mental illness. He had multiple suicide attempts and was lucky that one of the staff in the behavioral health unit on his last visit there was studying traumatic brain injury and referred him to a neurologist.

On the highest end of traumatic brain injuries from repeated blows to the head you get persistent vegetative state and death.

But hey, we all are going to die some day anyhow, right? This brings us to the knife and gun club portion of our talk.

First, let's talk about knives. For this discussion I am not going to use a fixed blade. I'm not going to use some Cold Steel hardware or the latest tactical, matte black, beltclip with half serrated edge. Nope, for this talk let's use the Schrade 1080t Old Timer Junior. You may recognize this blade as the one your grandfather carried around in his pocket. Three blades, fake wood body and a little shy of three inches long. I do believe the main blade was around 2.5 inches and pointed. And just for grins, let's not put this blade in the hands of a highly trained knife fighting expert, but just an angry guy with no training. He won't get in more than two good jabs or maybe a jab and a slice. I mean, you expect to get cut in a knife fight...right?

With the exception of the heart and the brain, there are not really any vital organs an untrained attacker *cannot* reach with such a blade. And to someone with knowledge of human anatomy and a desire to do harm, even those could potentially be reached. Liver, lungs, pancreas and kidneys are all close enough to the surface in a person of average build that it takes no more training than 'push the pointy end at them'.

Then there are the abdominal viscera. These are your intestines, large and small, and the surrounding fat and tissue. Once these are punctured, by bullet or blade, they have a nasty habit of releasing their contents into the abdominal cavity. This can have devastating consequences. This can release digestive juices into your abdomen capable of digesting your own organs to a degree and damaging everything. This can also release feces into the abdominal cavity thereby guaranteeing a nasty infection.

Once damaged these organs often never function correctly again. Kidney damage may put you on dialysis for a while, if not permanently. That would involve sitting in a room full of strangers with a needle in your arm for three to five hours between two and four times a week. Hit a liver and you will be lucky to live through it. Hit the intestines and you will likely end up with a colostomy bag. You see, while your intestines heal from the surgery, doctors don't want all that foul feces and bacteria processing through all of it. So to keep that from happening, they cut through a section of the intestine and then extend it outside your abdomen so all the feces can be deposited in a bag you glue to your belly.

I bet that girl you were fighting to impress will be really impressed with your colostomy bag. And we haven't even really talked about gunshot wounds.

Gunshot wounds are terrible. The projectile creates a hole, just like the knife, except it is usually much deeper. Once inside, the projectile can do any number of things.

Most times, the best hope you can have is for it to just go all the way through. That is bad, but worse is if it starts tumbling, ricochets off a bone or lodges against something vital or painful. If they can't remove it, you live with it, even if it hurts from then on. You could be in the hospital for weeks with months and years of follow up therapy.

This seems like the most appropriate place to tell you a little bit about spinal cord injuries. I had one patient who had a gunshot wound to the chest. In one respect he was lucky. He survived. On the other hand, the bullet hit his spinal cord, ricocheted to his shoulder blade and then went back and lodged behind his heart. Now he has no sensation below his nipples. For a few years after the injury he got depressed and gained some weight. It is understandable, after all. He chose to deal with the loss of bowel and bladder control with a colostomy and self-cathing every four hours, which involved sticking a tube into his penis to drain his bladder. That changed a few years later to a permanent catheter. He said it was better than the diapers. He came in to the emergency room because of the ulcers from sitting in the chair so much. He wasn't able to lift himself out anymore and his caregiver had gone on vacation to Las Vegas.

Just remember when you hear someone say it is better to be judged by twelve than carried by six that those aren't the only two options. Even more likely is it is better to leave the bar or run like hell than stick a tube in your penis every four hours for the rest of your life.

While I have seen some pretty amazing survival stories, they aren't all that cheerful. What many people don't realize – and I know I certainly didn't until I started working in healthcare – is the long-term toll both physically and financially.

Physically, once you have suffered a serious trauma, you often aren't the same again afterward. Many of our frequent patients are one-time victims of some sort of trauma. One man got stabbed over forty dollars in a bar. He has a long-term colostomy, kidney issues and chronic pain problems. One stab wound turned into eight to ten surgeries to repair the damage and all those surgeries took their toll on him. I saw him in the ER about every two weeks for some problem related to that event which took place years ago.

As much as it may seem I am trying to gross you out or scare you, this is only scratching the surface on the trauma one person can do to another. And we haven't even talked about money yet.

Let me give you an example from my own experience as a patient. My two-year-old fell and caught his chin on a bed frame. I was at work and my wife brought him in. He was seen in a minor care room by a nurse practitioner. No stitches, no staples, just some glue and steri strips. Cost? $800. Now, go spend some time in a trauma room with ER doctors, nurses, cardiac monitoring, and a trauma surgeon. One visit to the ED for a trauma can set you back tens to hundreds of thousands of dollars. A planned open abdominal surgery will cost upward of twenty thousand dollars. One night in the ICU can cost forty thousand dollars. And remember, everything is more expensive in an emergency. Don't forget the chance of a secondary infection like we talked about earlier. That will add days to your stay and probably result in at least one return visit through the ER. That doesn't factor in follow-up care, rehab or pain prescriptions you can take home. How good is your insurance?

Even if it is your opponent that takes the worst damage, unless it is clear-cut self-defense, you may be on the hook for the medical bills. Every single person I have seen who is in the hospital on someone else's dime has insisted on the best specialists money can buy. Every single one of them.

These are things your Sensei probably didn't tell you. They are real and they quite possibly await you in each potential violent encounter. So listen to your instructor. There can be great value to what they say and what they teach. Just understand that there are things they might not be teaching you about what can happen when you try to apply these techniques in the real world.

How to Read Your Opponent

by Terry Trahan

In this essay, we will be discussing things through two different outlooks, 'brewing' situations and 'flash' situations. This is also assuming, in a self-defense scenario, that the first layers of awareness did not work or your attempts at de-escalation were not effective.

A brewing situation is one that takes time to build, is longer lasting and involves many chances for observation before the tactical considerations take over and you must act.

A flash situation is an immediate action taking place with little to no warning and requiring immediate counter action.

A brewing self-defense incident is more common, as it includes things such as workplace/school shootings, inter-group rivalry, bullying or even mundane non-life-threatening aspects such as dominance games in work or social groups. The skills needed to read the attacker in a SD situation also work in the lower risk environments with some modification, and experimentation on your part will show you how to adapt them.

The skills, observations, and clues I am writing about in this essay are applicable to both situations, brewing and flash, but you must pay heed to the difference between them, *time*. In a flash incident, barring it being a total ambush, you still have some time available to read your attacker as he proceeds through the interview process, and the most important things to watch for are what I refer to as shorthand. Think of them as Cliffs Notes to personal survival. With practice, they will bleed over and be applicable to the brewing situation, and also to other facets of your life. It just so happens that the same skills in reading people and situations comes in very handy in navigating through work or other social events that don't include a large possibility for violence.

The other, not so obvious part of this equation is that you can take these observations and apply them to yourself. We should do this from time to time to see what kind of profile we are presenting to the public at large, and also to the pool of attackers we may come across in our daily lives. We can also apply them as camouflage in a way, to limit the appearance we may give of being an easy victim. If we can switch the odds in our favor by changing our appearance or demeanor instead of fighting, it increases our survival. And this is all about survival, not Monkey Dancing.

In any incident, your first line of defense is your observation skills and instinctual feeling or intuition. Do not discount how important these are to your life, whether in fighting or getting along at work. These skills are evolutionary and are still around because of their efficiency in keeping our ancestors alive and helping to grease the wheels in social circles. Have you ever met a new co-worker and immediately thought, "*What an asshole*" even though you only exchanged pleasantries with him?

That is your observation and intuition working together to warn you of a possible issue that may occur. Big hint: *pay attention to this*. We hear all the time that everyone is unique or special, and that we must treat everyone with respect, and this is true, I am not saying that you turn on your own asshole switch, I am saying pay attention to your gut. You are getting a warning, not confirmation at this stage.

A warning is just that, a warning. It means pay attention and look around the corners of the walls this individual has put up. People wear all kinds of masks and your warning picked up on the fact that this person has something hidden more than the others you are used to dealing with. At this stage, you have no idea what he is hiding. It could be a bad home life, his religion, alcoholism, or some form of sociopathy. It is all possible, and merits a closer look, but not paranoia.

For any of this to work for you, you cannot give in to paranoia or prejudice. Here is where you have to pay attention to the fact that each person is different, we have guidelines that will bump people up or down the scale of violence, but it is an art and not a science with lots of room for error or interpretation.

So, what to look for? I am so glad you asked.

First thing I look at is mode of dress. This goes beyond clothing, by the way. It can include what clothes or designer they wear, jewelry, how the clothing fits and how clean/dirty the person is. For shorthand purposes the things I pay the most attention to are accessories, jewelry, footwear, belts and watches.

Clothing is important, but so many people buy an identity that wearing a certain style of clothing does not mean that person is a member of a particular group. By this I mean some young male wearing baggy clothes with his pants sagging below his butt may be a gangbanger or he may be a middle class suburbanite who thinks this is a way to rebel/fit in with his peers. Seeing the same young man wearing baggy clothes, sagging pants, a colored bandana and an LA Dodgers jersey and hat, may very well mean you have a 'banger on your hands.

Here is a list of particulars that always stand out to me:

Rings. Most rings are decoration, but fighting rings stand out, as do affiliation rings. By affiliation rings I mean class rings, military service rings, or rings that will tie that individual with a particular group like the pinkie ring Joe Pesci wore in "*Goodfellas*" that showed mob ties. Some affiliation rings also act as fighting rings, like the big swastika rings certain skinhead groups favor, so there is a neat bit of symmetry involved sometimes.

Watches. Dress watches or plain watches tell me the person is not a very physical individual or does not lead a physically demanding existence. Heavy-duty watches like G-Shocks are an indicator of the need for durability, which might indicate a certain toughness about a person. Expensive watches like Sinn or the like generally tell me the person will not go physical for small reasons, but if they do it will be serious.

Belts. If you can see them, they can tell you a lot about a person. A heavy leather belt can indicate someone is a firearms aficionado. A heavy-duty leather or webbing belt with a heavyweight buckle can mean someone who will beat you with the belt. Someone wearing a rope as a belt in the middle of the city speaks of a desperation that may mean the person is very poor, very unpredictable, borderline or homeless, but it always means you should watch that person, even if it is for small level crimes of opportunity like stealing your bag.

Boots. Someone who wears boots in an urban area always stands out to me. I don't mean brands like Merrill or Danner, although that does say something about the person, I mean work boots and the like. Things like the wear pattern on the toe of the boot – is it steel-toed, overall condition of the boot and even any accessories like spike collars, spurs or such – will tell you something.

Accessories. This is a catchall that I will only briefly mention. Things like bandanas, wallet chains (or what appear to be wallet chains), fanny packs on a younger male, hats, and jewelry other than rings. For example, a simple bandana in the pocket. It could be for wiping of the hands while working, like a shop rag, but not generally in our society any more. I look for how it is carried. Are both ends hanging out of the pocket and the bandana appears to be twisted? That may be a weapon and have a padlock looped through it. That is a good thing to know. Or, is only one end hanging out with a knot tied into it? It may be weighted and used as a weapon also. Is it a particular color, carried in a certain area or manner, knotted in any particular way? This may inform you of the person's affiliation, outlook or other habits or lifestyle choices that can be important to your survival.

Unfortunately, the other things we have to pay attention to are not as obvious as the clothes a person wears. Most serious warning signs are almost subliminal, or can be explained away as something else if the offender is found out. It is always easier to do this in a brewing situation due to the time involved, but a lot of these can be immediate judgments in your intuition if you train yourself to pay attention, so are applicable even in a flash situation. So let's get the hardest one out of the way early: vibes.

Everyone has the experience of the creepy guy, whether at work, the bar, or the pervert on the bus. Everyone knows creepy no matter how hidden, but describing it is one of the hardest things you will try to do. Creepy does not mean violent, but it is an indicator that violence is possible. Creepy is just one of the "vibes" we pick up from other people.

If you think about it, we receive, evaluate, and act on vibes every day, and we, as a species are quite effective at it. Applying this to self-defense is not a new skill, it is applying a skill you already have in a new manner. Have you ever walked into your workplace and felt anger? Not anger at being at work, but anger in the air. You feel it, but have no way of knowing why or how. Your subconscious feels what is going on, and is warning you.

In the same way that you feel the anger, and can track it down to the person emitting it (like your boss)and you can sense the other vibes people put out, after time and practice, you can interpret the vibes and learn the best way to act on the information they give you. The reason I used anger and creepiness as examples is because they are universally understood, usually one or both are present from an attacker, and your radar has evolved to pick them up. It is a free gift you already have, even if it is atrophied from non-use. It does not take much to bring it back.

The most important things to keep in mind are to not deny your feelings, even if you cannot prove or explain them, and do not let others translate them for you. Different things have different meanings to different people. A warning sign to you might not register or not have the same meaning to the person next to you. Always go with the assumption that *your* intuition is correct. It can be disproved by further evidence or interaction, but it should never be dismissed. Remember, this is survival we are talking about, your survival or that of your family; do not pawn off the responsibility to others or think you cannot do this. You do it everyday, while driving, taking care of your child, or going for dinner. You know when something is not right, and with practice you sharpen this edge. Combined with effective de-escalation and physical training you are now more in command of your fate.

Now onto some physical clues that will help hone this ability you're working with. You know the common saying that the eyes are the windows to the soul? It is a common saying because it is true. You can tell a lot from someone's eyes. Mood, intelligence, level of intoxication... there is a lot of information available. Eyes also give away what someone is interested in. Women know this well. If a woman is on a date, and the male she is with insists he appreciates her mind, thinks she is smart, etc. but is continuously staring at her breasts, she knows he is full of crap.

The lesson here? Pay attention to whatever your opponent is watching. If it is you, you can kind of eliminate the assailant has any other target in mind. If it is your purse, you are now aware of what kind of crime is likely to occur. This may be personal, but if this individual is watching your genitals or other sexual area, you may be dealing with a sex offender, which ups the level immensely. And I am saying this to both men and women. Sexual assault happens to both genders, and not many predators are good at hiding their interest. Even if it flashes quickly, the interest is always present.

Some other things that are good to pay attention to and that increase the odds of survival in a physical altercation become very obvious with training. Yes, I am recommending adding an intellectual element to your physical training. Ultimately your mind and intellect are what saves you, your body is the tool it uses. So keep the tool in working order, but tune up the engine.

Things to look for: What side is prominent? In other words, what lead does the person use? This is an important clue to your physical response. How does this assailant position himself to you, is it chest out, arms waving? Is it square on to you or bladed off? Can you see both hands or tell how he is balanced? Is there a sense of competence or overconfidence present, maybe desperation?

An important one to me is general physical appearance. Is the person clean and well put together, or is he disheveled, dirty and desperate? Desperation can mean that the person is not in the greatest physical shape, but can be a much harder individual to fight. Ever stood between a spouse abuser and his wife? The man is so desperate to get his target, everything he does to you is inconsequential, but highly damaging. Think of a mama bear protecting her cub. That is the kind of desperation a junkie has to get his fix. If you are his chosen walking ATM, that desperation is now fixed on you.

Are there any obvious disabilities visible? If you are targeted by someone who is obviously disabled, he is probably going to be a tough nut to crack. Remember, there are cultures and sub-cultures you are not aware of, and people survive horrific, painful, debilitating things, and still operate in them. Know that some disabilities remove a person from the attacker pool, like blindness, but he may be faking blindness to get close to you. The disabilities I am talking about are things like prosthesis, someone using a cane, a severe limp or the like. One of the old foul dudes I knew when I was younger had a patch over his eye. It happened in a bar fight and just made him worse. This is what I'm talking about. You need to pay attention to all of these clues and intuitive feelings just to even the odds if you run into problems with people like this.

When you step into this world of self-defense, you begin to see many things, and you begin to see that many things are not as you first thought. None of this stuff is hard to learn or hard to do. Many people have mystified the subject, tried to capitalize on it by obfuscating things, or treating this information as secret.

Bullshit, it is the same as living. Driving relies on all the same reading of people and situations. It even requires reading lines of force, controlling emotions and seeing what other people project through what kind of vehicle they drive and accessories they add to their car. You already have the knowledge base to do this. It just requires applying it in a different venue, and in a manner that needs practice to become proficient. Do not let anyone convince you that you cannot do this, and just as important, don't talk yourself out of it either.

What I have tried to do here is lay out some basic information, things you can use as building blocks, and hopefully inspire some curiosity that spurs further learning and insights for you. Even if you never have to use this in the context presented, it comes in handy in everyday life. It also increases the pleasure of living. By making the problem of self defense take its proper place, and having these observational tools available, you will see more in life, appreciate more, and be more comfortable as you are out and about.

The Independent: A Variation of the Alpha

by Michael Johnson

In his first book "*Cheap Shots, Ambushes and Other Lessons*" Marc "Animal" MacYoung introduced the concept of the Alpha male and female as it pertains to self-defense and survival in the mean streets of America.

"*It was an attempt to explain,*" Marc wrote on his website[*] "*an important social dynamic that has a lot to do with whether or not violence erupts.*"

In another part of his website, Marc describes what an alpha is[†]:

Let's start with the fact that being an alpha is a whole lot more than just ordering people around or intimidating people with the threat of violence (that's called being a bully). And it's definitely more than just being able to beat people up.

Being an alpha has to do with one's involvement in a group. More specifically, it's about[the] helping develop and maintain[ing] ...a group dynamic, hierarchy and the functionality of the group. [...] Being an alpha is about leadership and taking care of others.

Knowing the nuances of how Alphas behave in certain situations can, and will, help people avoid most violent situations and the inevitable consequences that follow.

There is a variation of the alpha that is rare among group dynamics because most of the time, this person chooses to be alone. I call this person The Independent. This is someone who is very comfortable with walking the world, and living life, alone. Someone who enjoys his/her own company and is not afraid of being by him/herself. This person is

---

[*] http://www.nononsenseselfdefense.com/alpharespect.htm
[†] http://www.nononsenseselfdefense.com/alphabehavior.htm

neither anti-social nor asocial, however. That's a different kind of person altogether.

The Independent has no qualms about socializing with others. S/he will purposely seek social times with others when the spirit moves them because they do, in fact, enjoy people's company. Usually, however, it's with special people in their lives – family, and/or very close friends, and/or colleagues that they trust. Rarely will they socialize with total strangers.

When it comes to being part of a group or organization the Independent becomes extremely wary, bordering on suspicious. They want to make sure they don't lose their identity or their independent nature by becoming a part of said group or organization. Even if they find themselves leading the group. *Especially* if they find themselves leading the group.

Why are Independents so cautious? Because they've been stomped in the past by a group, or members representing a group – whether or not the Independent was a part of said group – and are not interested in repeating that experience again.

Rarely will an Independent remain a member of a group or organization for long. Even if s/he is leading the group. On that rare occasion that they do choose to be a member of a group or organization, it's because the Independent is allowed the freedom to leave for a time and return whenever they want. That kind of loyalty from the group or organization to the Independent will be returned in kind. If an Independent decides to leave, permanently, there is nothing that group or organization can say or do to change their mind. It's a waste of time to try.

I mentioned before about the Independent having been stomped in the past by certain groups or group members. That leaves such an indelible mark on their soul that some Independents teach themselves how to deal with such groups all by their little lonesome. Because of their life experiences, in a violent situation, Independents always expect to be confronted by an armed group, even if they initially face a single, unarmed opponent. At times an Independent has confronted a group head-on and won. Most of the time, though, they'll employ Sneaky Shit (tm) strategies and tactics, combined with the main principle of such encounters: "Exit. Stage left!"

However, the main strategy an Independent will use, more than any other, is the Awareness/Avoidance/De-escalation strategy. They'll live much longer that way. Some Independents can sense trouble coming down the pike from hundreds of yards away. That gives them more than enough time to avoid trouble by not being there. If they can't leave for some reason (and usually it's not an ego thing – remember, a group stomping is not their favorite pastime), ghosting is a viable option. Failing that, back-up plans A through E will be employed, with the "Exit. Stage left" strategy at the center of each plan.

This is usually the de-escalation part of the main strategy. De-escalation tactics range from the Independent finding a way for their opponents to save face and status, to alerting the authorities to their opponents' actions, to letting their opponents know, in no uncertain terms, that they (the Independent) will die killing their opponents. And that their opponents will be dead no less than ten minutes before the Independent dies. It all depends on the particular situation.

When it comes to protecting others, an Independent will do so with their entire being – after assessing the situation to make sure that kind of intervention is necessary. If it is necessary, the Independent will do so by any means necessary up to, and including, sacrificing their life to protect others. If they do sacrifice their lives, they'll be sure to take as many aggressors with them as they can. The Independents' decision to sacrifice their lives for others isn't done for heroic reasons, they do so because the trash needs to be taken out, and they've volunteered to take it out.

There are times, however, when an Independent comes upon combatants and realizes that either the combatants deserve what they do to each other, or that the combatants need to be separated. It depends.

Now here's a paradox. Sometimes an Independent needs help and is wise enough to ask for it. Sometimes an Independent needs help but doesn't realize it. That's when a family member and/or a close friend has to go "Oops" upside the Independents' head to get their attention and inform them that they *will* accept the family member and/or close friend's help. The truly wise Independent will see the light – or the star circling their heads from the "Oops," realize how foolish they've been thinking they can handle that particular situation alone, and accept the help that has been thrust upon them.

When the Independent opens him/herself to that help, s/he will discover that the love they spread throughout the world will return to them a hundredfold. And s/he'll know that s/he isn't as alone as s/he thought.

How do I know so much about Independents? Because I'm one. And I've known many others, male and female. We are, indeed, a unique variation on a theme.

Talking to Cops

by Marc MacYoung

I never really like looking down the barrel of a gun. It doesn't much matter who it belongs to. The last time I found myself looking down the barrel of a gun it belonged to a cop.

In the officer's defense, I was kneeling on a dude's head at the time. Also, it was the middle night, in a bad part of town, we were out on the sidewalk and there were two of us on top of this drunk guy. So the cop pointing a pistol at us is an understandable reaction.

The nice policemen suggested that my partner and I might want to stop what we were doing and allow the gentleman to get up. I held up my hands and said, "I *will* comply! But this guy is on the fight and, if we let him go, there's a good chance he'll attack us again."

Still, the officer was adamant about us letting the lil' feller go. While we were discussing his release, two more police cars arrived. We stepped back and the guy popped up like a jack in the box from hell.

We were quickly separated into two groups by the officers and questioned. As should be the case, we were facing the officer interviewing us with our backs to the other individual involved. (Getting people out of view of the person they're pissed at calms things down.) The other officers were talking to the Master of Drunken Kung Fu.

We told our story, who we were, where we worked, that this intoxicated individual had attacked two customers attempting to enter the business. We'd come to their assistance. He had fallen, yet retained a death grip on one of the customer's shirt. They couldn't flee. I'd used a knife to cut it, so they could jump in their car and leave. (There was the scrap of cloth on the sidewalk.) We'd waited until they had left, then we let him up. When we did, he'd attacked us. We'd put him down in a controlled manner and were trying to talk him down when they'd arrived.

The officer looked at me and asked, "Did you hit him?"

"No sir. I did a prescribed takedown to control him without injury. We never struck him. All we did was hold him down so he couldn't hurt us or the others."

About then the other party decided to offer a suggestion to a female police officer. Not only was the suggestion not polite, but it was loud too. As a final point, he called her a name. Women generally do not like being referred to as that part of their anatomy.

The officer in front of us blinked when he heard this. He quietly said, "You two can go."

We politely thanked the officer and returned to the business. We looked over to see our old friend now had new friends – who were also kneeling on his head.

The female officer seemed to really be working the knee. Women *really* don't like being called that.

This story exemplifies many different and important points about a violent encounter. First of all, odds are good you will be dealing with the police.

Second, this situation wasn't self-defense. Nor was it a 'fight' to win, dominate, prove whose pee-pee was bigger, teach someone a lesson or punish him. None of the normal definitions people commonly banter around in the martial arts applied to this situation.

It *was* a use of force situation with a clearly defined goal, tactics and integrated with verbal communication. "We don't want to hurt you. If you calm down, we'll let you up."

Third, not only would punching the guy have been inappropriate, but it would have gotten us arrested. The question of whether we had hit him was a trap to get us to admit excessive force. A trap that we hadn't fallen into *during* the altercation. A trap we avoided because we knew: use of force is a 'Goldilocks and the Three Bears' issue. *This one is too little. This one is too much. This one is just right.*

Fourth, our calm, professional and cooperative demeanor – as we articulated the facts of the situation – is what kept us from getting arrested. This, even though the situation had started with us looking down the barrel of a gun.

Had we jumped up and down, howled, screamed, made accusations and insulted the other guy, and demanded the police arrest the other guy and gotten angry when they didn't believe us, it wouldn't have turned out so well. We would have ended up, like him, down on the ground with someone kneeling on our heads.

Let me add, that incident wasn't the first or the last time I ended up dealing with the cops. (It was just the last time I had someone point a gun at me without pulling the trigger.) Cops have been – and still are – a major issue in my life.

Let me point something out: I am an ex-outlaw. That means something very specific where I am from. It also means I have a lot of experience dealing with the cops and not getting arrested. Cops don't like criminals and they're equally not fond of outlaws. That's because outlaws have their own rules and creeds and often those don't gel with the laws of society.

I've set aside my outlaw ways and not only have I become a respected member of society, I now teach cops. I not only teach them how to more effectively kneel on people's heads, but I also teach them how to keep their emotions under control. So when someone screams in their faces an obscene suggestion and refers to them as part of their anatomy they don't lose their cool and instead of just kneeling on his head, throw the guy a beating.

This gives me a unique perspective when it comes to dealing with cops. I cannot tell you how many times I have stood there handcuffed (or sat on the curb) while being questioned by the police. It was such common event, I honestly can't remember how many times it happened. I was a violent and scary dude so I didn't take it personally when the officers felt more comfortable talking to me in handcuffs. I can communicate just as well with my hands handcuffed as I can when free. Because of my outlaw lifestyle, I've had cops itching to arrest me and trying to find cause. I can also tell you I've met a brick wall for lipping off to a cop. Important safety tip, female cops don't like being called 'pigettes' either. (Hey, I was young and stupid OK?)

On the other hand, I've spent many a pleasant hour smoking cigars and drinking scotch with them. I've talked to officers about their stresses and fears about the dangers they face in their job. I've listened to officers in bitch sessions about how the department and society treats them and what insane restrictions they must operate under. I've helped them through time of emotional torment and trauma because of what happened to them on the job.

I tell you this so you will understand that I have dealt with cops under all kinds of circumstances – including from both sides of the law.

Therefore my first bit of advice to you when dealing with the cops is remember: *They are human beings.*

They are not your enemy. They are not your friend. They are not Nazi SS troopers, robots or clones in uniforms. They are not gods or lawyers. They are not out to get you, oppress you or take away your rights. Nor are they your whipping boy or your nigger.

Yet, that is how a large number of civilians treat the police. They'd never think about snapping their fingers at a waiter, but they'll treat a cop even worse.

Officers are human beings with feelings, thoughts, biases, frustrations and ways of looking at things *just like you*. They can make mistakes, lose their cool, be opinionated, angry and judgmental, *just like you*. Also like you, they can decide someone is being an asshole and that it's okay to make that person's life unpleasant.

I always preferred Hillel's version of the Golden Rule "That which is hateful unto you, do not do unto your fellow." Now if you want a cop to decide you're an asshole, go ahead and ignore Hillel's advice.

This should be common sense, but you can't believe the number of people who make cops the target of their anger, frustration and outrage because the cop is telling them 'no.' Most people don't ever go any further than being angry because they are being ticketed for breaking a traffic law. But believe me, it does go *way* beyond that.

Cops are constantly barraged by people calling them names, screaming at them, blaming them, snarling at them, disrespecting them, lying to them, spitting on them and even physically assaulting them. It's appalling, the petty stuff people fly off the handle about. Some people are outraged when police tell them they cannot go a certain way because of some issue up ahead.

So when I remind you that they are human beings, I'm pointing out something very, very important. Namely, that you aren't the only one there with feelings, frustrations and human limitations.

Here's my second bit of advice. How you treat the cops has a *big* influence on how they treat you.

This is critical to remember because if you're an unreasonable, obnoxious asshole to them, then that's going to come back on you. Whether it's them being an unprofessional asshole or a professional asshole—it *will* blow back on you.

Don't worry about being pepper-sprayed, beaten or shot for being a pissy little asshole. They save that stuff for people who are really working at being obnoxious. It isn't his gun you need to worry about if you're being a snot, it's his pen.

What he writes can turn your life into a living hell. So do yourself a favor and don't give in to your urges to be rude and obnoxious. I once had a girlfriend who insisted on her 'right' to tell the cops what she thought about them stopping us. That traffic stop ended up costing me over $1500, as the cop just kept on writing.

My third bit of advice is to understand that the police are, first and foremost, public safety officers. That is their *numero uno* job. And it's something they take seriously: stopping people getting hurt bad. The cop's job is to keep people from getting hurt.

That simple shift in perspective will save you all kinds of problems.

Most laws are based on known dangers and known problems that arise from certain behaviors. If people are doing this, sooner or later, bad things happen. Plain and simple.

Now, here's where something a friend from long ago used to say comes into play. *Just because something is dangerous doesn't automatically mean you are going to get hurt if you do it. I have noticed that the young, inexperienced – or simply imagination impaired – often take this to mean there is no danger at all.*

There are a lot of imagination-impaired people out there. Or to be more precise, there's a lot of people who willfully ignore the potential danger and damage of their behaviors. They think since they're having fun or profiting by it, it must be 'good.' (Better yet, that they have a 'right' to do it.)

An obvious example is a bunch of drunk teenagers deciding to go all *Fast and Furious* racing down the city streets at over one hundred miles an hour. People doing this kind of stuff *will* catch the cop's attention. Even if it's to scrape them off the traffic divider.

That brings us back to safety laws. If you're behaving in a way that runs afoul of these laws, the cops *will* tell you to stop. How insistent you are about your 'right' to behave this way is going to influence the outcome of the situation.

So too is how far out of bounds you've decided to go. *Fast and Furious* on city streets? Mandatory arrest at twenty miles over the speed limit in most states. Even if you don't get in an accident, you'll be facing the local equivalent of reckless endangerment charges. Get in an accident and kill someone? Vehicular homicide or manslaughter is in your future. That's if you don't end up with a telephone pole on your head after you wrap it around one.

However, long before you get to that potential road kill stage there's another aspect of public safety. That is fucking with other people and interfering with them going about their business. Now we're talking disturbance. This is actually a two-fold issue.

First, it is how most people encounter the cops.

Straight up, 99% of your dealing with police will be about safety and disturbance issues. This, whether getting a speeding ticket or your neighbors complaining about your barking dog. Or you complaining about your neighbor's dog or stereo. Generally speaking the easiest answer is stop doing whatever is causing the fuss. Oh wait, try not doing them in the first place. That works better.

But that brings us to the second issue: people get obnoxiously self-righteous about their 'right' to be an asshole, usually because of the following reasons:

1. they are having fun
2. they are emotional
3. they are intoxicated
4. they don't want to be told what to do
5. they feel entitled/oppressed
6. they get territorial
7. some of the above
8. all of the above

That means they're going to insist on acting the way they are acting. Odds are good they're going to get pissy when they get told 'no.' They don't see (or care about) the problems their actions are causing. It's all about them and their 'rights.' This is something cops get a lot of.

If this describes you then you're going to see the ugly side of cops.

Remember the officer's pen. It's going to become real important to, and expensive for, you.

Now let's say that the situation has gone past barking dogs or an illegal left-hand turn. Something has happened that looks a lot like a crime to cops. I'm not talking about you coming in and robbing the local 7-11. How about you and your neighbor get into a dispute over the placement of fence and it comes to blows.

When the cops roll up what they're going to see is 'two citizens in dispute.'

Well okay, that's the official version. Odds are is what they are going to see is two screaming, pissed off people who want the other arrested for assaulting them. Both of them are going to claim the other attacked him first and what they did was self-defense. In short what they're going to see is two assholes.

And if you were acting like one, they're going to be right. Odds are, both of you have crossed legal lines and are co-creators of this problem. Like 95% of the time, odds.

Here's an important safety tip: Cop's first duty upon arriving at an incident *is to investigate.*

Reread that again. It's important. That means to find out what happened. They're going to be asking questions. How well you communicate, how you conduct yourself, how calm, polite and respectful you are of them trying to do their job is going to have *a lot* to do with the next stage.

There comes a point in any investigation where the officer decides if a crime has been committed or not. From this point the focus shifts from finding out what happened to building a case for the prosecution.

You need to understand that the officer is not going to hold up a sign that says, "I'm now trying to build a case against you."

Nor is he going to tell you "I'm beginning to suspect that a crime has been committed and you did it." Which is less of a turning point than the 'I'm now building a case.' The 'I have a suspicion' is more of a veer in that direction. But if you are paying attention *you'll see the veer*.

Using the incident I mentioned earlier you could say the veer was the cop asking us if we'd hit him. The truth was however, the veer had happened when they'd pulled up and we were kneeling on his head.

I'd veered it back when I told them ""I will comply! But this guy is on the fight and, if we let him go, there's a good chance he'll attack us again."

In my initial communication, I'd given him multiple reasons to shift back into investigation mode. First, I'd told him we were going to follow his orders.

But most importantly, I'd given enough information to make it questionable as to whose name went in the victim box and who went into suspect/arrestee box on the police report.

Here's something to keep in mind. If the cops show up, there's usually a problem. Problems look bad. Thing is, this may be a first for you, but the cop has seen it hundreds of times before. Unfortunately, that can lead to bias and jumping to conclusions. So it's incumbent on you to communicate to him that whatever is going on is not just SOSDD (Same

Old Shit, Different Day). It's something that he needs to investigate instead of just going for building a case and arresting someone.

Going back to the kneeling on the dude's head incident. Fortunately, the drunk's outburst showed I wasn't lying about him being on the fight. All the other little details like us being sober, having legitimate business reasons for our presence, the scrap of cloth and cooperating all added up as to who was the problem – despite what it looked like when the cops showed up.

Now being polite, calm and cooperative during the investigation might seem like common sense, but when you're adrenalized, emotional and self-righteous, it's easy to fall into asshole mode. You'll want to tattle on the other guy to get him into trouble.

Another thing that gets people in a tizzy is they think the cops should be psychic. "Well, I'm obviously the good guy here. Why is the officer asking them questions about my behaviors? It's the other guy who's cause this problem. Why is the cop treating me like a criminal?"

But there's one special spot where people don't just step on their dicks. They start pogo sticking. That's when, confronted with statements and questions about your own bad behavior, there's a strong impulse to lie and spin the truth to make yourself look good. Ya know what? It's not going to go well for you if you do that.

It's definitely not going to help if it's true.

Here's a hint, if you crossed the line and know it, it's time to shut up and lawyer up. Don't try to lie. Don't try to talk your way out of it. Don't spin. Shut up.

Granted that isn't news to people who are professional criminals. But there's something you need to know. "Lawyering up" is the fastest way to get a cop to shift into building a case mode. It's a common criminal tactic and when cops see it, it is human tendency (remember, cops are humans) to jump to that conclusion.

This makes what I'm about to say a judgment call. You need to know when it's time to talk and when it's time to shut up and get your lawyer involved.

When you see that veer it's time to start being very careful with your answers. When you see the turn, it's time to shut up and get your lawyer there before you answer any other questions – even if you are innocent. *don't* try to fix it yourself. You're dealing with a professional with a pen and what he writes, *not what you say*, is what is officially in the record.

In a related venue, the more serious the potential charges, the more you need to have your lawyer present. Anything, and I do mean *anything* involving weapons and self-defense, and it's time for you to exercise your Miranda rights about having an attorney present during questioning.

Remember that turn into 'start building a case?' Well let me tell you something important about it. This has been court-tested and approved, so listen well. In the development of a case an officer can lie to you, trick you and ask you questions designed to get you to admit guilt without coming out and saying "I did it." Remember, cops routinely deal with bad people who are tricky and lie to them. They have to do the same to build cases against bad guys. They're good at catching bad guys.

This is why it is so important that you do everything in your power to keep the cop from deciding you're one of them! Being polite, cooperative and doing what you can to assist them in their investigation is a *really* good start to achieving this.

But if the cop decides that you're a bad guy then there really isn't anything you're going to say to change his mind at that moment. Here's the funny thing. If you're a bad guy, you need a lawyer. If you're a good guy in a serious situation you *really* need a lawyer.

If you've been paying attention there should be something that's bothering you. It's 'Marc, didn't you say that cops think you're guilty if you lawyer up? But now you're telling me to lawyer up."

Well, there's lawyering up and then there's lawyering up. Or to put it another way, it's a matter of style. Personally the best way I've ever heard of doing it comes from Rory Miller. "Officer, I want to cooperate and I will provide you with a full statement. But we both know about the risks of getting sued. Because it's so serious, I'd like to have my lawyer present when I answer your questions"

I could write an entire book about all the yummy goodness that is in this statement. But let me give you some highlights.

You're *still* cooperating – you're not telling the cop you ain't going to say nuffin'. Nor are you making his job harder. You're just rescheduling.

You're going to talk even with the lawyer there – lawyering up by the guilty usually means roaring silence. You want your side of the story to be heard. You are willing to help the officer in his investigation.

You are informing the officer you are exercising your Miranda rights – you will not talk about the case without an attorney present. Three subpoints come with this

1) You *have* to inform the officer you are exercising your Miranda rights otherwise they can keep on questioning you. Asking for your lawyer to be present before answering any more questions counts.

2) From the moment you ask for your attorney the officer *cannot* ask you questions about the case—without the presence of your attorney. If he does not only will anything you say not be allowed in court, but there's a good chance the entire case will be thrown out. Seemingly small thing from your side, huge issue from the cop's side.

3) Everything I have said is null and void, if *you* bring up the case again to the officer. Do not step on your dick about this. Not talking about the case without your lawyer present also means you don't talk about it.

If the situation is serious, expect to spend some time sitting in a jail cell while waiting for your attorney to show up. Well fine. I hope you like cartoons. Because you're going to be watching them. Oh by the way, you know the thing I said about not talking about your case without an attorney? Yeah, that goes double with the guys in county jail. Jailhouse snitches and all that….

In closing I'd like to give you some perspective. You know when the traffic cops walks up to your car and asks you "Do you know why I stopped you?" or "Do you know how fast you were going?" That is a very sneaky way to get what is known as an admission of guilt.

If you were 75 in a 60 zone, most people are going to try and lie it down. "I thought I was doing 65." Well guess what Brainiac? You've *still* confessed to knowing you were speeding *and* you lied to the cop. Guess what category that puts you in?

A-S-S-H-O-L-E

These days I deal with cases of people going to prison for the rest of their lives and in some cases facing execution. I grew up doing things that could have put me into prison for a long, long time. So you know what my advice to you about the small stuff like speeding tickets and a too-loud stereo is?

Man up about it.

Don't try to wiggle out of it. Don't piss and moan about your 'rights' or that you weren't doing anything. You know you were doing it. You know you're out of line so just take a chill pill. It's small time stuff.

Don't make an issue of it. This really applies to safety and disturbance stuff.

But most of all own up to it.

You know what? That honesty will help you. Last time I got a moving violation I was running late to the airport and the cop clocked me doing 63 in a 45 zone. Three more miles an hour and it would have been mandatory arrest. When he walked up to my car I had my license, registration and proof of insurance waiting. The first words of the conversation were "I was a baaaaad boy." He laughed.

He also wrote me up for doing 50. I sincerely thanked him for it and then I went and caught my plane.

What to expect after a traumatic event

by Dr. Drew Anderson

It Can (and Probably Will) Happen to You

Unfortunately, traumatic experiences are common. Several studies have found that more than half of all individuals surveyed reported a history of at least one traumatic experience, and many of those actually reported more than one such experience.[1,2]

Given these numbers, you should expect that you, or someone close to you, will experience at least one trauma in the future (if it hasn't already happened). The rest of this article will describe what to expect and how to deal with the aftermath.

First, Expect Distress

By their very nature, traumatic events are outside most peoples' everyday experiences, and extreme reactions are common immediately following a traumatic event. For example, one study found that 94% of rape victims experienced symptoms of PTSD in the week following their assault,[3] and another found that roughly 60% of individuals met criteria for PTSD within the first month after a nonsexual assault.[4] A study of individuals living close to the World Trade Center found rates of PTSD to be about 8% and rates of depression to be about 10% within one to two months after the September 11 attacks.[5]

So the bad news is, if you are involved in a traumatic incident there's a good chance that you will struggle to cope in the months following the incident. This can be a very trying time, any many people feel like they will never get over the experience. Fortunately, this isn't the case for most.

But Also Expect Resilience

Some mental health professionals have made dire predictions about the psychological resilience of those experiencing trauma. In one glaring example, it was estimated that over 9,000 crisis counselors descended on New York City to assist after September 11, and the director of one of the counseling programs predicted that 25% of the residents of New York City would need therapy for emotional problems resulting from the attacks. In hindsight, this was an obvious overestimation.[6]

We now know that despite the fact that many people show symptoms of PTSD following a traumatic event, many, if not most, individuals who develop severe symptoms following a trauma will recover on their own without treatment.[7,8] For example, one review found that that the proportion of disaster survivors who develop chronic psychological problems rarely exceeds 30%, and in most cases the proportion is much lower.[8]

Recovery also tends to happen fairly quickly; most studies find significant improvement occurs within three months to one year after the trauma.[7,9,10] Some theorists have suggested that recovery from traumatic events is a natural process and it may be best to think about diagnosable PTSD as a disruption or stalling out of this process.[11]

So the good news is that, even with no treatment, most people go on to recover with no lasting psychological harm. On the other hand, roughly 30% will continue to have long-term problems, including PTSD, depression, and substance abuse problems.[7,10] This brings us to the next question: how can you make it more likely that you or someone you care about ends up being one of those who recovers? That is, what makes people better?

How to Help in the Immediate Aftermath

Until fairly recently, crisis interventions like critical incident stress debriefing (CISD), critical incident stress management (CISM), or psychological debriefing (PD) were commonly recommended to help people immediately following a traumatic event. Without going into too many details, these interventions generally involve a group format in which all individuals affected process their thoughts and feelings related to the incident, guided by a trained facilitator. [12,13] These approaches are not recommended any more, however, because of research showing that they are ineffective or even harmful.[6,9,14,15]

As an alternative, psychological first aid (PFA) has been widely recommended as a framework for helping individuals in the immediate aftermath of a trauma or disaster.[8,16,17] PFA is a flexible approach that is designed to be used by anyone, not just mental health professionals, to help assist those in crisis. It has eight core actions:

Psychological First Aid Core Actions[17]

1. **Contact and Engagement:** To respond to contacts initiated by survivors, or initiate contacts in a non-intrusive, compassionate, and helpful manner.

2. **Safety and Comfort:** To enhance immediate and ongoing safety, and provide physical and emotional comfort.

3. **Stabilization (if needed):** To calm and orient emotionally overwhelmed or disoriented survivors.

4. **Information Gathering: Current Needs and Concerns:** To identify immediate needs and concerns, gather additional information, and tailor Psychological First Aid interventions.

5. **Practical Assistance:** To offer practical help to survivors in addressing immediate needs and concerns.

6. **Connection with Social Supports:** To help establish brief or ongoing contacts with primary support persons or other sources of support, including family members, friends, and community helping resources.

7. **Information on Coping:** To provide information about stress reactions and coping to reduce distress and promote adaptive functioning.

8. **Linkage with Collaborative Services:** To link survivors with available services needed at the time or in the future.

If you are interested in learning PFA, a manual is available for download at

`http://www.nctsn.org/content/psychological-first-aid`

and

`http://www.ptsd.va.gov/professional/manuals/psych-first-aid.asp`

and an online training course is available at

`http://learn.nctsn.org/course/category.php?id=11`

PFA is probably your best resource for dealing with the immediate aftermath of a crisis. But what if you or someone else continues to have problems? The next section will discuss options for longer-term help.

Longer-Term Help

If you or someone you know continues to have significant problems three or more months after the event, you may want to consider therapy for the issues. Fortunately, there are effective treatments for PTSD and the other issues that are often associated with trauma. For PTSD, the type of therapy known as cognitive-behavioral therapy (CBT) seems to be most effective. In particular, a couple of different approaches appear to work. First, a type of CBT therapy called prolonged exposure (PE), which involves repeatedly re-imagining the trauma in a safe situation, has been shown to be extremely effective.[18] Another CBT, cognitive processing therapy, which helps individuals process their thoughts and emotions about the trauma, is also very effective.[11] There are other variations on CBT that are also effective,[7,19] and some other types of therapy and some medications have also shown some promise.[20] In the interests of full disclosure, I am a CBT-trained psychologist, so my bias is for CBT-based approaches. However, they really are the most widely-recognized approaches as being effective for PTSD, trauma, and associated problems.

No matter what type of therapy you choose (or recommend), it is important to seek out a therapist with specific expertise in dealing with trauma. Trauma can be difficult to work with, and the treatments can be challenging to both the patient and the therapist, so it is critical that the person doing the therapy has some experience with it. Luckily, these types of therapy do work, and often fairly quickly – in months rather than years.

Conclusions

Trauma is something that most of us will face at some point in our lifetimes. Fortunately, most people will recover quickly, if not painlessly, from trauma. Even more luckily, help does exist for those who need it. Approaches such as psychological first aid can help in the short-term, and effective therapy can help for those who continue to have problems after the first few months to one year.

So while you should expect that trauma can cause pretty significant problems over the short-term, you should not expect that it will affect you or those close to you for the rest of your life or theirs. Full recovery is possible, and even expected.

References and Further Reading

1. Afifi, T. O., Asmundson, G. J. G., & Sareen, J. (2009). Epidemiology of traumatic events and posttraumatic stress disorder. In D. J. Nutt, M. B. Stein, J. Zohar (Eds.). *Posttraumatic stress disorder: Diagnosis, management, and treatment* (2nd ed., pp. 12-24). London: Informa Healthcare.

2. Kessler, R. C., Sonnega, A., Bromet. E., Hughes, M., & Nelson, C. B. (1995) Posttraumatic stress disorder in the National Comorbidity Survey. *Archives of General Psychiatry, 52,* 1048–1060.

3. Rothbaum, B. O., Foa, E. B., Riggs, D. S., Murdock. T., & Walsh, W. A. (1992). Prospective examination of post-traumatic stress disorder in rape victims. *Journal of Traumatic Stress, 5,* 455-475.

4. Riggs, D. S., Rothbaum, B. O., & Foa, E. B. (1995). A prospective examination of symptoms of post-traumatic stress disorder in victims of nonsexual assault. *Journal of Interpersonal Violence, 10,* 201–214.

5. Galea, S., Ahren, J., Resnik, H., Kilpatrick, D., Bucuvalas, M., Gold, J., et al., (2002). Psychological sequelae of the September 11 terrorist attacks in New York City. *New England Journal of Medicine, 346,* 982-987.

6. McNally, R. J., Bryant, R. A., & Ehlers, A. (2003). Does early psychological intervention promote recovery from posttraumatic stress? *Psychological Science in the Public Interest, 4,* 45-79.

7. National Collaborating Centre for Mental Health. (2005). *Posttraumatic stress disorder: The management of PTSD in adults and children in primary and secondary care.* London: Gaskell/BPS.

8. Watson, P. J., Brymer, M. J., & Bonanno, G. A. (2011). Postdisaster psychological intervention since 9/11. *American Psychologist, 66,* 482-494.

9. Litz, B. T., Gray, M. J., Bryant, R., & Adler, A. B. (2002). Early intervention for trauma: Current status and future directions. *Clinical Psychology: Science and Practice, 9,* 112-134.

10.   Rosen, G. M., Frueh, B. C., Elhai, J. D., Grubaugh, A. L., & Ford, J. D. (2010). Posttraumatic stress disorder and general stress studies. In G. M. Rosen & B. C. Frueh, *Clinician's guide to posttraumatic stress disorder* (pp. 3-31). Hoboken, NJ: Wiley.

11.   Resick, P.A., Monson, C.M., & Chard, K.M. (2008). *Cognitive processing therapy: Veteran/military version.* Washington, DC: Department of Veterans' Affairs.

12.   Mitchell, J. T. (1983). When disaster strikes. *Journal of Emergency Medical Services, 8,* 36-39.

13.   Mitchell, J. T., & Everly, G. S. (1995). *Critical incident stress debriefing: An operations manual for the prevention of traumatic stress among emergency services and disaster workers.* Ellicott City, MD: Chevron.

14.   Bisson, J. I., McFarlane, A. C., Rose,S., Ruzek, J. I., & Watson, P. J. (2009). Psychological debriefing for adults. In E. B. Foa, T. M. Keane, M. J. Friedman, & J. A. Cohen (Eds.), *Effective treatments for PTSD: Practice guidelines from the International Society for Traumatic Stress Studies* (2nd ed., pp. 83-105). New York: Guilford.

15.   Work Group on ASD and PTSD (2004). *Practice guideline for the treatment of patients with acute stress disorder and posttraumatic stress disorder.* Arlington, VA: American Psychiatric Association.

16.   Inter-Agency Standing Committee (IACS) (2007). *IASC mental health and psychosocial support guidelines in emergency settings.* Geneva: IASC.

17.   National Child Traumatic Stress Network and National Center for PTSD (2006). *Psychological first aid: Field operations guide (2nd ed.).* Washington DC: Author.

18.   Riggs, D. S., Cahill, S. P., & Foa, E. B. (2006). Prolonged exposure treatment of posttraumatic stress disorder. In V. C. Follette & J. I Ruzek (Eds.) *Cognitive-behavioral therapies for trauma* (2nd ed., pp. 65-95). New York: Guilford.

19.   Follette, V. C., & Ruzek, J. I. (2006). *Cognitive-behavioral therapies for trauma* (2nd ed.). New York: Guilford.

20.   Foa, E. B., Keane, T. M., Friedman, M. J., & Cohen, J. A. (2009), *Effective treatments for PTSD: Practice guidelines from the International Society for Traumatic Stress Studies* (2nd ed.). New York: Guilford.

Section 2: Training

Regardless of style or system (even if you don't give a Tinker's Damn about martial arts) here are some things you might want to know. Some are about life, some about the process of teaching, some about the process of learning.

Do You Want to Win? Learn How to Lose.

by Dan Gilardi

What follows are the details of a single minute of time that happened some years ago

Ding
60 seconds.

Finally, a break. I try to keep my composure as I walk to my corner and lean my back against the ropes. My body hurts, and my lungs are on fire.

I'm in a hard sparring session at the tail end of a Muay Thai kickboxing workout, and I've been getting the crap beaten out of me for what seems like a never-ending series of rounds.

There is nothing I want more than to get out of this ring and lie down on the mat. Possibly in the fetal position.

45 seconds.

I spit my mouthpiece into my glove so I can breathe easier, but I'm still sucking in air. I can't believe I still have one round left to go after this break.

I feel like a 6-year-old girl could take my lunch money right now.

30 seconds.

The guy across the canvas from me is far more experienced, and he has much better boxing and head movement. I have been trying to keep him on the outside with kicks to his legs and body, but many times during the last few rounds he was able to close the distance and slam me with punches to the gut and jaw.

I can feel myself slowing down. My opponent looks like he doesn't have a care in the world; he might as well be taking a one-minute break from crocheting a trendy yarn scarf. Fantastic.

15 seconds.

Holy crap, this rest period is about over and I feel almost as exhausted as when the last bell rang. One more three-minute round doesn't sound like much, but when you're tired, hurting, and dodging punches it's the longest three minutes of your life.

5 seconds.

I put my mouthpiece back in. It tastes like a combination of stale sweat and futility.

1 second.

Meh.

Ding

I would love to tell you that I pulled myself up by my metaphorical bootstraps that day and put a severe (legal) beating on my experienced adversary. The truth, however, is that I got my ass handed to me for another three extremely long minutes.

No, I didn't just stand there and take the punishment. I fought as best as I could, but there was no classic Hollywood ending to this one. And you know what?

That's a good thing.

Why is it a good thing? Because sometimes *life is hard*. You have to learn to bounce back from failure, even when it hurts and you feel like you're full of suck.

Failure allows you to find where your limits are, so you can eventually break those brick walls down and grow. The next time I sparred with that same fighter, it got a *little* easier, because I was able to calm down a bit and deal with the pressure better.

The real benefits showed up months later when I had my first Muay Thai match. The *huge* adrenal crash left me gulping air halfway through the fight, but I didn't lose my composure. I was able to push through the fatigue, stay aggressive, and win.

If you *never* fail, you might not be pushing yourself to the edge of your abilities. Of course, you don't want to get shin splints because you are trying to break your personal running records every day and you don't need to bust your shoulders by constantly trying for a new max on bench press.

Sometimes, however, it's good to take a risk and challenge yourself. You might be surprised at what happens.

"I've missed more than 9,000 shots in my career. I've lost almost 300 games. 26 times, I've been trusted to take the game winning shot and missed. I've failed over and over and over again in my life. And that is why I succeed."

-Michael Jordan

Louis, The Legionnaire

by Wim Demeere

I met Louis right before a Pentjak Silat class a friend of mine taught. I spotted him straight away and saw he was in essence a human fighting machine. He was tall, muscular and had that tough-as-nails attitude soldiers sometimes get. He exuded that special kind of confidence born of surviving dozens of scrapes, knife fights and worse. But what stood out even more was the vibe he gave off of somebody who just loves to fight.

I later learned that this was true: he was a former Legionnaire with combat experience along with a checkered past as a civilian. This isn't uncommon for men entering the French Foreign Legion. One of the benefits of joining is that you can get a new name and basically a new life after you leave the service. So the Legion tends to attract people who have no choice left but to start over. Turns out this was exactly the way it went with Louis.

As we were standing in the bar before class, I kept a low profile and gave him plenty of space. When it got time to change into our training gear, I had to pass him because he was blocking the hallway. I calmly but confidently gestured that I intended to pass and smiled. He looked straight at me with a challenging stare, held that look for a second and then stepped aside.

When the class started, I made sure we were on opposite sides of the training hall, giving him all the space he needed and no reason to notice me. As it so happened, the instructor teamed us up, together with another partner. I arranged it such that he worked with the other guy first because I wanted to see him move. As I had figured, he did so very well. He was perhaps a little rigid, but he demonstrated tremendous power and had that glint in his eye street fighters get when they are having fun mauling somebody. He also clearly enjoyed intimidating the much smaller partner that we worked with.

After he'd done the technique a few times, it was his turn to attack me. He came at me relaxed the first few times and I responded in kind. As I expected, he suddenly launched a full-power, full-speed attack, but

I was ready for it. I accelerated to match his speed and performed the technique with sufficient impact so each hit would sting and hurt but not cause damage. He took it without flinching and as he stepped back into his ready position, we exchanged smiles.

The question he had on his mind had been asked and answered: If we'd really go at each other, it might be fun but also painful.

The rest of the class, he was fun to work with: co-operative and mindful of both me and the (now very scared) other training partner. But he kept me on my toes by throwing non-compromising attacks and also pointing out if he didn't feel a technique was placed well enough. Meaning, if he felt it wouldn't have done sufficient damage to him had I thrown it for real. This feedback helped me a lot in not only learning the new techniques we were practicing, but also as a benchmark for other training I would do later on. If he hadn't insisted I land my shots hard enough so he could gauge their effectiveness, it would have taken me a lot longer to get them down.

The class finished without incident and we ended up talking for a while in the changing room. I had apparently passed his test and been deemed worthy to share his thoughts with. When I had to leave for home, I shook his hand and smiled on the inside as he came just shy of trying to crush it. I'd expected as much and had tightened my hand before he touched it so I just smiled as I said my goodbyes.—————Over the years, I met many men like Louis. They routinely came from a similar background to his and were (to some degree) still living a life of danger and violence. In their mind, you aren't a man until you've proven yourself to them in some way. Sometimes this meant we had to rough each other up a bit in training. Other times, it meant a full on fight or a verbal sparring match to prove I wasn't intimidated by their taunting.

Sometimes this testing ritual annoyed the hell out of me when it felt like a waste of time or worse, risking a trip to the hospital. But I came to understand the lives these men led and how judging somebody's character and motives is an essential survival trait in their world. So I never held it against them, especially because they often proved to have valuable information for me: once the test was over, they shared critically important knowledge few people have and I always ended up learning something when we'd train or talk.

I don't want to give you the impression that you should seek out such men and ask them to fight a bit, just so you can afterwards get access to their hard-earned experience. What I do mean is this:

When such a man crosses your path, don't immediately discard or avoid him because of his background and demeanor. Neither do you have to befriend him. But if you can gain his respect, you might receive some unique training that ends up saving your life.

I know, because that's exactly what happened to me.

Teaching, Training and Conditioning

by Rory Miller

There are distinct differences between teaching, training and conditioning, with different uses, different strengths and different inherent weaknesses or dangers.

Teaching is passing information from brain to brain. I can tell you that 'colors are how our eyes perceive different wavelengths of light,' or I can teach you the formula to convert Celsius to Fahrenheit. Teaching can be entirely cerebral.

It can go wrong in a lot of ways.

First and foremost, teaching lends itself to 'knowing' and knowing has little to do with understanding. Like illiterate medieval monks copying the Bible or some modern Afghanis who have memorized the Qur'an but do not understand the Arabic they are reciting, it is very easy to have a store of knowledge that you cannot use.

Teaching does not necessarily have an automatic reality check. I can give you the formula to convert to Celsius, but if you calculate incorrectly it doesn't mean anything. A wrong number at the pure teaching level is just a squiggle on a piece of paper that doesn't look like the squiggle the instructor wanted. You can know that the earth is round or the earth is flat, and outside of a handful of professions, whichever you believe will not affect your life or anyone else's in any way.

Because there is no reality check, there is no inherent difference between good and bad information when it is taught. As long as it stays at this level, you can get a child to believe almost anything. Santa Claus and the Tooth Fairy are *teachings*. Most of what we think we know, most of what we have been taught, may be no more true. Because most of the things taught are not tested.

And this becomes dangerously bad, because we then believe these things we were taught are *important*. Sometimes worth killing over. You can be taught, as an obvious example, that your religion is objective truth, all other religions are lies created by an evil Adversary, and killing over this is a duty....

You can *feel* very sure about your beliefs at this level, but you cannot *be* sure...any more than a child's insistence in the Easter Bunny makes him hop.

'Knowing' in actual application, does not even *imply* truth.

On the good side, teaching allows us to transmit a huge amount of information, and to think through connections that would take lifetimes to try out in the real world. It allows us to imagine possibilities and juggle symbols. And teaching compounds over time. From simple sums to Pythagoras, Newton and Einstein, every advance is built on others. The questions that inspired Aristotle's "Metaphysics" have been outgrown.

Validity does not imply truth, however, only internal consistency. And bullshit can compound like any other information.

Training is guided practice in how to do stuff. I can tell you the Celsius formula, but you have to put pen to paper for a while to become proficient at it. I can tell you what to do if you are ever attacked by a right over-hand punch from a taller person... but if it is only taught, not trained, you will think and not act and you will eat that slow, clumsy punch.

Sometimes training has a touchstone to reality and sometimes it doesn't. This is crucial to understand. Training always has a touchstone (unless you are really doing it wrong) to *something*. You train to move a body by moving a body. You train to swing a stick by swinging a stick. If the touchstone is real or simulates reality closely, no problem. You hit a guy hard enough, he goes down....

It goes to shit when the touchstone doesn't mirror reality. You hit a guy lightly or miss him entirely and he goes down because he is 'supposed' to.... Or you spend your hours training against the way the instructor imagines bad guys attack instead of the way that they do attack.

It can also go bad when the metrics are wrong – when you measure success (one form of touchstone) by a poor standard. How a technique *looks* is not a tenth as relevant as how it feels on the receiving end, but if 'proper form' is measured against a picture, you will get, and I have seen, instructors who pick themselves up and say, "You didn't do that right." Or, to dust off an old memory of a wrestling champion choked out: when he came to, he explained to me that he had "won on points" before he lost consciousness.

Training is critical, though, in teaching us how and when to move. And when done right, it gets us used to the conditions we will face.

Conditioning affects a deeper part of the brain. It is how animals learn. In many ways, it is how we all truly learn. We are creatures of sense and motion, constantly watching the world, constantly affecting the world. A part of our brain, the one that learned 'stove-hot' is always watching what we do and the effects it has.

Do *this* and things get better, do *that* and things get worse. Do *this*. X hurts, Y feels good? Do Y. A flatworm, with a single neuron, works this way. Under immense stress, we might freeze, thinking about what has been taught. We probably, for the first several incidents, won't remember our training. We will respond with our conditioning.

"You will fight the way you train" is a lie, and I am just as guilty of mouthing it as any other instructor. You will respond to any high-stress, low-time stimulus the way you have been conditioned.

Conditioning is natural and has an automatic correlation to reality. Your shooting form is good and you see the center of the target disappear in a ragged hole. Your form is poor and your shots don't connect, dissatisfying and embarrassing.

But conditioning can go wrong even under good intentions. If you yell at the poor shot, increasing the embarrassment, do you empower the conditioning? Or do you instead condition the student to avoid the situation altogether, to avoid *you*? Conversely, if the students *always* win in scenarios have you 'programmed for success'? Or conditioned the hindbrain to know that results are always good and effort and judgment are wasted resources?

Under bad intentions....

We have all seen the instructor who makes an example of any student who does well. Training to win, but conditioning to lose. The hindbrain remembers, and learns/knows that losing is a safer strategy than winning. That's screwed up, and the ultimate example of training to fail.

Conditioning can be complicated as well. Even simple organisms will move towards pleasure and away from pain, but a child can be conditioned to some mighty strange definitions of pleasure and pain. Confuse the two in just the right way and a child can be groomed into an eager and permanent victim. In individual cases it is not automatic that rewards are as we expect.

Three avenues to make your students better: teaching, training and conditioning. All have uses, all have potential pitfalls. The most important thing, in my opinion, is that the approaches be congruent. That what you teach and train and condition all work via the same tactics towards the same goals.

There Are No Secrets

by "Denton Salle"

That advice has probably been passed along by martial art instructors since the only weapons were sharpened rocks and burnt sticks. Attributed recently to Chen Man-Ching, it reflects a truth most people want to ignore.

Most people seem to want to believe there is a fighting art with secrets that make you invincible. Through my lifetime, it's been karate, kungfu, ninpo, taichi, and Brazilian jiujutsu. It's not a recent thing either: going back through the manuscripts and writings on martial arts over the centuries you see people have been seeking a secret technique or the magical charm for centuries. Gladiators' graves have been found with charms to assure victory. Human nature seems to seek the gain without the pain. Sadly, it doesn't work.

Conceptual errors always come in pairs, it seems, and with the idea that there are secrets to martial arts that will make you the incarnation of the death god, comes the idea that "a punch is just a punch."

As with other philosophical error pairs these concepts are really different sides of the same coin. It's been said that when the devil pushes a vice, she also exaggerates the opposite virtue. That probably makes more sense if you've read Dante's "*Divine Comedy,*" which you probably should.

Substitute 'society' or 'martial artists' for 'devil,' and it's pretty close to what we see today. Both sides of this coin are looking at the complex set of skills we call martial arts, and trying to somehow take the work and discipline away.

One wants a magic key – the power that clouds men's mind – that makes everyone else's techniques meaningless. The other wants a set of simple principles that underlie everything so you don't really have to learn all that stuff. Both share a common root in our psyche and both tend to lead to the same messy painful place…possibly on the floor of the bar looking for your teeth.

The problem with the first side of the coin, the secret art or the secret method, is that humans are humans and that a technique or principle based in human physiology is going to be the same for all of them. Reaction time is about 0.06 seconds to a stimulus and that's a function of the physics of our neurology. Muscle and joints can handle a certain amount of load before tearing and bone has a specific breaking load. So nothing exceeds the limits of our biology – it's a hard lesson, as a lot of career women are discovering when they attempt to get pregnant in their 40s or old guys when we try to keep up with the kids at the gym. There is skill, and it can make things appear miraculous to someone unaware. But seeming miraculous doesn't make it so. The thousands of *fouette* thrown in practice before a young woman kicks a cigarette out of her boyfriend's mouth on a moving train don't show up. You just see the shapely leg snap out with amazing control.

Systems talk about chi, intent, fa-jing, or some other "magical" effect and the desperate seeker (who if he had just picked something, stuck with it, and put in the required hours of focused practice would be a master), runs from one to another looking for the magic key to power. He never finds it because he never stays long enough to learn that the secret doesn't really exist. One reason is that human aren't really good at keeping secrets and if someone had a super method that worked for everyone*, it would be common knowledge in a couple of generations. If someone could make supermen with their training, they would be dominating the world by now.

So the mystic, the secret, the unfamiliar attract him because he doesn't understand it and therefore it must be better – because '*if we don't understand, it must be difficult*' remains a common logical fallacy.

Never mind that some of the talk comes from poorly translated concepts, a culture where information is passed in stories and analogies rather than instructions, or way too often marketing fluff. Another believer is made and he sticks until reality inserts itself. If that happens, and in our relatively non-violent society it might not for years or decades, off we go looking for the next secret method.

---

* I'm going to ignore genetic variation here, but we should note that elite athletes come from a very small part of the human distribution and that the gifts needed for a boxer, a runner, or a swimmer are all different. Bruce Jennings would not have been a successful runner. We should note, however, it appears the variation is greater in males than females and therefore trying to train like Arnold just might kill you instead of making you stronger.

Actually we know the secret…10,000 hours of serious practice. 2 hours a day for 10 years will just about do it. Heck, you can get passable competency for an hour a day for 5 years. It's a question of how bad do you want to be good and how good do you want to be.

The idea that mastery requires a certain amount of practice is well documented and it depends on a good teacher, your ability to listen, and your ability to focus in your practice. When asked by his students if anyone really got taichi, Man-Ching reputedly replied that one person did and it took him a year because he listened. Kenny Gong used to claim that if you worked with him for one year, his system would work and it didn't matter if you believed, just that you did the exercises. I don't think either of them meant being a master, but that you could learn to be competent and at that point mastery is a question of commitment.

There is a Chinese saying that talent gets you 5%. Now on the master's level, say like Yoyo Ma, 5% is a lot, but for most of us it just isn't a big deal. Practice seems more important, which may be why careers track in families: the majority of both scientists and musicians have parents in the field. It's amazing the advantages that learning violin at 2 or 3 or hearing discussions of science at dinner confer. When my own were young and we wanted to start them on music, my professional musician friend asked whether we wanted them to be able to consider music as a career, because the starting age and expectations would be different than giving them a lifelong hobby would be.

Focused practice is expected for a beginning musician, a shingyi player, or any skill you really want to learn. This means you are there doing the drill with concentration and intent. It's harder to do and rarer than you think: look at the local gym – people read while they run, listen to music and yak while they lift, and they wonder why improvements are so small. One doesn't focus or work very hard when multitasking. Compare that to someone whose cardio comes from doing front squat Tabatas. It's not surprising most people fail.

The second side of the coin is almost a reaction to the failure of the first. 'Human bodies are the same, hence all actions must be the same.' Never mind centuries of different tradition, ignore those genetic differences, forget about how dress, social class, etc affect how you move. We are all humans, and particularly we all want to be white, middle-class, secular Americans. After all, the movements come from the same joints and muscles so there can't be any real differences between, say, Isshin-ryu and boxing or Tai Chi and freestyle wrestling. We're all the same and therefore every striking technique using a fist must be a punch and I can mixed and match as I please. (Okay. I'll hold your drink. Want a baggie for your teeth?)

The number of fallacies this includes is like saying all food is limited by what human can ingest and hence there are no significant difference in cuisine in the world. It's closely tied to the general American bobo worldview and it fails as dramatically here as it does in foreign policy. The influences of society, social class, religion and culture are much stronger than we in the secularized west accept.

One of the most effective weapons for martial arts is the firearm, to the point that the rich tapestry that was western martial arts is lost and currently being resurrected as some half-rotten zombie by various groups of re-creationists. Yet, the Japanese gave up the gun, after successfully conquering Korea with it, for two reasons: one was the political calculation that a weapon which made a peasant equal to a warrior was a bad idea and the second, which from period sources was equally important, is that using a gun was so inelegant. You had to stand and move like a peasant to do so, and the early manuals used commoners as illustrations. It was considered insulting to a gentleman to draw him like that.

Contrast that to the longbow in England, where it became required that the commoners practice a certain amount every week from ages 12 to 60 to make sure there were always enough bowmen.

Dealing with just the techniques, the simplification also fails. Let's look at that punch. Are you throwing a boxer's jab, a karate front punch, or a wood strike from Shing Yi Chuan? In all cases, you are going to hit with your fist. After that, the similarity fades out. First of all, even the striking surface is different. Then, the stance you need to transmit the power is different. Try altering the stance of the karate-ka to match the boxers and watch him fall over. Similarly, throwing a jab from a rooted stance in boxing is called being a punching bag . Different body movements and stances develop to generate the power needed for similar-looking strikes because of different strategic and cultural reasons. Even in one system as simple as boxing, with 5 main strikes, there are different methods of generating power. Dempsey in 1948 discussed 4 or 5 methods of power generation, each specific to a strike. O'Donnell discussed many different fist and arm rotations depending on the angle needed to strike the target. Some of this has been lost with modern gloves, but not all.

So even within a system, the urge to reduce body movement to a single type represents a "lie to children." I've been guilty of it myself by reducing *savate*'s movement to the pivot. Teachers do this because it's really important and because if they correct everything you do wrong at once, your brain melts. So we tell you a small lie and then add pieces when you are ready. However, when you pull things together from very diverse systems that were never intended for the same thing, based on a year or two of experience in multiple systems, it doesn't work.

While there is no royal road or shortcut, the changes that occur when you really try for something are magical. Whether the first time you snap out a *fouette* to kill a flying bug or shut a door by just tapping the knob, the first time something shatters and you wonder where all the power came from, or when you just step out of the way of something without thinking, there is this moment of realizing that it's not that hard. Well, no, not assuming you put the time in and sadly today that is the problem. Few folks anymore say if I train hard, maybe someday I can do that. Heck, most people want to learn it in a week, never mind a year. Lovett's story of seeing a swordmaster sitting after a form and thinking if he could train long enough, he too might be able to sit like that just doesn't click anymore. Personally, someday I want to be able to catch a butterfly but I'm not there yet. I've got more work to do because there is no secret except practice.

Breaking: Why We Fail, How We Can Succeed

by Jesse J. Alcorta

I was at a Tae Know Do test many years ago. I think it was the spring of 1988 and I was testing for a green belt at the time. I remember one student in particular. He directed his holders to where he wanted them, set up the height of the boards and lined up for his break. He obviously knew what he wanted to do and was ready to demonstrate his technique.

He drew back his hand and a *kiap* split the silence. The hand and board met in an obnoxious thud. At one time or another we have all had this happen to us. He re-chambered his hand and struck again. And again. And again. One of the master instructors yelled "*Goeman,*" meaning "stop" but the student being more focused on the board thought he heard "Go Man" or "Come On" and proceeded to whack on the board several more times. While this was happening more of the master instructors started shouting as well. This only spurred the student on further.

To keep the story short, the student did not break the boards, didn't pass his test, and embarrassed both his instructor and his master instructor. I'm sure his hand hurt like the dickens too. So the question is: what went wrong here?

What You Should Know About Breaking

Breaking is both an art and a science. The laws of physics and engineering will help get you through more breaks painlessly and without embarrassment, and you don't need to know a lot of math. It is an art as well because you need to select the proper breaking material, employ your mental strengths and demonstrate that you have learned your lessons well.

You need a few things to begin with to make a break happen. You must have:

1. **Technique:** without proper technique you shouldn't even try

2. **Speed:** speed rules, physics proves it

3. **Focus:** if you aren't mentally present, who is performing the break?

4. **Breathing:** if you don't relax and breathe you'll choke

5. **Kiap:** the verbal expression and explosion of power

The Set Up

Once you have decided that you want to be better than "Karate Joe" on the other side of the dojang, dojo or kwoon where you practice then you have taken a very large step indeed. You have selected your breaking material and found a couple of holders to assist you. You must now do two things. You must decide what technique to use and how to set up your holders.

The Power Stroke

Ever play baseball, lacrosse, swing a stick or a Bo? Well there is a "sweet spot" that you must travel through. This sweet spot is the peak of the *power stroke*. It is a point where power is neither increasing nor decreasing at any great rate. If you hit too soon then you haven't generated all the power you are capable of. Of course, if you hit too late your power stroke is lost and you don't have the power you did before.

Stand in a natural stance; feet shoulder width apart and hands at your side. Raise you right hand straight out to your side, shoulder level. Move your arm from your side to straight out in front of you. This semi-circle describes the power stroke. Power builds up, holds for a period and then decreases. Place the breaking material or yourself so that contact is made at the peak of the power stroke. The same concept applies to the leg as well.

Your power stroke will almost always be in an area covered by about 30° of arc. I always suggest that people stand at a 45° angle to the target for any strike that comes around in a semi-circle motion. Experiment with this idea on a heavy bag and you'll get the idea of where the power stroke peaks. For a punch I suggest that you try positioning yourself so that your lead knuckles penetrate about 1½" inches beyond the back of the target. The power stroke is different for a punch and it occurs in the last 4-6" of the strike and ends very abruptly.

I always tell beginners not to have the board too high when kicking. The board should be placed at a level that allows a sidekick or round-house kick to be parallel with the floor when contact is made. This same idea should be kept in mind for hand techniques as well, at a comfortable level for the technique. Once you have established yourself and the break then you can move on to changing the height. Techniques that either rise up from the floor or come down from above have a special place that you should try to center them in as well. That place depends on your technique and where your power stroke peaks.

Finally, you want the strike to come straight through the target. The target is only 1" thick. If your strike comes in at an angle to the board then you are actually trying to penetrate through more than the original thickness. An adult can easily compensate by putting more of their mass or muscle into the strike. A young adult, child or slightly built individual may not be able to do this and has only technique to carry them through the break.

A Word About Holders

Holders have a difficult job. They don't want their fingers smashed or toes stepped on. They don't like to have their wrists and elbows jammed. Your holders are likely to flinch. Your holders are doing you the courtesy of holding a board for you so you should do everything you can to make their job easier. Try the following checklist:

1. Place the target at a comfortable level for you and them
2. Get a second holder if need be
3. Remind the holders to look away once everything is a "go"
4. If it's a power break, or you're not sure, I suggest a third person behind the first two
5. Tell the holders that you plan to take two practice strikes and do so as any more is a waste
6. Then tell the holders to "Lock up"
7. Break the target

In regards to the employment of a third holder, I have found that many people like to lean on the backs of the two people holding the target. I say this is a waste of effort. I suggest that the third holder hug the shoulders of the first two people bringing them closer together instead. There are several reasons for this based on engineering and physics.

The power or energy from the break is transmitted to the target by the strike. Most of it is concentrated at the center of the board, we hope. A portion of the energy is transmitted up the arms of the holders though. The target is only about 11" wide. The shoulders of both holders, side by side, are probably closer to 45" across. This taper means that the energy is going out in a cone instead of straight ahead. In other words the power is becoming unfocused and diffused. By bringing the shoulders of the holders together more of the power is concentrated in a straight line where is should be.

This also brings up the concept of trying to match your holders in size and shape to reduce this cone. Two holders, equal in size, work much better than two mismatched in height. The taller person places extra stress on the shorter person by virtue of arm length. This is difficult to correct when employing a third holder behind them.

Always bow to your holders before the break and bow to them after. If you set up the boards and the holders properly and did your job correctly then the impact that they felt hopefully wasn't too jarring. They will be more likely to hold for you again because of your more professional approach.

The Technique

Your technique is one of the key things that you can bring to a break. A former wrestling coach once told me "If you have technique, speed, and strength then you can expect to win regularly". While I didn't list strength as one of the things that you need to accomplish a break it certainly helps. Good technique is vital though. You should be prepared to tell everyone your break well in advance of the day you must perform.

Proper Striking Surface

For instance, in a step behind sidekick, if your foot position is wrong then you may strike the target with the ball of the foot. This is a quite common mistake for everyone to make, lowly white belt through black belt. It comes from being too far away from the target or failure to recognize proper distance. You must strike the target with the base of the heel or the blade of the foot. When striking with a foreknuckle punch most schools teach you to keep the wrist down and strike with the first two knuckles. Many people strike with the fingers, too many knuckles, too few knuckles or too much surface area of the hand when contacting the board.

The idea is to minimize the surface area that you strike with and thereby concentrate more power in a smaller area. Which would you rather do: Drive a pipe in the ground with a hammer or drive a nail in the ground with a hammer? The nail is easier, of course. More force concentrated in a smaller area results in better penetration, greater energy concentrated at one point rather than spread out and greater energy transmitted to the target more efficiently.

Speed Rules, Slow People Drool

There cannot be a bigger reason why we fail most breaks, children and people of low body mass not withstanding, than a genuine lack of speed. We just don't put enough speed into the technique. Everyone seems to remember the basic equation from Physics class in high school and it gets repeated plenty:

$$Force = Mass \times Velocity$$

The equation explains force – how fast you move multiplied by how much you weigh. The problem is that the equation doesn't tell the whole story but just makes it easy to explain for most people. The fact is that the equation is really like this:

$$Kinetic\ Energy = \tfrac{1}{2}\ Mass \times Velocity^2$$

This equation explains kinetic energy or energy in motion. In other words, changes in mass make a little difference but changes in speed make dramatic differences.

Changes in the speed of the strike make a huge difference. To illustrate the point, we have two students, Adam and Zeb. Adam weighs 150 pounds and Zeb weighs 200 pounds. Both want to break a board with a step behind sidekick. Both travel at 2.5 feet per second or about 1.7 miles per hour. Using the second formula Adam hits the board with 468 foot-pounds of energy while Zeb strikes the board with 625 foot-pounds. Looks like Zeb can break more boards because he has more force in his strike.

Now let's say that Adam learns to be quick with his technique and moves at 5 feet per second or almost 3.5 miles per hour. Zeb will gain 50 pounds because he hasn't been working out a lot lately but still can move at the same speed. Adam is now striking the board with 1875 foot-pounds of energy. Even though Zeb has gained 25% more mass he can only hit the board with 781 foot-pounds of energy. You would have to gain *a lot* of weight to make a significant change in the force you could generate. When you learn to move correctly, moving in a coordinated manner, then you can generate more power than you might have imagined in the first place.

Now the numbers I used here only illustrate the point and should not be used to determine who has more power because the units are incorrect. This is also a simple explanation because we haven't discussed deposition of energy or energy lost in the break. I simply used numbers that make sense to people. The fact remains that increasing the speed of your technique gives you more power. It's a very simple thing to change and accomplish. *Period.*

Body Mechanics

When you walk, you place one foot in front of the other. You repeat the process. You move. Right? Yeah, as if… it is more complicated than that. From a standing position, you shift your weight to one foot. Pick up the other foot and move it forward and set it down. Shift your weight into both legs and then completely to the front leg. Pick up the rear leg and repeat the process. Again, that is the basic process; it's more complicated than that.

Breaking is the same deal. You have to break down the mechanics of how you move and correctly sequence the process and then speed it up until you can break. When you make a mistake, slow down again and repeat the sequences until you can speed up again.

I know I said that speed was everything but if you have little to no mass behind the strike you will have poor penetration. So you need to incorporate more of your mass into the strike. Even if you weigh 98 pounds you must incorporate the mass that you have available to make the best of the technique.

What does this have to do with breaking? It makes it more efficient for you to transfer more weight behind the strike. Remember Adam and Zeb? In reality, they might only get 10% of their mass behind the original sidekick. Ten percent of the power in the original equation isn't bad but if they could get 50-60% of their mass behind the strike….look out! You'll have plenty of firewood. With some techniques, particularly jump spinning kicks, you could increase your power by over 200%.

Take a roundhouse kick for example. The knee comes up, then one hip comes forward and one hip moves back. The foot arcs up and over then penetrates the target. If you counter-rotate your shoulders at the last instant you will have added mass to the strike. *All* **techniques must have some hip motion and that can be translated to added mass in the technique.** Even the simplest hand strikes have some body mass behind it. You need to work at a coordinated movement to make the most of it. You will find that this is the basis for the simpler accomplishments of beginning (3-5 years) Tai Chi practitioners – well-coordinated movement.

Offsets
When you offset yourself from the target you are no longer lined up with it. It's the biggest problem people have. **Many techniques require you to offset to strike the target correctly with power.** Techniques that travel in arcs or circles benefit from this because it permits you to bring the power stroke into correct position with the board. Techniques that travel in straight lines can benefit as well. If your body's centerline is in line with the centerline of the board, as in a punch, and your fist comes in correctly, you will have formed a triangle of sorts. This beats trying to punch straight off your shoulder.

I would be willing to bet that better than 75% of the people I see doing an elbow break fail. The elbow break is one of the simplest breaks we teach and one of the most powerful in our arsenal of self-defense. By using the offset to reset or realign the power stroke these numbers would dramatically change.

Did You See a Stop Sign?
People must see stop signs or they wouldn't stop at the board. There are various reasons for stopping short on your technique. Fear of the board, failure to understand how much power you really need, failure to employ correct technique, lack of previous successes all come to my mind. Success breeds success. I suggest focus and visualization to help improve and eliminate this problem, coupled with plenty of practice. In bowling we see a lot of five pins, the pin in the center being left over. The ball is deflected around this critical pin by the first contacted pins, result-

ing in no strike. The old saying "…no five, no drive…" says it all. You must drive through the board/target and not be deflected from your goal

Focus, Grasshopper, Focus

Mentally you have to be in the here and now. Concentrating all your effort on what you are preparing to do cannot be underestimated. When your mind wanders you're more likely to make mistakes. Those mistakes will lead to a failure to break or worse yet, you might break yourself.

I like to get the breaking material set up and take a couple of practice strikes to ensure that I'm lined up correctly. Then I stop for a moment to clear my mind and picture the break happening mentally. I literally play the break on a mental video camera. Many professional sports teams and Olympic athletes use this visualization technique. It shows you every detail if you let it. A quick mental review may be all you need.

On a few occasions, as I focus on the task, I have experienced a calming sensation that leads to a perception of time slowing down and then speeding up again. The best that I can describe it is to watch large waves build up very slowly and then suddenly speed up and crash. A drop of water falling into a pond in slow motion and large waves being generated at a high rate of speed is another analogy.

Now I am not talking about Chi breaks or internal energy or anything like that. I am talking about a straight-forward, hard-style, physical break. Plain and simple and nothing more. If you are distracted or mentally unprepared then you need to take a step back and gather yourself together before you attempt a break. Chi or internal energy does play into your break but that is not what I am discussing.

Tunnel Vision Good for Lizardbrain

When sparring with a partner you tend to become very focused on that person. Tunnel vision is the term we use for when your brain drowns out everything else. You miss a lot of the peripheral things around you, including the second attacker coming in on your right side. That is motion-induced blindness. Breaking is the one time you need to create that effect.

You are actually focused on one spot on the target. Sometimes I'll draw a spot, circle or X for the student to concentrate on. I'll tell them to put their foot on it. The board or brick appears too small or too large but the *spot* changes the appearance of everything. It gives tunnel vision a chance to work for you rather than against you

I'll Huff and I'll Puff and I'll Blow the
House In

Okay, so I said it didn't matter but it does and no discussion is complete without some mention of internal energy. As strange as it sounds, breathing plays a critical role in your break. Your body consumes oxygen. If you don't breathe you will pass out, then you'll breathe again. Seriously though, it goes further than that....

Stand in a natural stance; feet shoulder width apart and hands at your side. Take a deep breath and then extend your arms out from your side. Twist from side to side and note how far you can rotate. Exhale and note your ability to rotate. Try the same exercise while exhaling and inhaling. You should note a decrease in rotational capability when you inhale.

The exhalation that you perform allows your body to rotate a maximum amount about your torso. This is another key to getting more mass into the technique that you want to perform.

Breathing also helps to calm the body and mind and allows you to focus on a single task or point more efficiently. This is referred to as deep breathing and should come from the **Hara or Dan Tien**, a point three inches below your navel. This point has historical, cultural and metaphysical significance in many cultures and is viewed as one's seat of power where your **Chi or Ki** is stored.

I teach several breathing exercises for a reason. I want people to be well balanced and centered, especially for their breaking or if they are handling weapons. This centered feeling, once you get used to it, can be summoned prior to sparring, forms or self-defense. I practice different breathing patterns while cutting the grass.

Then Thunder Split the Air

You yell when you're in pain. It doesn't help much. You yell to get the kids attention and it doesn't help much. Your boss comes in at 4:30 and indicates that the proposal you're working on needs more work and you want to yell, which doesn't help. You're on your way home; someone cuts you off and then jams on the brakes. You want to yell and you know that won't do any good either. So why does it pay to yell when you are breaking? Well, that is a fine question.

A yell is an exhalation of air. A very violent exhalation of air. It provides the little extra umpf needed to empty your lungs during the power stroke and allow that last bit of rotation during the break. It is also a concentration of all your energy, a primal release of energy that helps trigger a release of adrenaline. It brings everything together.

There are many ways to yell and one way that is very dangerous. Unfortunately most people yell the incorrect way. The yell should never come from the throat. If you had to yell for an entire class and yelled from the throat then you would know it the next day. Your throat would be sore and raw. You would lose your voice or tear a vocal cord. Now if you were a politician I could teach this to you in about 30 seconds…

The best way starts with *dahnjeon* breathing, deep powerful breathing. And then the exhalation, using the tremendous strength of your abdominal muscles. I always tell people yell like you had bad fish for dinner and you're about to throw up. Sounds gross but that is about it.

I use another visualization technique here. I take air in through my nose. I let the air in and visualize my chi flowing up over my face and the top of my head. My chi flows down the back of my head and down my spine to my *huiyin*. The Chinese stylist understands where this point is located. I then continue to visualize this energy flowing upward through my *dahnjeon*, lower abdomen chest and throat. As I exhale the air/chi is permitted to flow out through the mouth. Sounds mystical but there must be something to it. It doesn't matter if you practice Taoist or Buddhist breathing exercises, just breathe.

You okay? You sound funny

Some people have noted that I yell oddly sometimes. It is true that I make a number of different sounds. I have one sound for punches and another for kicks. I have a very distinct yell for breaks and another for self-defense and one for attacking sequences. In breathing exercises I have several sounds that I make just while standing still. Breathing and yelling are esoteric arts unto themselves that are becoming lost.

For instance say "*ha*" in a normal voice. Now take a deep breath and say it with a forceful breath from lower in the abdomen but without yelling. It feels more powerful. Now try the same thing with the sound "*he*". These are Yin and Yang sounds my friends. Different sounds for different techniques and I'm here to tell you it is *Oushi*. *Oushi* is Japanese for deep truth…

A Standard to Measure Yourself Against

The board you break today is different from the board you break tomorrow and is different from the board you broke yesterday. To determine your progress you must have a standard to measure yourself by. The best way to start is by choosing a standard breaking material. It doesn't matter if you like brick, wood or whatever – you must make it standard for every break.

Hey, Watch This!

In working with Master Charles Lewis I saw plenty of breaking going on. We broke all sorts of things. I learned to standardize my material several years earlier but he drove the point home vividly one day. He brought in some kitchen tiles, approximately 8" x 8" square. Now you might think a kitchen tile is tough considering the abuse it takes. We thought it was pretty tough stuff. So we wanted to try a couple of pieces.

He set one tile up on a pair of concrete blocks. The attacking implement was a foreknuckle punch. He drew back and punched straight and hard. The tile broke; more appropriately, it shattered. It sliced his knuckles pretty good. Ceramic materials are like razors when they splinter. The point was we wanted to know if this was difficult material. The answer was a resounding no. It shatters very easily when supported on the edges. It looks spectacular as the material shatters but it is dangerous, as the results proved.

A Standard Board

My first instructor, Master Mark Weber, taught me to standardize the board. I start with a 1" x 12" x 6' board of #2 White Pine. I actually will go and pick out my own boards for breaking. Back in Wisconsin, there were two lumberyards that we dealt with. They either knew us by sight or knew who we were once they heard our order.

I look for boards that do not have splits, a minimum of knots and are clear and free from defects. Sometimes this is easier said than done. A six-foot board gives you an optimum number of pieces for the best price with minimum waste. I have each board cut to 11" in length. This gives me a board that is almost square. It is still a little taller than it is long. I get six boards and that is usually enough for a demonstration.

Unless you learn a bit about lumber you have no idea of what a piece of wood really is. I pick all lumber that is four sides square and kiln-dried. This means that the piece I buy is square and surfaced on all sides, and is generally smooth. It's good for you and your holders. Kiln-dried means that it has been dried in a large oven or area to control the moisture content. Most of the lumber sold these days is kiln-dried and has an average moisture content of 14-18%. Kiln drying helps control splitting, checking, warping, cupping and a host of other dastardly things that wood does.

Sometimes you can get a board that has a large amount of residue and sap. The board feels heavy, sticky or wet. If this is what you want fine but it will be hard to gauge the moisture and the sap when you get one. You really will generate different results each time you break. What breaks easy today might be real hard tomorrow. Standard boards and something from the back of the lumberyard are two different creatures.

The average board I described breaks with about 12-16 pounds of pressure. The average pressure to break a wrist or elbow joint is between 12-16 pounds of pressure when properly set up. The forearm bone is approximately equal to little more than one board. Ribs are equal to one board. The biggest bones in the human body, the femur or thighbone, is about equal to four boards. The skull is equal to about three boards but it is a tough nut to crack. If you break open a coconut you can see the similarity to the skull. The grain is crisscrossed or in woodworking terms "roey" or interlaced.

Standard boards break the same every time and give you a gauge as your power and skill develop. It also takes away any excuses for failure if you break consistently otherwise.

Multiply Your Troubles

Okay you got the one board done easy and want more. Pile on the boards! Most of the rules discussed so far work up to about four boards. Why? That is about the maximum of some power strokes and tends to be about the maximum of most handheld breaks. Some people use spacers for various breaks and types of breaks. I've seen a lot of different objects used over the course of time. All are good; if that is what you use or taught to use then so be it.

My personal choice is the ubiquitous pencil. A pencil is cheap, comes in packages of more than several, are hard to lose and can be used for other purposes; weapons, eye/ear/nose pickers and when all else fails, for writing. Since I am picky, I choose Dixon Ticonderoga Pencils. These are made of cedar rather than the sawdust and plastic composition you see today. They are also still made in the United States and I believe in buying American when I can.

The pencil also provides support across the entire end of the board rather than just the corners. I don't think it makes much difference but that is the way I was taught and it works well for me.

The Water Principal, Sort Of

The Water Principal doesn't get discussed much any more in Hapkido, where it was very popular. You almost never hear about it in Tae Kwon Do except in passing. The theory is best explained like this:

Take a bucket of water and gently push your fist into the bucket. The water moves to the sides and your hand effortlessly enters into the water. Now make a fist and punch your hand into the water. Suddenly the water is quite hard and more force is required to make the water yield to your hand. What happened?

You must be like water and permit yourself to yield to forces acting on you, take the energy when pushed and when something pulls, you push it out of the way. This give and take, yin and yang, is the basis of the water principal.

The same thing happens to body parts striking targets. A slow-moving attack implement will crush under the tremendous force being applied against the target. The target may break but the attack implement will suffer damage also. An attack implement traveling at a high rate of speed doesn't experience the crushing force and the target collapses.

Look at it like this – the body is almost 90% water. The water in the hand represents a hard compressed force under a high rate of speed. It hardens the strike and helps to protect you. Remember the bucket of water earlier?

Fakery Pointed Out

I saw lots of fakery over the years and some texts point it out. Baking boards in the oven or microwave is one way to fake a break. This dries out the board even more and damages the fiber. Storing boards in your garage does not dry out a board any more than it already is after being kiln-dried. Soaking bricks in water for 24 hours prior to breaking softens the concrete and makes the brick break easier. Another trick is to place a splinter, a toothpick for example, in between a stack, and claim to break a specific board through the use of Chi. Master Lewis showed me a clever cheat for a construction brick that involved holding the brick a short distance from the block on which it rests and then breaking it. The edge of the block knifes the brick and you really just accelerate the brick. There are a great number of ways to fake the break. Watch for them and avoid them if you can. Hold to your standards to gauge yourself.

So What Is Your Point?

Much of the time we stress out over which breaks we should do. We don't want to do what everyone else has done or is doing and we want to look good doing it. I would take three simple breaks with good technique over a couple of fancy single boards any day. Especially when the person demonstrates a solid grasp of what needs to be done. But I think that many people fail the mental checklist of everything that needs to be accounted for prior to the break.

As black belts, instructors or as students we need to pass a lot of information and sometimes we forget to pass things along or information doesn't get transmitted. The days of the live-in *deshi* are fading. The *deshi* is a follower or practitioner of an art. Many people just can't live like that so we catch things on the fly.

Sir Francis Bacon said, "It is not so much that we need to be taught these things as we need to be reminded periodically". A gentle reminder of these things is what we need once we have been instructed. We can give the next generation of students this information so that they can be successful. Whether the information is in print or verbally given does not matter but it does need to be reviewed periodically. The two combined make things easier for all I'm sure.

Breaking need not be feared, difficult, painful or dreaded. We just need to make sure that we are armed with everything available to make it a pleasant experience. It can be a stress reliever or a demonstration of proper technique and not just an act of luck or body mass. To quote The Doors "...Break on through to the other side..."

Interlude: Fiction

Just for your amusement, Barry Eisler (best-selling author of assassination thrillers) thought it would be fun to write up a meeting between the fictional (we assume; Barry has a sneaky streak) John Rain and the very real (we assume; he has a sneaky streak, too) Marc MacYoung, a pioneer of reality-based self-defense training.

So, Marc and Barry wrote this interview, where the format enabled them to go into territory usually off-limits in non-fiction. Read it. You'll see what I mean.

Marc MacYoung Meets John Rain

by Barry Eisler and Marc MacYoung

I don't much like bars. At best, for me they're a busman's holiday. At worst, the smell alone kicks me into work mode. Hard to relax. Lot of bad memories and awareness of how stupid people can be while drunk. But Barry had set up a meeting with John Rain. A chance, he said, to "talk shop." The meeting was in the bar of one of Denver's fancier hotels, so I didn't have to worry too much. Sitting down at the table with a professional killer wasn't much of a concern. Professionals are predictable – don't do anything to piss off them or the people they work for, don't make yourself part of the job, and you're pretty safe.

. I had to blink before I saw Rain. He was sitting where I would have—his back to the wall and with a view of the entrance. He'd also kindly left a seat where I could watch the door, too.

Marc: John?

Rain: [Indicates a chair] Marc.

Marc: Nice seating choice. And from where you're sitting, I take it Barry told you about my bad ear?

Rain: He told me your right side is your good side, but he didn't say why.

Marc: I was sort of in the middle of an explosion.

Rain: What were you doing there?

Marc: Causing it.

Rain: Yeah, minimum safe distance isn't always what they tell you.

Marc: I wish I had a story about mercenary work in a distant land. Actually, I was lighting a water heater. Funny thing is, I've had a number of people try to kill me, but my worst scars are always from self-inflicted wounds.

[Scotch arrives on cue—a Highland Park twenty-five-year-old, neat with a glass of water on the side]

Marc: I see Barry did tell you about me.

Rain: He did. I can't help but be intrigued by a guy who back in the day earned the nickname "Animal."

Marc: Yeah, you really have to do a lot of stupid things to get a moniker like that.

Rain: Well, you're still breathing. You must have been doing some smart stuff along with the stupid.

Marc: Do fast reflexes count?

Rain: I hope not. Mine aren't quite what they used to be.

Marc: Neither are mine. I just make it a habit not to piss people off like I used to.

Rain: Anyone who stays reliant on the reflexes he had when he was a teenager isn't going to age well in this life.

Marc: You could fill encyclopedias with what I didn't know about violence when I was younger.

Rain: You more or less have. You know, I've read all your books. Starting with *Cheap Shots, Ambushes, And Other Lessons* all the way back in 1989. I thought, this guy knows his shit. He's lived it.

Marc: I started writing as the guy who lived it. You got Barry to convince folks you're a fictional character. Nice move that, by the way.

Rain: Shit, even Barry thinks it's fiction.

Marc: Well, I won't tell him if you won't.

Rain: He probably wouldn't believe you anyway. But yeah, thanks.

Marc: That does bring something up. First off, I don't want to talk shop about what it is you do, but I do want to talk to you about something you must have mentioned to Barry because he puts it into the books.

Rain: Okay.

Marc: There's things I can't really talk about in non-fiction because they seem woo-woo and out there. But the truth is, it's stuff that kept me alive. I notice some of that stuff shows up in the stories Barry writes about you.

Rain: What are you thinking of?

Marc: Well, in one of the books I remember reading that you'd pinged a bodyguard's radar. The dude came up to you and you psyched him out.

Rain: Ah, I see what you mean about "woo-woo." Yeah, this stuff can be hard to explain. But if you've felt it, you know what it is. I'm sure there's science behind it, actually, though I don't know what it is. The guy you're talking about came over for a closer sniff, and I knew I couldn't just act like a civilian—I could feel he was good enough so he would have seen through that. I had to be a civilian. I had to think civilian thoughts, feel like a civilian, wall off everything else or he would have felt it. Is that what you're talking about?

Marc: If I remember right, you totally changed your vibe by turning into someone obsessed with your coffee.

Rain: You've got a good memory. That was it exactly. It was the nearest thing at hand—a Styrofoam cup of coffee and a wooden stirrer—and that's what I focused on.

Marc: That's when I decided I wanted to meet you. That's one of those details that a pro knows exists, but you can't talk to civilians about.

Rain: Some civilians you can. Barry's actually a pretty good listener. I find he's open to things a lot of people would instantly write off.

Marc: Is that because he's a writer, or because of his previous … ahem... occupation?

Rain: I'd have to attribute it to both. What about you? Where did you learn this stuff? The hard way, I'm guessing.

Marc: Honestly? From a Disney movie.

Rain: Snow White? I wouldn't have guessed that.

Marc: Good guess, but no. It was a 1972 movie with Kurt Russell called "Now You See Him Now You Don't." They talked about becoming invisible by bending light around you and then reassembling it behind you. I was twelve years old and I didn't know the laws of physics say you can't do that. So I just went out and started doing it. I learned how to become invisible.

Rain: I've got a friend who's damn good at that.

Marc: Big loud fella by the name of Dox?

Rain: You guessed it. Loud and obnoxious. But when he wants to go quiet, he's just gone.

Marc: Same thing. I make noise so people see me, so when I have to go into stealth mode, I'm gone.

Rain: The contrast. The Soviets used to do something like this with surveillance back in the day. They'd deploy a big team, some of whom were deliberately obvious. You'd get clear of the obvious ones and think you were clear entirely. But there would always be a ghost you hadn't noticed because you were distracted by the ones you were supposed to see.

Marc: Ghosting is the term I use for it. It's hard to describe, but something that has always fascinated me is where psychology stops and something else starts. I seriously doubt I'm actually invisible, but somehow I can fall off people's perceptual radar.

Rain: I know what you mean. You think this can be taught, or only experienced?

Marc: I don't know. I once knew two brothers who loved to play hide and seek. I told the younger one how to do it and he said, "*cool*!" His older brother sniffed and said becoming invisible was impossible. Three weeks later, I saw them again and the older brother asked me how to see someone who is invisible. Their mom told me the older brother was going nuts because his little brother was unfindable.

When he asked, the younger brother told him he was just turning invisible. The older brother didn't believe it. Yet the younger brother, who didn't know any better, could do it.

Rain: How'd you teach him?

Marc: Same formula as in the movie. Except I told him to bend his brother's attention around him. The funny thing is when I told the brother what to look for, he started finding his brother again.

Rain: Okay, what did you tell him?

Marc: If I tell you, you're going to start pissing off Dox, you know.

Rain: Like I don't already.

Marc: Good point. It's hard to describe, but it's almost like heat waves coming off the desert that cause a ripple in your consciousness. You can see what's behind it, but it's distorted. The trick is to shift your consciousness and look through the ripple to see what's there.

Rain: I call it looking for the absence, but I think we're talking about the same thing.

Marc: Actually that's a different way to disappear.

Rain: How do you mean?

Marc: I suspect this is what you do. When I walked in, I knew where to look, but even then there was a cognitive hiccup. I had to focus to see you. I know two other ways to disappear. I'm just not sure which one I saw before you decloaked.

Rain: I was just minding my own business, enjoying the thought of a 25-year-old Highland Park, killing a little time after a long day at the convention.

Marc: Well then, let's just say the essence of "chair" was particularly strong where you are sitting.

Rain: Hah. Not much you can do when someone knows to look for that.

Marc: If you know how to disappear that way, you know what to look for. That's you taking on the vibe of the item you're next to or the background. I suspect Dox is really good at becoming one with the tree or the lump of grass he's hiding in.

Rain: He is. Most people, if they notice it at all, notice it as an area of uninterest. Nothing there. It's not that they can't see it, their brain just tells them they have no reason to. So it's functionally invisible even though not literally so. With some experience, though, those areas of absence can cause a ping. Especially if they're combined with other indicators of a potential problem, like a strategic seat or other position.

Marc: That's more how the snipers I know describe it. And part of that ping, I call leakage. There's something in the grass that is leaking predator. If you know what predator feels like and it's on the clock, that leak may be the only warning you get. Bushes don't leak predator. Neither do chairs, by the way.

Rain: True.

Marc: The other way I know is to pull into yourself so deeply that you become a blank spot. This one is really hard to describe. But my wife and I had an experience that sums it all up. We were having coffee on the Santa Monica Promenade. All these people were busy going about their business and inside their heads. When we both focused on a spot of silence—except it was flowing through the crowd. Another shift in focus and we both saw a small gray-haired guy who was invisible to the people he was flowing around. He moved through them and they didn't even notice him. I mean, this guy was smooooooth. When we fixed our attention on him, he immediately locked in on us. It was like having a machine gun trained on us. I smiled and lifted my coffee in salute. He relaxed, smiled and just kept on moving. My wife turned to me and said, "He was trained." I replied, "Operative." He saw us as fast as we saw him.

That's why I'm not sure which one you were using. You may have been zoning out, but when another predator walked into the room and pierced the veil, you magically appeared before my eyes.

Rain: It's funny the way these things work. Like tends to recognize like. Little kids key on each other but not on adults. Dogs ignore all sorts of things, but home in on another dog. If you've been around long enough, you can pick up the vibe of...well, if not another predator, then at least someone who's tactically aware of his surroundings.

Marc: Yup. And you recognize the significance of the fast scans people do to check the room. Like you've been doing since we sat down.

Thing is, if that blank spot is coming to do you, you need to see it before it gets to you.

Rain: If Dox were here, he'd tell you he was just looking for the ladies. Thing is, he half would be. He has an unusual capacity for multitasking.

Marc: Gotta respect that in a man. But that's another way of being invisible. Be so obvious that you're immediately forgettable. Or so that what they are seeing doesn't register. I learned that from my dad. Guys he'd want to bust would see the FBI cars coming down the street so they'd drive over the lawns and right up to the guys. They'd just stand there wondering what was happening as my dad drove up and busted them.

Rain: Yes, that's another strength of Dox's. He can hide in plain sight. No one that loud and seemingly full of himself could be trained, or dangerous.

Marc: Wanna bet?

Rain: No. I know better. But even I have cognitive dissonance watching him in action sometimes.

Marc: That brings it back to "what is this?" Is it messing with perception? Is it how the human brain works that we don't actually see what's in front of us, but are searching for known patterns? In which case, that big loud horn dog can't be dangerous; he's just looking to get laid. Can we control the messages we send out? Does stuff leak from behind the mask? Or is it woo-woo magic? Are we throwing spells and curses on our targets?

Rain: Arthur C. Clarke said, "The supernatural is only science, not yet understood." I think that's what's going on here. There's a lot about the way perception and the unconscious work that we don't really understand. Which is fine with me. I don't have to know how something works to be able to use it.

Marc: That may be why you're still alive. All I know for sure is that there comes a point where this stuff becomes a lifesaver to people in the life. Yet you can't explain it or really even teach it. But it's saved my ass on numerous occasions.

Rain: What else have you relied on for your longevity? Aside from gaining some physical distance from the things that were causing you problems.

Marc: Well, if I said my charm and good looks, you'd know I'd be lying.

Rain: Suspicious, at least.

Marc: (Laughs) Yeah well. Seriously though, I think in the end it had a lot to do with learning to pay attention. I often joke that I stopped drinking after my first black out. I don't remember the '80s. But in truth, I discovered something very strange about being blasted. I didn't jump to conclusions or judgment. I sat there and observed the whole process. Probably because I was too baked to jump ahead. In doing that, I found out how most people just stop paying attention to what is really happening and start telling themselves stories about what they think is happening. When you learn to wait before you judge, make a decision or act, you see other elements that influence your decisions.

Also, after a few times of folks trying to gut you like a fish, you start noticing little details. Then you learn to recognize what ones are important. Like his hand slipping out of sight.

But hey, I've been doing most the talking, what about you? How do you describe disappearing and all this woo-woo stuff that keeps you alive and breathing?

Rain: Not as well as you do. I just... feel like someone, or something, I'm not. I have a feeling it's a lot like acting, though I haven't ever acted. At least not on a stage. Some guys can't hide themselves at all. Most that can, do it in a way where you can sense something is off—it's as though, okay, I don't know exactly what's being concealed, but I can sense the act of concealing. I think of those people as bad actors. Maybe you don't know what they're like in real life, but you can still tell they're acting. There's something obvious about it, something artificial.

But the really great actors disappear into a role. The really great actors, you have no idea what that person must be like when he's not in character. No, it's more than that. When you're watching an actor like that, you assume what you're seeing is the real person. You couldn't imagine someone could act that realistically. It must just be someone who's being himself on stage.

But it's not. The really great ones have such complete mastery of the craft that they don't just act, they *become* the character they're playing. They feel like that character. While they're in character, they *are* that character. Deep down, they still know who they are, but it's walled off and unknown, unseeable, to anyone but themselves.

That's what it feels like to me. But like you said, it's a hard thing to teach.

Marc: It's a hard thing to even talk about. We have to use known topics like acting and weird stuff like "essence of chair" to even get the idea across.

But I like that you brought up the idea of walling that part of you off. Because that may be what I can see and yet it's hard to communicate to people about. See that friendly smile on the dude who's coming at you? It's what's leaking out from behind the wall. What he doesn't want you to see, that's what you need to pay more attention to.

Rain: The guy you just described I would describe as a B actor. Good, but not great. The hard part is, keeping the truth walled off, submerged, until the last possible instant. Too close to the surface before then and it'll leak through. Not so much so that most people would notice, but the top talent would. And you don't want to go after top talent with amateur skills.

Marc: That's a really good way of putting it. In fact, most people can't really tell bad acting so the actor doesn't have to improve his craft. They're good enough for dinner theatre. Thing is, if you go after a major player, you'd better realize he's looking for that leak and he knows what it means.

Rain: Exactly. Some of it is a question of motivation. If you want to be a big fish in a small pond, and you're sure you're never going to enter a bigger pond with bigger fish, you only have to be so good. If all you want to do is win the district wrestling championship, you only have to be so good. If you want to win the States, you have to be better. Want to prevail in the Olympics? You are talking about a whole different level of competition, and of the skills you need to have if you want to survive it.

We were talking about secrets of longevity. I think this is one of them. Don't assume the opposition is only going to be so good. Assume the opposition is going to be *superb*. And be intent on being even better than that.

Marc: Actually, you just opened up another can of worms there. It isn't *just* about how good you are. It's also very much about accepting you're going up against people who are just as dangerous as you. Then comes in the added challenge of, what can you do to reduce their effectiveness? And assume that's what they're going to be trying to do to you, too.

Rain: Yes, a solid ability to think like the opposition is a critical foundational skill. But then it's a question of thinking like the opposition, while knowing the opposition, if it's worth a damn, is doing its best to think like *you*. How would you get to you? It's something like shad-owboxing, but it's not physical. It's more... imaginative. Perceptual. And over time it becomes reflexive, too.

Marc: At the same time, it's also knowing how to jam their skills. You got Dox after you, don't spend a lot of time out in the open. They have you after them, don't spend time alone or let strangers get close.

Rain: Judo is like this, along with any other one-on-one sport. What's your opponent's strength? What will he be relying on? Deny him that. While remembering that, if he's good, he knows you're going to try to deny him that, and will be devising ways to prevent you from denying him that, while trying to deny you your strengths, too.

Take this a little further and start thinking outside the box, and in-teresting possibilities open up. "My opponent is a puncher, I'm going to try to make him grapple." Okay fine, but wouldn't a gun be even better?

Marc: Heh. That's against the rules.

Rain: My favorite kind of tactic. "Shit, you weren't supposed to do that!"

Marc: Not only that, but I'm a big fan of denial of what he needs to either attack or resist. Rommel had better tanks, experienced troops and awesome tactics in North Africa. Yet the allies took out his supply lines by torpedoing anything that floated in the Mediterranean, blowing up the supply depots and ambushing supply caravans. Rommel couldn't fight without supplies. I like to target those things people need in order to attack. People don't guard their supply lines well enough. It makes them vulnerable. That's the biggest "you weren't supposed to do that" I get.

Rain: The old, "No, you attacked me wrong," martial arts school response.

Marc: Oh, you've encountered that too?

Rain: You can't mess around in martial arts for as long as we have and not encounter it. What people have to remember is, any worthwhile opposition is looking to attack you wrong. That's the whole point. What's that Joss Whedon line? "Well, I'd kill a man in a fair fight..."

Marc: "Or if I thought he might start a fair fight." Dear old Jayne. Guided muscle as my wife calls him.

Rain: Right, that guy. Reminds me of Dox at times. But that's the concept—fighters want fair fights, and their longevity reflects the men-tality. Hunters, survivors, predators...these types all want fights to be anything but fair. Hell, they don't want to fight at all. If the fight looks fair, you find a way to avoid it. When you can fix the fight, okay, you're in.

Marc: I think you just identified a major problem with not only what is being taught, but what it takes to survive. Guys who are fighting are trying to prove something. If not to themselves, then to an imaginary audience.

Rain: I think I remember you saying in one of your books, "Amateurs ask, 'Could I take him?' Professionals ask, 'How would I take him?'"

Marc: Which I actually got out of an old Joel Rosenberg book called "Emile and the Dutchman." The guy is talking about meeting Avi, a mercenary from a planet Israel colonized. He describes Avi looking at him like having a tank turret turning towards him. I recognized the concept and said to myself, "Self, that's important, remember it." It proved to be oh so true.

Rain: Proving, along with the Disney example, that wisdom can be found in the most unexpected places.

But yes, this concept of "fighting." You even hear people talking about "knife fighting." Off the top of my head, I can't think of something I'd rather not do than get in a knife fight.

Marc: Oh gawd, if we're going to talk about this, I'm going to need another scotch.

Rain: Good idea.

[We order another round of the Highland Park]

Rain: By the way, no disgrace to your book about street knife use. You were describing reality, not a macho "fight" fantasy. Especially your coverage of assassinations. Knifers, as you call them, don't want to get in a knife fight. They just want to knife you and walk away clean. Like the saying, "A bully doesn't want to fight you. He just wants to beat you up." In this case, with a blade.

Marc: Yep. That's the only book that describes a knife fighting technique of calling the bouncer and saying "Hey, this guy's giving me trouble," and then going back to flirting with the sweet young thing. I can't believe all the macho crap that is out there about so-called knife fighting.

Rain: A while back, Barry told me there was an Internet discussion about who would win in a fight between me and a guy named Jack Reacher. He wanted to know what I thought.

Marc: I'm listening. Do tell.

Rain: I asked him, why would I want to fight Reacher? He's 6'4", 250 pounds, a former military cop, tough and experienced. Why would I want to fight someone like that?

I think Barry was disappointed. He kept trying to come up with scenarios where I would have no choice. Finally I told him, look, if I had to go up against someone like Reacher, I would use stealth, surprise, and a tool. And if he saw me coming, I'd run away.

Marc: I take it having Dox shoot him didn't satisfy his curiosity?

Rain: Completely valid option, but no, I don't think that would have satisfied Barry. I tried to explain to him that people like Reacher and I don't get in fights. When we see each other, we instantly recognize what the other guy is about, nod politely, and go about our business.

Marc: That's something a lot of folks don't get. Fighting for pride is for amateurs. If there's no benefit or there's no reason, don't do it.

Rain: Right. I got in a lot of fights when I was a kid. Most of them were stupid. I'm not sorry – I learned a lot from it and it gave me a lot of confidence that I could handle myself. But you get to the point where you don't have anything to prove anymore. And that's especially true if you've been in not just a lot of fights, but in combat, too. You just want to live and let live.

Well, to the extent that attitude is commensurate with certain aspects of the life, anyway.

Marc: I often say that most violence is over things you can't put in a wheelbarrow. You can't put pride, emotions, or social status in a wheelbarrow. But you can put money into one.

Rain: All true. It's too bad, most of it comes from insecurity. Sometimes I think it's a shame boys aren't allowed to get into fights anymore. They can't get it out of their systems, can't prove themselves to themselves. Then the insecurity festers, they go through life feeling like they have something to prove, and maybe, as an adult, they pick the wrong moment to do it.

Barry once told me he had to get in a few fights before he felt confident enough to start avoiding them. I understand that process.

Marc: It's all part of a giant spectrum. When you're young, you want to prove yourself and get status. As you get older, you should grow past that. That tracks back to what you just said in that I strongly suspect that not allowing boys to fight not only doesn't teach them the rules about violence, but also never teaches them that there really are better ways to handle stuff. Without that cache of "violence sucks" data, it always has a siren's call.

In fact, it can become an obsession with some folks. Yet their fixation is always on the low end of the spectrum. They don't realize there are serious predators out there. Guys who aren't doing violence for the reasons they did in high school.

Rain: You talk about this in at least one of your books – the game of "*escalato*". You want to play that game, you better be ready to play it all the way to the end. Because the other guy might force you to.

Marc: But when you know the stakes could be your life, you're not likely to get sucked into *escalato*. Most people who are playing that are playing for the bluff. They keep on raising the stakes to get the other guy to back down. I've long maintained that the stupidest last words on this planet are—when looking down the barrel of a gun – "you ain't got the guts." But people in *escalato* do it all the time.

Rain: Even worse than "Hey, hold my beer."

Marc: That too has a high fatality rate.

Rain: I have a feeling you've seen the movie, "*Roadhouse*."

Marc: Okay, I want you to recognize my self-control here. I'm sitting next to a very dangerous person and I didn't scream when you mentioned it. Just sayin'.

Rain: There's a line I like: "Be polite. Until it's time to not be polite." Say what you like about the movie, but there's a lot of wisdom in that line.

Marc: It's a good line. And his advice to the bouncers when he takes over is really well informed. It's good professional standards. That having been said, I tell people to turn the movie off after the topless dance in the bar before the fight. Past that, the movie deteriorates into fantasy. But the first part of the movie really has good stuff. Including the opening scene where he tells the guy "outside." Then once he gets the guy out he turns and walks away. I really like that.

Unfortunately, in a lot of action movies, they have to have a gratuitous fight to show what a he-man the character is. Here's the stud beating five or six guys. Now you know how tough he is.

And by the way, the cause of my discomfort about that movie tracks back to something a friend did to me. I'd returned to LA and taken a job bodyguarding strippers, and my quote unquote friend told everyone the movie "*Roadhouse*" was about me. He used the line "I thought you'd be bigger." as proof. The joke leaked out and I'm still trying to live that one down.

Rain: Suddenly I feel better about my relative lack of acquaintances.

The reason I like that "Be polite. Until it's time to not be polite." line is because it's good professionalism, it's a good philosophy, and it's good tactics. I don't want to fight anybody. I'm done with all that. And if someone treats me rudely, or gets in my face, or whatever, mostly I find it amusing and I'm happy to let it go.

Marc: Can't imagine that happens very often.

Rain: You know how it is. There's always someone too stupid to spot the subtle warning signs. But when it happens, I'm always happy to let it go. If there's a real problem, the switch gets thrown and I click from relaxed, deferential, and polite – even meek – to something very different. Nothing in between that could escalate things or turn it into a fight. Or that would give someone a warning or an opportunity to prepare.

Marc: Well, there's a few things there. First, unlike you, I've managed to go about sixteen years without having someone try to kill me.

Rain: You're making me feel wistful now.

Marc: Have some more scotch. It'll pass.

Rain: Appreciate that.

Marc: But the simple truth is, when I had people trying to kill me, I was in the life. It was a cost of doing business.

More than that though, the people who were trying often knew how. Sure, there was the obnoxious drunk who wanted revenge, but when people are hunting you, it's a flat-out different game. Namely because they're likely to have it together.

But the key point here, and this applies to the individuals you're hired to…have conversations with, are up to something they shouldn't be. Even then, though, you piss off a lot of people in your line of work. The folks coming after you, or to be more precise, the folks who are sending folks after you, have reason to be cranky.

Rain: I never take these things personally. Life's too short to complain about it being unfair.

Marc: But see, it's not unfair. Those are the stakes you're playing for. And maybe the people you're visiting didn't think so, but that's the stakes they were playing for, too. That level of the game is a contact sport.

Rain: Agreed.

Marc: When you play for those stakes, social violence is…well, stupid. You understand what the guy wants and if it makes him feel all big and bad, then so what? It's no problem to you to give him that, because you know what high stakes are.

In contrast, when you've done all the social scripts that will make the guy either feel he's won or not given him any excuse… *and* he still keeps on coming at you. Well, something ain't right. He's not looking for a fight and your response shouldn't be to give him one. Because if you do, he'll win.

On the other hand, if you've given him every off-ramp and he didn't take it…well, it sucks to be him because now you're going to drop him. Now, your form of dropping tends to be more permanent, but you can leave the country afterwards.

Rain: I know a lot of people will find me insensitive for saying this, but for me, whether it's going to be permanent or not is just a logistical question. "Is it worth the paperwork?" Usually, for what we're talking about, it won't be. Which is fine, because at that point all I want to do is make the problem go away. I don't know the guy, it's not like he's in my life—at least for the kind of scenario we're discussing—so I can get permanent relief from him with something less than a permanent move, if you know what I mean. Usually it takes anywhere from one to three moves of sudden, no-warning violence, and I can leave the guy where it happened. He'll recover later, more or less, but by then I'll be gone and he's not my problem.

Marc: Damn, now it sounds like you're channeling me.

Rain: You know the mentality. You called it social violence—that's exactly it. For amateurs, it's social. A kind of interaction and communication. When you get to a certain point, and maybe this isn't a good thing in terms of your overall humanity and your appreciation of the oneness of the universe etc, but when you get to a certain point, you don't look at certain people as people anymore. You don't want to engage them or interact with them. They're just a problem to be solved. It's almost mechanical. I don't know about you, but I find this attitude avoids a lot of problems, and, for those it doesn't avoid, it's a good way of solving them.

Marc: A lot of people might find this particularly stupid, but I'm going to argue with you. And what I'm going to argue is semantics and something else that's going on.

Rain: Please do.

Marc: Notice that I'm smart enough to mention it beforehand.

Rain: I like people who know they're bad enough to be polite.

Marc: Thanks. In a lot of ways. I not only know the mentality you're talking about, I understand and agree with it. Part of the reason why the name "Animal" stuck with me is that I was raised in a barrio. I learned how to get angry like a Mexican—after all, my first stepdad had grown up in East L.A. Thing was, people would come up to me and say, "Animal, you just went off on that guy." My response was, "No. I warned him." They'd tell me, "All you said was, 'you're pissing me off.' Then you hit him."

Apparently, "Yeah, like I said, I warned him," wasn't considered fair enough warning.

Rain: No doubt, a lot of this is affected by culture.

Marc: Very much so. In fact, I had to learn how to get angry like a white person when I moved into white culture. That included learning to scale the violence to what was appropriate. In the barrio, if you didn't know the guy, you went in to hurt him. Up to and including reaching for a weapon.

Rain: In an office setting, that wouldn't go over as well.

Marc: Now you see my problem trying to fit in with nice, civilized folks.

Rain: I feel your pain.

Marc: I thought you might. You grew up stuck between two cultures and not accepted by either one. So you were always the outsider.

Rain: Classic case of "what does not kill me makes me stronger." It was a pretty rough ride at the time, but when I look back, I realize it was an invaluable experience. It might have melted me, but instead it... forged me, is I guess how I'd put it. If you know at least two cultures, you can recognize what's culture and what's more likely hard-wired human nature. And the kind of acting skills we were talking about...also invaluable. You spend a lot of time learning to be whichever type you're supposed to be in that setting.

Marc: Exactly. And at the same time, the kind of violence that comes at you as an outsider tends to be a much higher level. It's what we call asocial. You're not "one of us." So your response to that kind of violence is a lot higher. I had to learn how to scale back my level when dealing with people who I wanted to peacefully co-exist with.

Rain: Same. And you know, there's one type of outsider who gets it even worse than the usual outsider.

Marc: Half-breed.

Rain: You know it. An outsider is distasteful enough. But an outsider who looks at least half insider? For whatever reason, people can find that to be an intolerable threat. Almost like a disease they feel they need to cleanse from the system.

So in my generation, a white kid growing up in Tokyo wouldn't really have been on the radar. But a kid who looked at least half local, and with a funny accent? Doom.

Marc: Yep. Isn't it funny how racism is a human trait? Not specific to any one race?

Rain: Sure seems to be hard-wired in my experience. Not that that makes it good – violence seems universal, too – but it seems to be in the DNA.

Marc: It is and it isn't. Children don't show signs of racism until they're about 5 or 6. But that often eclipses a much bigger issue. We humans are incredibly tribal. Are you in my tribe or outside it? As humans, we don't like those outside our tribe. Skin color and eye shape are just the easiest identifiers.

But when you get deep within a group, you realize that the tribalism goes even to those who are supposedly inside the same group. This whether it's social class, sub-group, or even doing different jobs for the same company. Humans find ways to "other" each other.

Rain: There are things we couldn't do to each other otherwise.

Marc: Yet if you don't dehumanize that person, you're considered a psycho for being able to do it. That's the real ironic part.

Rain: There's a lot of what I would charitably call confusion about these issues on the part of people who have no firsthand experience with them.

You remind me of something Reinhold Neibuhr said: "Perhaps the most significant moral characteristic of a nation is its hypocrisy. We have noted that self-deception and hypocrisy is an unvarying element in the moral life of all human beings. It is the tribute which morality pays to immorality."

Marc: Oh yeeeeah.

That's something that never ceases to amaze me about people and violence. Of all people, Gloria Steinem said about violence, "From pacifist to terrorist, each person condemns violence—and then adds one cherished case in which it may be justified."

It's wrong when other people do it, but it's okay when we do it.

Rain: Yes, that's something else that seems fundamental to human nature.

I think my biggest shortcoming in this business is that I don't like the weasel words and doublespeak and rationalizations most people use to "other" the enemy. Even "the enemy" is a phrase designed to other. I do what I need to do psychologically to get close and to finish things, but I don't want to pretend afterward it was other than what it was. I don't know why. Some kind of perverse pride that I'm more honest with myself than most. Whatever it is, it's a lot to carry.

Marc: I know. That takes it back to the woo-woo. I always knew what it was that I was doing. I couldn't hide from it. It hit me like a bomb blast.

Rain: Well, if that's part of what got you out of the life, maybe it's good news for me, too.

Marc: It is. But it's not always a comfortable realization about yourself. You can do what needs to be done, but that's not all of who you are. The most dangerous trap is when you start defining yourself entirely by that definition. You become nothing more than a means of destruction, pain and death. As human beings, we're a lot more than that.

Rain: Thanks for saying that. It's something I know, but that I need to think about more.

Marc: Well, glad Barry got us together. Hope whatever business you're out here for goes well.

Rain: It already did.

Marc: In that case, let me know next time you're back in town. Always good to bounce ideas around with a pro.

Rain: Yes it is. And yes, it would be good to get together again. I'd enjoy that.

[I put a few bills on the table for the booze and got up to go. Better to leave first. Given Rain's profession, he tends to draw the kind of attention I've worked hard to leave behind. And if it happens, I'd rather not be around for it.

I knew he wouldn't take it personally.

Section 3: War Stories

True stories from the field(s). Stadium security, bar fights in Korea, dealing with an unstable student… enjoy. You might even learn a thing or two.

Guards and Rails

by Lawrence Kane

I was walking along the upper concourse when a call came over the radio. Dianne, one of my captains, was freaking out (again) and screaming into the mic, so I could only understand every third or fourth word. Nevertheless, I clearly caught 'fight' and 'end zone.' "Crap," I thought, "Not again." As I sped that direction, I grabbed a couple guards along the way figuring I'd need the help.

Perhaps I should back up and set the scene: I used to work as a security supervisor at a Pac-12 stadium. That should have meant that, in essence, I got paid to watch football, but in practical reality some yahoo (several yahoos actually) would invariably start a fight, puke all over themselves, pull a knife, smuggle in a bottle of gasoline, riot, or otherwise do something stupid that would make me earn my paycheck. Over the 25 years I worked there I witnessed, interceded in, and stopped or prevented hundreds of fights. I lost count at 300 altercations…

This game was no different. It was late in the third quarter of the Apple Cup, the season-culminating battle between cross-state schools University of Washington Huskies and Washington State Cougars. The rivalry alone assured high emotions amongst the fans, but the stakes were raised even higher that year because if the Huskies won they'd earn a spot in a post-season bowl game while the Cougs, who were not bowl-eligible, were doing their damnedest to assure that wouldn't happen.

Heading down the stairs I discovered that the fight wasn't actually in the end zone, but rather behind it, on the landing of the stairwell that separated the football stadium from the softball facility. I couldn't see the combatants until I got close because of the crowd of people at the nearby concession stand, but I could discern reactions of the bystanders and knew that whatever was happening couldn't be good. I couldn't spot Dianne either. Rather than worrying about where she'd disappeared to, I simply radioed dispatch, asking them to send officers to help.

Finally, I spotted the fight. There were only two guys involved, one Coug fan and one Husky, both bloodied but going at it fast and fierce.

129

The Coug fan was wearing a crimson football jersey, while the Husky wore a white one with purple lettering. As I shoved my way through the crowd and approached, Coug threw a haymaker, putting his full body-weight into the blow. Unfortunately for him, Husky twisted out of the way just before it landed, so instead of striking his adversary Coug hit the steel handrail that ran down the middle of the stairs.

And shattered his fist.

There was a spray of blood. Two of Coug's knuckles broke loose and were shoved an inch or two down the back of his hand. When he raised his fist to throw another blow I could see white shards of bone sticking out. But he didn't even notice.

Snarling, he continued to pummel his adversary. By the time I reached him there were three or four bloody fist-prints glistening on the other guy's white jersey. They looked just like the fist symbol that some karate schools use as their logo.

Lovely. Dude was not only enraged and/or drunk enough not to feel pain, but now I had to worry about bloodborne pathogens in addition to everything else. My hepatitis vaccination was up to date, but that didn't really make me feel any better since it wouldn't do anything to protect against HIV.

I should probably point out that as event services personnel we did not have arrest powers. This meant that while we had the same rights to defend ourselves as any other citizens, we weren't supposed to fight with the fans. We were supposed to contain situations, keeping control until law enforcement arrived, without physically intervening. Nice thought on paper I guess, but not horribly practical in reality, especially not in the student section or end zone where the majority of altercations oc-curred. Regardless, I wasn't about to let these two bozos keep fighting in the stairwell. I figured that sooner or later, probably sooner, one of them would do a header down the concrete steps and break his neck during the fall.

I directed two of my guys to pull the Husky fan out of the way while the third helped me with the Cougar fan. Thankfully Coug was paying more attention to Husky than he was to anything going on around him, so it was relatively easy for me to get him on the ground and roll him onto his stomach. I was able to hold him there without getting blood all over myself, a definite plus. Despite practicing judo for eight years as a kid I'm really not that great at grappling, but I was a lot more skillful than he was which is all that really mattered. And I had a couple guys watching my back while we waited for the officers to arrive.

Officers from the University of Washington Police Department got there first, followed closely by a couple of state patrolmen. I briefly explained what had occurred before letting Coug go so that the officers could take control of him. Unfortunately he had a lot more fight left in him than I'd thought. After a scuffle, he wound up face down on the ground again, this time in handcuffs.

Officers separated the two combatants and spent the next ten minutes or so sorting out what had happened. Somewhere along the line they decided that Coug had settled down sufficiently and let him sit up. Suddenly he stiffened, sat up ramrod straight, and started shouting, "Oh, my hand. My hand! What are you doing to my hand!" He clearly hadn't realized what happened during the fight, and with his hands cuffed behind him he wasn't able to see what condition his fist was in.

I wasn't called to testify, so I assume that Coug copped a plea. Perhaps his bloody fist prints on Husky's jersey helped make that decision. Nevertheless, I suspect he needed major surgery to repair his fractured hand. And, it likely never worked quite right again. Important lesson, that…

Any time you get involved in a physical altercation odds are good that someone's going to be hurt. Perhaps seriously. Perhaps it'll be the other guy, but it just as likely could be you who's injured. Before you take a swing it's worth thinking on whether or not it's worth it. Beyond medical concerns like surgery and rehab, repercussions can involve lawyers, lawsuits, and jail time…

Is a fight over a sports team worth all that risk? In a sane, sober world, probably not, but in the heat of the moment it's easy to make the wrong choice. That's why thinking about what is and isn't worth fighting over ahead of time is a worthwhile exercise. This includes the decision to get involved when someone else is threatened. I could very easily have yelled at those guys to stop then waited for the officers to arrive without doing anything further. Instead, I put my job at risk (I didn't get in trouble, but I easily could have) in order to physically intervene because I knew I wouldn't be able to forgive myself if one of those guys got killed or paralyzed while I stood by and did nothing.

A second lesson is the fact that Coug did major damage to himself yet felt no pain. That usually doesn't happen in the dojo, but it's relatively common on the street. With enough alcohol, drugs, rage or adrenaline the other guy may not feel a thing when you hit him, unless you do physiological damage, an important consideration not only in whether or not to get involved but also in how to proceed if you do.

Most fights end when someone gives up, not when they can no longer continue. It's easy to hurt someone, as in cause them pain, but humans take an awful lot of breaking when pain does not work. Most folks don't think about what that really means. For example, growing up I lived across the street from a guy who had stepped on a landmine during the Korean War. I didn't hear the whole story, but I did learn that he had continued to fight for close to an hour without noticing that his legs were missing until he tried to stand up.

With good situational awareness it's possible to avoid most confrontations. Decent people skills can help you de-escalate many others. This means that oftentimes there is a choice of whether or not you're going to fight. Going in with your eyes open can help you make good choices.

The O Menace

by Bert Bruijnen

Short History

Through the mists of time he appeared, playing a *shakuhachi* (Japanese flute) and burned the incense stick before drawing his sword…

Though this could have been a wonderful beginning of an ancient saga, the story below is more recent. I run a school for Historical European Martial Arts (HEMA) in the Netherlands. This is not an ordinary martial art and it's a martial art where much research still needs to be done, so it attracts a very broad range of different people. Some of them are, let's say, a bit special.

I happen to live in a neighborhood that can sometimes be disturbed by rather odd people, it is not that much of a problem when these individuals keep to themselves, but sometimes one needs to keep them at bay. Having been involved in different martial arts, I had been searching several sources for information about realistic dynamics of self defense. During this search my eyes opened in relation to the dynamics of violence.

The Odd Individual O.

One day, O. enrolled in my classes. He was a bit of an odd type, but he didn't openly do anything wrong, so I decided to allow him into the school. With weapons training involved, a teacher has to be somewhat selective on who enters the school. I saw him train, and do his best, he paid the class fee on time, but my gut instinct kept warning me about him. This grew stronger when he took a razor sharp steel sword into class and was very adamant to practice with that sword.

I found it too dangerous, so I forbade it. He turned angry, but didn't say or do anything. This also meant that he was on my 'watch out list'. Sometime after that he insulted a female teacher and when I approached him to confront him with that behavior, he reeked of wine. That was it! I told him to leave the school.

He was out.

The Letter

The week after the expulsion of O., I had to ask the lady who keeps the key of the training hall something about the rent, so I rang her doorbell. She opened, let me in, and she gave me a letter. It was handwritten by O. The handwriting was very inconsistent and hardly readable but it came down to sending a letter to me by a third person.

That alarmed me a bit, for I have a responsibility to my remaining students. The letter, for example, which he sent by a third person, was not just a threat, but it was, as people explained: 'plowing the field'. Some of the contents of the letter were phrases like: "I've got very serious traumas, and you won't touch these!"..."I am *not amused* by what you did to me!"... And "...I 'only' drank two glasses of wine...."

To me 'only two glasses of wine' means: he consumed alcohol before class, while he knew that he had to train with weapons. So that admission affirmed that my decision was a good one.

The Confrontation

Then, a few days later it was time for the class that O. was expelled from (I teach multiple classes each week). I didn't have a good feeling before going to class, something in me told me that I had to go to the training hall an hour earlier. I don't know why I felt like it, but it seemed a good idea at the time. An hour earlier I wandered to the training hall and to my amazement O stood there, waiting, looking tense and angry. And a bit surprised he said, "oh, ehhh, you are ehhh... early!"

I replied, "Yes, and you are still expulsed and you have to leave now" I set the bag with equipment against a wall.

Then he approached me, while he was talking to me, closing the distance. As I saw him closing the distance I recognized the situation and from several sources I learned that 'closing distance' is quite a clear attack indicator. I had read that a good action in that situation would be to verbally and sharply command that person to 'back off!!'

I did so, and, well, he didn't just back off, he jumped back! This, to my jaw-dropping amazement. I even continued and said, "Stand there where I can see you and keep both of your hands in my sight!!" Which, again to my amazement, he did. After that he stepped on his bicycle (this is in the Netherlands, so bicycles are a standard means of transport) and he rode away, still verbally trying to save face and get under my skin.

The showing up early was so that he could pump himself up to a boiling point and when I would arrive in calm mood, he could overwhelm me with his fury. This was quite some preparation by O. Closing the distance while talking was not only a huge attack indicator, but the talking was to distract me from noticing the attack coming.

However, the factors that screwed up his filthy little plan were my showing up early too; this prevented him from getting to the 'boiling point'. My sharp, verbal command to 'back off!' told him I noticed him getting too close, my one step forward accompanied by my pointing hand, let him know that if he kept approaching, he would be in trouble.

The fact that I also told him to stand where I could see him and to keep his hands in my sight, told him that doing anything unexpected or grabbing a concealed object out of his pockets, was not possible and would get him in trouble. His babbling and calling names while riding away is called 'woofing,'; that is, to keep saying things that seem quite 'macho', but are actually 'to save his face'.

As the distance between us was getting larger, I let him go. I entered the classroom and it was a wonderful class.

Having said the above, in retrospect, I must say that a simple verbal command to 'back off!' prevented the situation from escalating. I finally understood what it took to not have to fight anymore. I used to get in trouble occasionally, because I simply didn't know the dynamics to prevent it.

What I finally understood as well, was that a prevented fight is a won fight. You win by de-escalating and taking control of the situation so that it is you who decides what the outcome of the situation is, not him. That – and getting home in one piece, and not ending up in prison – is where the victory is.

Zero to Sixty

by Alain Burrese

The two behemoths strutted in, pinging my radar immediately, and walked past tables and the dance floor to where they could order another drink. While the first in this bar, it was obvious the two had downed a number of drinks elsewhere before arriving at this club. I noticed the giant in the corner by the door also observing the pair. He was the only one in the bar bigger than these two, and from his vantage point, he didn't miss much. I shook my head as the two tried to be cool—one even had a pair of sunglasses on.

John and his girlfriend headed toward the dance floor, John motioning for me to follow. I reluctantly got up and did so. I was there to be the "fourth" since John's girlfriend had a friend visiting from Seoul. Normally I preferred the smaller, quieter places that had pool tables rather than dance floors. I liked the little joints in Kwangamdong, just outside of Camp Hovey, but John liked the larger clubs outside Camp Casey in Tongduchon, or TDC as it was called by most GI's. So, there I was, on a dance floor, feeling almost as uncomfortable as the Korean girl I was dancing with. She spoke very little English, and was obviously intimidated by the loud soldiers that filled the bar. But we were both being good friends by accompanying the two who were enjoying the place.

The pair of gorillas reappeared as they pushed their way through the crowd on the dance floor. They were intentionally bulling through, not even trying to be polite. As one walked behind the girl I was dancing with, he grabbed her behind. Not a mere brush, but an intentional grab that made her flinch away like a scared animal. I immediately stepped toward him and grabbed his wrist. Mr. Sunglasses had pushed the eyewear up into his hair line, so I was staring up into his eyes as I said, "You don't do shit like that."

It must have been the paratrooper-sniper bravado that kept my voice steady, because as I looked up at this guy I started wondering just what I'd gotten myself into. He was huge! That was the last actual thought that I remember, because everything else came in a blur. I still had my hand grasping his left wrist that had grabbed my dance partner, stupidly thinking he'd back down and apologize, when his right hand reared back to throw an overhand right that most likely would have sent me into orbit if it had connected.

Now remember, we were still out on this crowded dance floor, so there was nowhere to move, let alone run. (As if running would have been in my paratrooper-sniper vocabulary.) I knew I didn't want to be hit by that humongous fist, so I just acted. I didn't think, I didn't plan, I didn't use any fancy martial art techniques. (While I'd studied various martial arts up to that time, I'd basically collected a variety of colored belts.) Actually, I don't even remember exactly what I did. I do know this though. I attacked. I charged. I went forward with everything I had. I exploded into him with a flurry of knees, elbows and fists and found myself on the floor, on top of him, pounding on whatever I could pound. I do remember hammer-fisting his sunglasses into his head and smashing them. I remember hitting him with everything I had and thinking, "I can't give this guy a second chance."

Unbeknownst to me at the time, his buddy, equally huge, tried to join in the fight and pull me off of the guy I was pounding. John had stepped in and told the guy, "It's a one-on-one, stay out of it." The guy didn't listen, telling John what he could do, and went back for me. John stepped in and rearranged the guy's face with the class ring he was wearing. While the fight started with me and the lumbering, ass-grabbing behemoth, by the time I stopped pounding and got to my feet, the entire bar had erupted into a massive brawl. It took me a couple minutes to find John and the girls. During that time, I don't remember everything, but I do remember the Korean bouncer of the place grabbed me, saying I started everything. I pushed, threw him to the floor, and continued looking. Someone grabbed me from behind and I turned swinging. At the last moment, I recognized that it was an American woman I was about to clobber, and I turned the hammer fist to the head into a push to the shoulder by opening my hand and lowering my swing.

When I reconnected with John, he was with the two girls who were both crying. As his girlfriend sobbed about the blood, he tried to reassure her by telling her it wasn't his. It wasn't working very well. People were still fighting and all we wanted was to get out of there before the Military Police, who were surely on their way, arrived. We ushered the girls out the front door, and as we exited, the big guy in the corner, who hadn't moved, nodded his approval as I went by. We got into an alley and hid behind a couple of shrubs and bushes as a group of MPs ran past on the main sidewalk. When they went inside, we did some E&E (Escape and Evasion) back to John's girlfriend's hooch. Once there, the girls stopped crying, but were not too talkative. John and I were still amped. While the ring he was wearing did a number on his opponent's face, it also broke his finger. I splinted it with a broken chopstick and an elastic hair band. It worked till he got to a medic the next day.

We found out later that the pair had been Tankers stationed at Camp Casey. Both had been taken to the hospital that night for stitches. The few in the bar that knew our names had kept their mouths shut. At least to the MPs. When we got back to the barracks the next morning, the tale had been told. It probably grew a little here and there too, raising John's and my reputations as brawlers. There was a reason we called each other "squash partners" after the "squash" Clint Eastwood and William Smith played in "Any Which Way You Can."

The two things I attribute to my success that night were my physical conditioning and the ability to go from zero to sixty in a heartbeat. When I was in the military, I considered maxing the PT (Physical Training) Test as a minimum standard. Strength and conditioning go a long ways in a physical encounter, especially against larger opponents. Yes, I know about technique, but size and strength do matter. But most important that night was being able to launch immediately into my counterattack when he started to rear his arm back to pulverize my face. I do believe that if I'd have done anything else, he would have hit me, and that could have changed everything. While I've taken some good blows in my day, I can't say for certain what would have happened if he had connected. I don't think anyone can. I'm just grateful I didn't find out.

Many times, when violence happens, it erupts explosively with no time to think about what you are going to do. Sure, there are often many cues leading up to an attack, and through being aware, you can circumvent or prevent the altercation altogether. But other times it all happens blindingly fast. In those instances, you must be able to go from a dead stop to full speed without thought, without hesitation, and with full commitment. Anything less might not get the job done, and in these situations you cannot afford to fail.

Sometimes I think that certain people just have this ability inside them. They are able to process and react quicker than average. They don't freeze in the headlights, so to speak. Others develop this trait through certain training procedures, especially scenario training that incorporates adrenal stress responses. Unfortunately, some people never develop this ability, and others who perform exceptionally well one time may not in a different situation. Therefore, all we can do is recognize that not only is it extremely valuable to be able to "turn on" instantaneously, but in certain circumstances it is critical and may mean the difference between life and death. And then train to be able to do so.

Scenario training, stress inoculation training, and mental imagery training are all methods that can help you learn to go from zero to sixty without hesitation. Incorporate these into your training regime, don't go grabbing gorillas, and then hope you never really have to find out.

Sensei and the Hockey Dad

by Lawrence Kane

There's an old joke that goes, "I went to a fight and a hockey game broke out." It's funny because it's true.

I'd won half a dozen free tickets to the Seattle Thunderbirds home finale of the season. Despite attending several games in college, I've never been much of a hockey fan; don't even understand most of the rules. Nevertheless, this one sounded like an exciting matchup—if the Thunderbirds won they would earn a shot at a playoff berth whereas their opponent, the Portland Winterhawks, could clench a postseason slot with a victory. Emotions would undoubtedly run hot, leading to some good fights both on and off the ice. What red-blooded American male wouldn't enjoy watching that?

I talked it over with my son who thought it would be fun to go, but he wanted company, so I agreed to bring him along with a few of his friends. The boys were twelve and thirteen year-olds, mostly students from my karate class. Since their parents already knew and trusted me it was easy to get them to agree to my taking care of the kids for the day. I bought them lunch and headed for the arena.

When we arrived we found that we had pretty good seats, but quickly discovered that everyone around us was cheering for the visiting team. In fact they seemed to know all the players by name. Talking to the lady in front of me, I discovered that these folks were the Winterhawks players' parents (and a few siblings). I didn't really care who won, just wanted to enjoy the game, so she and I got along really well. She explained some of the particulars of the game, things not obvious to the casual fan, as well as interesting facts about the players. She not only knew every one of the Portland players, but most of the Seattle ones as well.

Surprisingly there were no fights, not even on the ice, but her color commentary made it a very pleasant experience, for a little over half the game anyway... Shortly after halftime the Thunderbirds scored a goal, pulling ahead. The kids were celebrating along with the rest of the home crowd while I was still chatting with the lady in front of me when suddenly I heard a guy roaring, "You want to take it out on the ice, kid? We can go right now. I'll fuck you up!"

Startled, I looked over to see a 40-something-year-old guy at the far end of the row snarling at the kids behind him. This guy, a Winterhawks fan, looked like he was about to take a swing at Bobby. Given the group he was seated with, he must have been the father of one of the players.

"What's going on?" I asked.

"You've got to control your fucking kids. He does that again I'm gonna fucking take him out!"

Wow. That was unexpected. I'll admit to hanging out with my fraternity buddies, drinking heavily, and picking fights with other fans at hockey games in college, but this guy was my age (mid-forties) and woofing at kids who were barely into their teens. He was big, at least half a head taller than I was, and in pretty good shape. He also had a beer in his hand, but appeared more angry than drunk. Working stadium security I'm used to dealing with drunks, but something else was going on here. The lady sitting next to him, his wife I presumed, looked more embarrassed than surprised so perhaps this was a regular occurrence in their family.

In the half second or so I took to respond several things flashed through my mind: I could see the kids getting excited. Ooh, sensei was about to go off on this guy. They wanted to see a fight. And this bozo wanted to give them one. Me, on the other hand, I flashed on all the bad things that were about to happen. If I got arrested my wife would kill me. And, Joey's friends' folks would never trust me with their kids again. How the hell could I arrange to get them safely home? What if my boss found out? I needed to either deescalate this or, failing that, create witnesses who would testify on my behalf, a not insignificant challenge since they were all friends with the guy causing the problem.

"What, you're threatening a little kid. Really?" That was aimed more at his wife than him. She pretended not to notice. Others seated nearby got the message though. I could see them shifting uncomfortably in their seats.

"Damn right I am!" Wow, he admitted it.

"What did he do to piss you off, man?"

"He was screaming, clapping in my fucking face."

"Did he touch you?"

"Huh?"

"Did he touch you?" Reason wasn't working, perhaps a small show of force to back it up. I de-cloaked a little: weight shift, deadeye stare, slight edge to my voice.

"No." He quickly turned away, pretending to be engrossed in the game. Success!

I let out a sigh of relief, but continued watching him out of the corner of my eye. Things went okay for a while as the Winterhawks scored a couple of goals, but then the Thunderbirds tied things up again. And the kids jumped up cheering.

As I feared, he started to react. I glanced over at his wife, cocking my head and doing the raised eyebrow thing. She gave a slight shake of her head, rolled her eyes, and with a disgusted look on her faced grabbed a hold of his thigh, digging her fingernails in. He gave a little snarl, realized what was going on, and

slumped back down, sheepishly looking at his feet. I could pretty much guarantee he wasn't getting any that night. Perhaps not for quite some time…

The Winterhawks took back the lead. Finally there were a couple fights on the ice, but surprisingly none in the stands even when they held on to win, spoiling the Thunderbirds chances of making the playoffs. The old dynamic must have changed. Nevertheless, the game ended uneventfully for the kids and me.

I kept a wary eye out for the other guy in the parking lot, but nothing happened there either. On the way home the kids started razzing me about not beating up the hockey dad. As I'd imagined, they really did want to see a fight. I turned the discussion into an impromptu class about self-defense, describing intent, means, opportunity, preclusion, and justification.

To be a legitimate threat in the eyes of the law, the other guy must have intent (desire), the means (ability), and the opportunity (access) to hurt you. If you wind up in court you must be able to show all three to justify using force for self-defense. And you must be able to explain why what you did was appropriate; martial artists tend to be held to a higher level than everyday citizens. Even if intent, means, and opportunity are clear, there is one other requirement (for civilians and in most states) to satisfy. You must be able to show that you had no safe alternatives other than physical force before engaging. That's the real bugger for self-defense, preclusion.

Could I have taken the other guy? Probably; I'm a karate instructor. But, he was big, strong, undoubtedly a former hockey player, and still in good shape. That means he was used to fighting and unafraid of being hit. And he was surrounded by friends and family members. Could I have beat him wasn't the right question; should I have tried was. And the answer to that categorically was no. In that case deescalating was the correct response.

I went to a hockey game and nothing bad happened. And the kids even learned a valuable lesson in the process.

A Little Social Violence Over Who Gets in the Last Word

by D.J. Dasko

I'm an old man. I'm supposed to be mature and not get involved in stupid shit like this, right? What business do I have at 43 getting involved in a fight in the wee hours of Sunday morning?

Some say that I'm going through a mid-life second childhood and I suppose there is some truth in that. I figure it's just me enjoying myself and screw social convention. I'm divorced now and as long as I keep my shenanigans away from the kids, no foul.

Out one Saturday night with my regular drinking buddy, a mutual friend from out of town, and two of his friends. We did the standard Saturday night bar crawl except with no women to temper things, I imagine more alcohol was consumed than normal. Still, I knew that I'd have to drive eventually, so I had quit some time earlier and was letting my liver deal with the dregs of the dregs.

After the bars closed we headed up the pedestrian mall to get some pizza on our way back to my buddy's condo. Hell Yeah!! Pizza shop was still open and we had ourselves a feast. Of course, that means it was about 3 am as we left the pizza joint and continued on our way East toward the condo.

Now, apparently my friend Brad has been picking on his friend Jake about his height, Jake being only about 5'6". After we left the pizza place it seemed to Brad and Jake's other friend Kevin that it was now his time to pick on Jake. Pretty quickly Kevin has Jake in a headlock as we all continue to amble up the mall. As we walked past this group of 5-8 guys, one of them breaks up this little fight. Err, it wasn't really a fight, it was Kevin dragging Jake up the street in a headlock. However, it seemed to me at the time, no big deal and we kept walking.

Right then, in that instance, it was no big deal.

However, someone said something. I don't know if it was one of the guys who just broke things up, or Jake or Kevin or Brad, but somebody said something, and it was no big deal except that they had to get in the last word.

We continued East and the dialogue continued as the distance between our groups grew. By this time, I realized that in our party, it was Jake who was quite clearly drunk and insistent on getting the last word. This continued through three or four exchanges, and then I remember hearing, "Well, I'm right here!" and I realized that some of the context of what had been flying back and forth was challenging and then here it was – a clear challenge.

Some little voice in my head said that I should probably look back up the pedestrian mall. I did and saw this group of 5+ people running toward us and I didn't figure they were coming to chat.

Without consciously recognizing it, I was clearly taking to heart something Peyton Quinn talks about. I certainly wasn't denying something was happening.

I took a large step to the right to gain separation from the rest of my group and took up some kind of a defensive stance. The first guy was probably 6" shorter and 50lbs lighter and threw a looping overhand right hand punch at my head. Not in range, his punch missed and then I stepped in and without looking where he landed, I grabbed him with both hands by the shirt and using his momentum, picked him up or at least lightened his gravitational pull and threw him about four feet away and onto the ground.

The next attacker was similarly sized and he also swung a big right hand punch and missed. I swung and missed and I'm really glad I did because while the memories are a little fuzzy, I'm pretty sure that I swung for his head with a closed fist. He swung again and missed, but then was in range for the same treatment as his friend. I grabbed him by the shirt and tossed him to the ground roughly where his friend had landed.

At this point, I figured I'd better gain some awareness and look around, so I stepped back with the left leg in a move that allowed me to pivot and see what was going on with the rest of the group. I could see that Kevin and Jake and Brad were either on the ground, or part of a tangle, but I didn't have time to really investigate what was going on there because another of their group was walking toward me.

I had my hands up ready to defend myself and the conversation went something like this:

Him: "Do you want some of this?"

Me: "No. That's why I've got my hands up."

Him: "Yeah, then you need to keep your fucking mouth shut."

I continued to retreat with my hands up. He stepped over and collected the guys I'd thrown to the ground and they all left.

Start to finish, I estimate it took thirty seconds to one minute max.

Brad, Jake, and Kevin got punched a few times. My regular drinking buddy, who is pretty small himself and had been in the lead, had adopted a defensive position near the rear and was keeping watch on my back.

Sure, stories like this are cute and it's fun when you're the one tossing people around and not getting beaten upon. A nice little episode of Sunday-morning-after-the-bars-closed social violence because Jake couldn't keep his mouth shut and let them have the last word.

It was about an hour later when I got home and was taking my pants off that I noticed I had very shallow surface cuts on both shins right below my knees. The only thing I can figure is that the shoes or legs of one or both of the guys I tossed into a heap hit my legs with enough force to break the skin. My jeans were still whole.

In the days and weeks after this happened, as I reflected on things, I still can't help but feel a certain satisfaction in how things turned out. Seriously, I tossed a couple of guys into a pile and had no ego involved and was thus able to keep my own mouth shut and not escalate things further. At the same time, I was horrified at how easily things could have gone horribly wrong. The pedestrian mall is paved with bricks and the guys I tossed ended up right next to a brick planter. There are far too many stories including one from a city about an hour North of where I live of people getting hit, falling and hitting their head and dying and then the other person is well and truly screwed. I'm not going to say that it was fate that protected me that night. While I have no numbers to back this up, I imagine that the number of times someone is permanently injured or dies from this level of social violence is small. However, small is not zero.

It's easy to say that I shouldn't have been there, that I should have been home asleep, that I should have told Jake to shut up earlier, that I shouldn't have been drinking and thus have been capable of these things, that we should have all run off, etc. Truth is, given the situation and how quickly things developed, I'm not sure what I would have done differently.

It's darned tempting to end this with a nice morality tale about how I've reformed and become a fine upstanding follower of social convention who never goes out drinking and stays home watching the television, but there is no truth in that. I've become more discerning about who I go out with, and I drink less. The end.

Even in Small Town, Louisiana

by Michael Johnson

It was the end of a long day and I decided to drop by the Texaco station across the street to buy a couple of things before walking home. Inside the store were three pre-teen boys who were a little rambunctious. The store clerk was fussing at them to behave and I was keeping an eye on them. But nothing happened. As I left the station and walked across a parking lot I hear, "Mister! Yo, Mister!"

I turned to the voice and saw a man about my age and size about 30 feet away.

"Can I talk to you?" He said.

I just stood there looking at him, astonished that I was being confronted by a street hustler in small town Louisiana. But I quickly got past that and started surveying his hands. They were empty and in plain sight. Good. He was wearing a brown shirt, brown pants, a dark cap and sneakers. There was a pair of glasses hanging from his shirt. And I could tell in the fading sunlight that his eyes were bloodshot.

"I said, 'can I talk to you?'" he said as he slowly approached me.

"What do you want?" I said.

"Good. Now that you answered me I can come closer. I didn't wanna come closer until you answered me."

He took two more steps toward me before I raised a finger and told him that was far enough. That stopped him in his tracks about 20 feet away. It was clear he didn't expect that from me. I could tell he was taking my measure and saw that I would not, in any way, be an easy mark. I, on the other hand, was making sure I still saw his hands and was scoping out how many targets on his body were open to me. I was also assessing what weapons I had available at that moment, besides my body, that I could deploy. I had an open bag of candy corn in my sweatshirt pocket that I could use as distractions if things went south. I palmed a handful.

In spite of the negative energy I was giving off, he continued.

"Could you loan me two dollars?" He said.

"No." I said.

He started walking away cussing under his breath.

I started walking away as well.

He started yelling and cussing at me, which I ignored. Then he yells, "I'm gonna kick your ass!"

Now maybe there was another way for me to react to that, but I must admit, I was in a bad mood at that point. So I turned around and looked at him.

"That's right," he said, "I talkin' to you!"

I shake my head and continue on.

"You wanna make somethin' of it?" he says.

"No need to," I said. And kept walking.

Now in my experience, most of the time a hustler will drop it and bask in his disillusioned glory that he had taught me a lesson. My ego has no problem letting people like him think this. No skin off my nose – figuratively and literally. This, however, was one of those other times.

For lack of a better word I "felt" him following me. I turned around... and, indeed, he was following me. I heard him cussing up a storm over the din of the traffic. But he was far enough from me that I turned around and continued walking. I still "felt" him following me. This time, I turned around, slowly, to let him know that I knew he was following me and I wasn't happy about it. I finished my slow turn and continued walking.

He was yelling at me now. Threatening all kinds of ass kicking.

I needed to change my strategy.

I was coming upon a building on my left that is detached from the one next to it. A plan popped into my mind.

I quickened my pace and rounded the corner to my left. Then I did a little jog behind the building while drawing one of my...toys. My plan was simple – circle around the building and wind up behind the man so I could do whatever I wanted to him should the situation warrant it. The main reason why I drew my...toy...is to be prepared should he turn out to be as smart as me and circles around the other end of the building to try and cut me off. No use in being empty-handed should that happen.

Fortunately, Home Slice wasn't that smart and as he rushed around the corner, I was sneaking up behind him.

As I sneaked around behind the man, I saw that he was very confused because I was nowhere in sight. He was so confused, in fact, that he was standing some 50, 60 yards from me looking all around for me...

except behind him. I was peeking around the corner of the building looking at the silly expression on his face and I thought, "If he decides to give up looking for me and goes his merry way, I won't have to do any kind of damage to him at all."

So I watched him. He stood there looking around for another minute or so and then decided to go his merry way. The direction he was going, however, would allow him to see me if I stayed there. So I ghosted to another spot of the building and watched him walk away and turn a corner.

Unpleasantness avoided. But I decided to be cautious.

I was wearing black jeans, black boots and a bright blue sweatshirt with a white stripe down the arms. I needed to get rid of the brightness. As it happened, I had a dark brown sweater in my black back pack. I took off the sweatshirt and put on the sweater – all the time looking out for Home Slice lest he appeared around the corner again. He didn't. So I slung my backpack over my shoulders, continued to palm my...toy...and walked home in a different direction.

While I was walking home, I checked my six several times. I also scoped out the places I'd chosen – during the many times I'd walked to work – that I could hide and launch an ambush, should I need to. Thankfully, Home Slice didn't show up again and I made it home safely.

During the next few days I decided to keep an eye out for Home Slice, just in case...

Section 4: Places You Don't Want to Go

OMFG. Of all the sections in this book, this one gave me the most pleasure to edit. This is information available nowhere else. Getting along in a secure psych ward. A Gaijin in Kamioooka prison. A year under a medical sentence of probable death. An insider's look at one of the most famous martial arts cults.

And possibly the only person who has ever performed kata at the South Pole.

Bouncer Advice: What Your Sensei Didn't Tell You

by Clint Overland

I was working this little biker bar in Lubbock, Texas. No big deal – been in the same place in 20 different cities. Same crowd, same problems, same bullshit every night, monkeys throwing feces at each other and me trying to play zookeeper/babysitter.

Noticed a situation arising in the back corner and head over to see what is happening. Two frat boys are in an argument over Golden Tee (a video golf game) and things are getting a little heated. I step between them and ease the bigger one back a few steps and position myself between them. "This is not happening," I tell them and ask them to slow down and tell me what is wrong.

They both start talking at the same time and I quiet them down and tell them that if that can't play nice then they have to leave.

The smaller of the two steps back and says I can't make him do anything and throws two nice snap kicks in the air and then says, and I quote, "What do you think of that!"

To which I reply by kicking him as hard as I can in his forward leg, right at the ankle, and drop him like a stone. I grab him by his hair and drag him out the door. All the while he's crying about how his ankle is broke. Oh, well, I really don't care. He made the mistake of not hitting first.

What's my point in telling you this? Read on, Horatio, read on!

There might come a time when you have to use what you know. All the bullshit has been said. De-escalation is flown its way south for the winter and you are standing there with your dick wagging in the air and the choice to either take an ass whipping and get hurt, or step up and let it rip. Nothing else is going to work, it is time to fight.

You need to accept these things:

1. You can and probably will get hurt

2. The cops are going to be a part of your life before the night is over

3. What you have gotten yourself into will affect you for a period of time to come

4. Be willing to pay the cost or do the time, the next few minutes can and will change your life!

5. The real world has come knocking with a positive pregnancy test and a lawyer!

Don't be deceived by all the glitz and glamour in movies and on TV; this isn't a fucking duel. It is not a Mixed Martial Arts match with rules and a referee. It's going to be brutal, nasty and over a lot quicker than it started. You will either be laying there with your ass stomped flat or standing there just goddamned amazed at what you did. When and if it comes down to this, then you had better be ready to back up everything you claimed, or you will be the one on the floor. Also understand that you need to be able to explain to a jury why you acted like this and what your intentions were when you didn't walk away. A lot of folks are doing time who claimed self-defense but were prosecuted for attempted murder!

Don't talk! Talking has done you no good up till now, act! Use what you know will work the fastest. Avoid trying to look pretty or like some Van Damme wannabe. High flying kicks and showy Martial Arts moves are great in a sports sense but a head butt and knee stomp work a whole lot better in these situations. You are not trying to score points on a mat, you are trying not to spill your intestines all over your nice new shoes.

Be aware of your surroundings. Use what is on hand to give you an edge. Oh, look! An ashtray full of butts and ashes. Boom, right in his face, blinding him for a sec while you kick his balls up to his solar plexus. What, that's not the honorable thing to do? *Screw that.* You are trying to survive against someone that very well may be willing to bust you open with a beer bottle and cut you from your balls to your brisket!

Honor and fair play are all good on paper but worthless as tits on a boar for trying to stay alive. (I am not saying to kill the guy, by any means. That's a great way to find out that you never ever want to shower with a 350-pound sex offender named "All-nighter"!) What I am trying to stress is that when it is time to act and the seconds count, use them wisely!

Chances are, what you have just stepped in is not self-defense, but a monkey-brained dick-wagging contest that has gone out of bounds. You are not trying to protect yourself from a mugging or stop an attack on a group of school kids. No, you've more than likely let your alligator mouth overload your jaybird ass and now it's time to find out what you can and are willing to do.

My advice is to run the hell away, and go somewhere else if at all possible. Hell, no one has ever gone to jail for *not* being in the wrong place at the wrong time. But if you can't do that, either from a safety aspect (leaving may put you in more danger from being alone with no witnesses) or because that speed freak monkey inside your head won't shut up long enough for your rational brain to take back the steering wheel, then just be ready to pay for everything you do.

Focus on the job at hand – staying alive, and getting away! You have nothing to prove other than you can whip this guy's ass and are a bully, or you are a pussy for getting your ass whipped! Pride is all fine and dandy, but being alive and still having the ability to make your own choices is priceless.

Don't understand that? Let me put it in terms that you may be able to understand. If you hurt him, you are going to jail. Then you will start your amazing ride of a lifetime dealing with our judicial system. Bail bondsmen, lawyers, court clerks, and court costs, time off work, possible civil lawsuit, and jail time. Yoo-hoo! Now if you go to prison you will be told what to wear, what and when to eat, where you will be staying. And if you're lucky somebody will *not* try and knock your front teeth out so that you can't bite their dick when they are gang raping you.

Option two: you're on your way to the hospital with possible life-threatening injuries, spending time in rehab to learn how to function again. You know, the simple things like walking, eating, not pissing on yourself. All those fun things you used to love. It's either that or you're being buried and leaving your loved ones behind to deal with the aftermath.

I am not telling you that you shouldn't defend yourself but always keep in mind that there are thousands of costs involved in getting into a bar/street fight. Are you willing to risk it?

Oh yeah, just a quick side note – a good prosecuting attorney is going to check you out thoroughly and find out that you've been studying martial arts (and your level of training) and use that against you.

Sweet dreams.

How to Stay Out of Trouble—As A Psych Ward Patient

by "D. Osborne"

Editor's note: This was written by a UK citizen and some of the details will pertain most accurately to the British NHS, or National Health Service secure facilities. Similar facilities in the United States, for instance, are unlikely to allow smoking at all. – RAM

Despite what you might think from watching TV, civilian psychiatric wards are, in general, not particularly dangerous. I've benefited greatly from my multiple inpatient stays for relapses of chronic illness, making a full recovery each time. There are things that can, however, make your stay a little or a lot tougher.

The main thing you need to remember is that generally, mental illness takes away verbal judo skills. I found that I had to do other things (claim I couldn't sit still, pretend to be on heavy meds) to avoid getting into arguments and rows, which could escalate into screaming very quickly due to everyone else being just as socially impaired.

You are, effectively, shut into a set of rooms 24/7 with twenty to thirty people, each with their own severe mental health difficulties, social skills drastically compromised by illness. Most of you do not want to be there. You cannot get away from them. This can lead to high emotions much more rapidly. Some people will resort to personal nastiness, drama, threats or even violence a lot quicker than they might if they were fully well.

Your usual ways of mediating social conflicts won't work either, because you aren't mentally healthy enough to use those skills. You have all regressed to having the social abilities of a 4-year-old. You can be aware of this, but not be able to do anything about it.

159

I have, over the course of fourteen months of inpatient time in my lifetime, worked out a few tricks that mean that all the above just completely bypasses me and I remain a character on the sidelines.————-

What kind of ward is it?

There are two kinds of adult civilian (as opposed to forensic) psychiatric wards in the UK – those where the staff do their jobs, and those where they spend all day shut in the nurses' office reading magazines, gossiping and filling out forms. You will have a more difficult time staying out of trouble in the latter case, because the staff are not going to do anything to help you until someone actually physically assaults you. Unfortunately, under the NHS, it's a crapshoot which you get.

To be fair, I have only ever been a patient on wards with a continual presence of alert, caring nursing staff, but I've heard about the other type from friends. If you end up stuck on the "endless dart tournaments in the office" ward, you need to be more careful in your dealings with the other patients as no-one is going to do anything to help you if you are unlucky enough to tangle with someone unpleasant.

Smoking Area Drama and Teenage Antics

The vast majority of psychiatric patients smoke. I don't know why (I don't smoke and never have), but they do. You will find the corridors of the ward completely empty during the day as the 30 or so patients squeeze into one tiny balcony area or ventilated room to get on with the essential business of getting through 40 Marlboro Lights a day.

Stay the fuck out of the smoking area. With everyone crammed in there, you get endless drama. A thinks B is looking at him funny, because A is paranoid. B gets really aggressive about this because he isn't able to control his emotions well due to illness. C starts shouting at them both to can it, because he can't hear the TV (there is no TV). D and E get stressed out by the noise and start screaming at everyone. F puts his hands over his ears and tries to hide under the table, spilling the contents of the massive ashtray everywhere...

UK mental health activist and author Seaneen Molloy refers to the above as the game of "Mentally Ill Dominoes," which as well as being really funny is quite accurate. There may also be schoolboy and schoolgirl bitchery, as one patient decides he or she wants a clique, and passes comment on everyone else. You get the picture.

The smoking area is the source of 90% of all ward drama. If you have a falling out with someone in there, you have to cope with being in the presence of that person all day for maybe several weeks until one of you is discharged. They may decide, for example, to make their distaste at your existence abundantly clear on a daily basis, screaming at you to get out of their space whenever they see you. This makes using any of the common areas of the ward very stressful.

Avoiding the smoking room cuts the probability of having this happen to you right down. You'll be alone a lot, but that's better than pissing off someone who spends the next 2 weeks roaring at you whenever they see you. Remember what I said about no-one having any social skills?

If you must smoke, go in there, stay really quiet, and if anyone says anything, mutter, "I'm not feeling well today, the walls are closing in on me" and then leave when you have finished your cigarette, citing that you feel paranoid. No-one will question this, regardless of diagnosis.

Watching TV

The advice about drama above also goes for the TV room. TV is the other way people pass the time in hospital and a big source of arguments. Don't get into fights about which channel to watch, instead find out which nurse likes your favourite program (e.g. "Mad Men") and ask them if they'd like to come watch it with you. If there's something you really want to see, it also helps to take over the TV room 20 minutes early, so that you have already picked your channel and others are less likely to overrule you. If other patients start to argue and it's likely to escalate in any way, get up and leave. No-one will care and a big row erupting around you is bad for your mental health.

The 250mg of Chlorpromazine Walk and "can't sit still" excuse

If for any reason you are in one of the common areas and someone you don't want to be near comes in, or drama starts, or someone looks like they are about to target you for drama, wait about 30 seconds and then say something like, "dammit, I can't sit still today, bloody medication," get up and leave. No-one will question you on this one.

You can then wander off doing what I call "the 250mg of Chlorpromazine walk" (Chlorpromazine is the generic name for Thorazine). This is where you imagine you're full of anti-psychotics, and shuffle along slowly with a blank, slightly confused expression on your face.

You sort of blend in as part of the furniture and people tend not to notice you. I'm serious, it works a treat. It's the ultimate get out of jail free as regards getting away from troublesome patient-related situations.

The Nasty Piece of Work (NPW)

There is always one. This is someone who is, outside the hospital, a social predator who spends their time living a life of petty crime, exploiting and intimidating others, and usually also abusing drugs and/or alcohol. These people also get mentally ill. They tend not to control their condition very well as their lifestyle doesn't really help matters, and so end up spending quite a lot more time in hospital than me or you. In the UK they will be on the civilian ward unless they are sent to hospital through the courts. They are very bad news.

They are used to the environment and have lots of practice. Therefore, they are in a position to exploit people they see as vulnerable for money and cigarettes and will go after anyone they see as a threat to their position as king/queen of the ward.

This person will likely immediately try and see if you can be intimidated into handing over cigarettes, or, if you don't smoke, money. In any case, you should never carry a full pack of cigarettes with you because it is a major hospital social faux pas to refuse to give someone one if you have a spare one on your person. Instead, keep your stash in your bed space, well hidden, and carry the single cigarette you are going to smoke with you to the smoking area. When this person asks you for a smoke, say, "Sorry, I only have this one on me".

If they try to get you to give them that one, it is *essential* that you not do so. Otherwise you mark yourself as an easy victim for the duration of your stay and this person will not back off. Just flatly state, sorry, I'm smoking this one now. No matter what kind of tantrum the person throws, or how much they scream in your face, just stand there and keep repeating yourself. With luck the staff will come running anyway and your problem has gone away – he or she knows you are not to be picked on and so they will interest themselves in someone else.

Another tactic is for the person to come to your bedspace and demand cash or cigarettes. This is a much more aggressive tactic. Again, repeating, "I'm sorry, I'm not willing to do that" over and over is what you need to do. You are being sounded out for intimidation purposes; don't give in this time to make it easier, as it'll get worse. Keep all your money and cigarettes on your person for a few days, but don't let anyone know (see one cigarette only above). Then report this person to nursing staff.

The good news is that the nursing staff know this person (almost certainly a "frequent flier") and hate their guts. They won't be able to do anything, though, until a patient complains, at which point they will take steps to have the NPW removed.

A woman threatened to kick my head in in 1998 because I objected to her stealing chocolate from my bedspace. I sent a letter signed by 3 non-delusional witnesses to my Resident Psychiatrist, the hospital's Chief of Nursing and a few other people. I pointed out that if they didn't act to stop her harming me I would take legal action, as they would have failed in their duty of care. She was moved to a different ward immediately and 2 days later discharged for continuing to try to intimidate others. So believe me, there is back-up available – especially when it's a known trouble-maker and the staff are fed up with them already.

Don't be tempted, though, to "police" the behaviour of this person with regard to others. If you do that, and continually report them, this person will start to see you as a wider threat and that's somewhere you probably don't want to go. You can't fix everything that's wrong. Leave it to the staff, they've seen this person many times before.

Your problem will be if the ward staff never leave the office and don't give a shit – so you have no backup and the NPW knows this – I am not qualified to advise you on what to do when violently threatened in that case. Marc Mac Young's *No Nonsense Self-Defence* website* is a good place to start if you think this is likely to happen to you.

The Violent or Threatening Because of Illness Person

There will also be, most of the time, someone who is potentially violent or who is overly lecherous because they are ill. The overly lecherous while manic thing is so common that this is why many wards have a women-only section as otherwise us ladies all have to hide in the dorms all day from one hypersexual bloke after another. It's trickier if it's a woman harassing males or a same-sex issue, but the same principles hold.

Avoid this person. Yes, you may feel sorry for them, but they are *not* your problem. The staff are there to assist them with their recovery.

* http://nnsd.com/

You, look after yourself. If they come and sit down beside you, do the 'can't sit still' excuse followed by the 250mg of chlorpromazine walk. If they are behaving really erratically or in a threatening manner, tell the nursing staff and let them handle it. Just stay well away from them and concentrate on your own recovery.

Loudly saying "I don't belong in here"

This goes down about as well as in the *Shawshank Redemption*. You may feel that you've just landed in a ward full of hard-core mentally ill who have all been hearing voices since birth and have been fully "in the system" for most of their adult lives whereas you have been depressed for precisely 6 months and have a nice job and family to go back to – and this is possible. If you landed on a kidney unit you'd meet all the people who have had dialysis 3 times a week since they were 6 years old even if all you needed was 2 days of treatment. Nonetheless, although these people are sicker than you, you are all mentally ill or all have diseased kidneys and that is why you are all patients on that ward.

Patients are very sensitive to any suggestion that someone is "too good" for them or that the severity of their illness makes them a lesser person, because they will be dealing with depressive and paranoid thoughts that tell them this already. So, no matter how scary you think everyone else is, do not express this view to them in conversation, not even to a patient who seems "normal". It will not make you *any* friends and will probably create drama.

Stay away from any commotion

If you hear alarms, staff running down the corridor, shouting and swearing and the like – don't run out to see what's going on. Stay well away and let the nursing staff deal with the problem. All that'll happen is that you'll get a punch in the face from someone who thinks you are trying to kill him, or get bodily fluids – including blood—from someone with unknown HIV status on your person. You'll also get in the way of the staff doing their jobs. You can satisfy the urge for gossip later on.

Colds and Flu

Bring your own *plastic* mug in with you - some wards ban ceramic mugs for health and safety reasons. Wash it yourself and don't let anyone else use it. The communal mugs tend to be washed by hand quickly under the tap so using them is a good way to pick up every cold and flu bug that is going around. If anyone questions you, tell them that you get paranoid about germs on your mug and they will leave you alone. If the staff say anything, tell them frankly why and they will be fine with this (and will also wash the staff mugs more thoroughly in future too).

Personal Belongings

Do not bring anything at all in to the hospital with you that you would mind losing. Everything, even used socks, is likely to get stolen. You'd be amazed what will get nicked. This includes your laundry – get family or a friend to visit you to pick up your laundry and get it done or just take it home. Seriously. A lot of "theft" of things like laundry occurs because confused or highly medicated patients wander into your bed-space and are incapable of understanding that the clothing or toiletries are not theirs. Although this is not people calculatingly helping them-selves to your things, the end result for you is the same.

Some other patients, however, do steal anything that is not nailed down. There will be people of all backgrounds admitted to the ward, including those for whom stealing is second nature. Keep things like mobile phones and their chargers, cash and cigarettes in your designated locked drawer when not on your person at *all* times. When charging your mobile phone, sit beside it for the duration. Consider switching off data if you have a smartphone so the battery lasts longer, thus reducing time spent babysitting it while charging.

It's not just other patients who steal things, it's their visitors. This is especially true if the hospital allows visitors to come up to the dorms to visit patients in their bedspace. Criminal patients have criminal friends.

Romantic Interludes

Do not have an affair with anyone while a patient. It's unlikely to end well as you have nothing but illness in common. There are excep-tions, but generally, this is not going to be conducive to your recovery and it will piss your doctor off.

Alcohol and Illegal Drugs

If you see anyone taking these in to the hospital, stay well away from them for at least 24 hours. This is actually a really common occurrence – a "friend" visits and brings drugs or alcohol in to their "friend". My local ward has a notice up at the door saying that anyone who brings in drugs to patients gets the cops called on them – they got so fed up with it. Severe psychotic illness + heavy meds + drugs or booze can *really* turn some otherwise ok people into total violent assholes. Tell the staff discreetly – make sure you aren't seen doing this! – and stay well away.

Handing out your cellphone number

Don't. Unless it's to someone you really think is going to be a friend after discharge. I am good friends with 2 ladies from my last stay, but we had a lot of things in common other than mental illness and illness isn't what we talk about when we get together. In particular, don't give your cellphone number to anyone who does things like bring booze in to the ward, who tends to be aggressive and unpredictable, or who seems to have a criminal lifestyle. They will try to hit you up for something later – money, a place to stay – and you don't want that.

In conclusion, I'd like to emphasize that Britain's psychiatric wards are, in the main, places of healing where people get help and get better. The problem is that being stuck around all these random people is an unfortunate side. Most of what you risk encountering is simply schoolkid social dynamics, but that wasn't any fun when you were 8 and it won't be fun now that you're 45 and ill. I hope this guide helps you avoid these annoyances, so that you can concentrate on working with your medical team on your recovery and your good health.

Martial Arts Cults

by "Chop Ki"

Over time I've had many people ask about cult experiences, specifically Martial Arts (MA) cults. I've also heard people wondering how or if such a thing—a Martial Arts cult—could exist. Well, I'll go on record and say that they are a one hundred percent certainty. What follows is a description of how cult behavior manifests itself in the MA setting, at least in my experiences.

Before we get to experiences we need to define a couple of things.

The word "cult" has a few different meanings. If you look it up in just about any dictionary, and I've looked it up in many a dictionary, the first few definitions usually have to deal with religion. It's worded slightly different from dictionary to dictionary, but they usually have to do with splinter groups of a main religion, something that I would call a sect. Then the definitions usually turn to something on the order of obsessive or faddish devotion to some person, principle, thing or idea. In the modern sense, when most people hear the word "cult" this is what they think of.

There is an extremely wide range here, from the mild "we think X is the best forget the rest" when applied to a single topic, all the way up to the full blown "don't drink the Kool-Aid" cults that grab all the headlines. Such it is with a MA cult as well.

In fact, most of the groups out there are on the mild end of the spectrum and I don't really think of them as cults, but rather groups that exhibit cult-like behavior. These are what a lot of folks call "personality cults"; however they really can be not strictly associated with a person (usually an instructor). Quite often when talking about the MAs, they are associated with a style. These are the typical "my instructor is the best, our style is the best" McDojo groups where the particular style and/ or instructor is seen as the be all and end all. While they can get rather fanatical about this (and fantastical as well), unless the subject of MA is being discussed, such as when they're rattling keyboards on multitudes of forums, they go about their normal lives until they strap on their gear and head to their particular temple, I mean dojo (or dojang, quan, school, whatever).

Yes, they can get quite rabid about the subject. Yes, they are very fanatical about the object(s) of their adoration. To me however, these are just groups exhibiting cult-like behavior for one simple reason: it's just one aspect of their lives, it's not what their *entire* life (at least their life at the time) is based on. Quite simply, they don't live it.

Yes, of course there are differing degrees and there are some who are fanatical enough that when they are away from the group they only have thoughts of when they will be with the group next. They go to school, or work, or home – most probably all of these – but just can't wait to get back to what they love and think about all the while they are gone. These are individuals however, not the group. Where things start to move farther up the scale is when it starts to be not individuals doing this on their own, but as a group.

The next defining characteristic is when the group starts to demand it from the individual. It's one thing for an individual to become fanatical on his own, another when a couple of people do this in concert (most likely on their own until they discover that there are others who feel as they do), quite another still when larger percentages of the group join in this adoration. A critical point is reached when it is the majority of the group – and by majority I mean much more than not, which is different than almost all. It does keep progressing until it gets to the point of almost all, if not all, of the members are in agreement. There is one thing still missing though: the group doesn't *demand* it. They might think a certain member is odd, they might not be able to understand how someone doesn't see it the way they do, but they do not *demand* that this thought be there. These are why I call them cult-like groups.

To me a true cult:

1. Demands that the member(s) think and act in accordance with all of their beliefs, and

2. The member(s) lives are totally dominated by their association with the group.

That is what I meant before when I said they did not live it. Their time away from the group is just as much a part, and has just as much influence on their lives, as their time with the group. In fact, for a lot of these folks unless the specific subject, MA in this case, is being discussed, it really might have little influence on the rest of the areas of their life. This is as opposed to living solely for the group, with your time away from the group being some sort of direct contribution to the group (more on this later).

When I see these two things, I switch from saying a group is cult-like and begin to say that this is indeed a cult. I base this on having been in and lived with a cult for fourteen years from the ages of nineteen to thirty three. My association with them ended eighteen years ago.

Of course I usually don't go around stating that fact in public discussions for the simple and obvious reason that quite often it gets what I call the "Alice's Restaurant Massacre" response ("...and they all moved away from me on the bench there, with a hairy eyeball and all kinds a mean, ugly, nasty things..."); Arlo Guthrie fans of that particular song will know what I mean immediately. As for the rest of you, suffice it to say that most folks look at you like you're a very odd duck, which I suppose in comparison to the general population you are, but I think this is based on numerous misconceptions. Most people just can't fathom how such a thing can happen.

They will look at you as if you are naïve, weak minded, gullible, foolish, and even stupid. I mean really; how could an intelligent and mentally well-adjusted person get sucked into such a thing!?!

Once they learn I was nineteen they say, "oh yes that must be the reason, a young foolish lad," but there were members who didn't come into the group until they were in their sixties.

Yes, but how intelligent were they?

Well let's see, there were doctors (MDs from all specialties of medicine) and lawyers and PhDs in psychology from major universities that you know well, and accountants and IT professionals and CEOs of major corporations that you know well, and just about anybody from any walk of life you could think of, including politicians from very high up in past and present administrations that you know well on down to nineteen year old music majors like me

To the folks who have the thought, and trust me I've seen it on their faces many a time, that *they* couldn't possibly fall for such a thing, I simply smile and think to myself, "I hope you never fall in the crosshairs of a con man, my friend," because let me tell you there is a con for everybody and that's exactly what this is, nothing but a con game. Those who think they're immune will fall the hardest (more on this in a moment).

A lot of the reason for the misconceptions, at least in my opinion, is that most folks just don't have any idea of how the game is played.

They have this thought that the person jumps into the group with both feet, knowing full well what it looks and feels and sounds and smells and tastes like, when that's not it at all. It's like the old saw about the frog and the boiling water. I have no idea if it's true, but the tale is that if you throw a frog into a shallow pot of boiling water it will immediately jump out because of the pain. If on the other hand you put the frog into a shallow pot of nice cool water, then start to heat the water up slowly, the frog will not try to escape, even though it is very easy to do so by simply jumping out, and will happily remain there until he is cooked. It's immersion by degrees. Little by little, slowly over time, little details change until you are not in the same pot any longer and you are had.

Some folks like to call it the weird-shit-O-meter. Slowly, over time more and more things are introduced. Things that get progressively weirder, but none too much weirder than the last, until you arrive at some monumentally weird shit. The thing is that because every incremental step is just the most miniscule amount weirder than the last, nothing seems outrageous. If someone were to be given situation A, which isn't really too weird at all, and then immediately plunged into situation Z, which is monumentally weird, they would say "holy shit, that's just too weird!" However, if situation A led to situation B, which is just the slightest amount weirder, and then to situation C successively on through all the way to situation Z, with every situation getting weirder as we go, they, like our little frog, would never see a reason to jump out of the pot because it's never very much weirder than it was just a moment ago. Situation Z doesn't seem all that weird when compared to situation Y if Y is your "normal". Through immersion by degrees, which most likely also has the inclusion of the passage of time, every step of the way becomes the new "normal". What was once an outrageous thought, now becomes a normal thought; being that Y is "normal," Z is not so far away. It is from A, though.

OK, back to the con game. Before when I said there is a con for everyone, and that those who think they are immune will fall the hardest, this is because not every con is for everybody, but there *is* a con for you, my friend. The reason for this is because in order for a con to work, the person being conned has to be an active participant. They have to *want* to go along with the con or it will not work.

Now it's easy to say, "well who would do this if they see it coming," but that's just it, the con man is playing off of what *you* want and when it comes to getting what they want, humans are capable of ignoring a lot of weird shit; things that would set off the weird-shit-O-meter of other folks are ignored. This is because it's not what *they* want, but rather what *you* want. Those that want the same thing are blinded by the same thing; those that don't want that thing aren't blinded by it.

Most con games are financial and work because of the greed of people, hence the saying "you can't con an honest man." The "mark" is given the illusion that they can have something for nothing, or at least at a "steal" (there's even a theme to the slang) and jump at the chance. They know full well that there's no such thing as a free lunch, but the temptation to get away with something is too great and "wham," they're stung.

Greed is the hallmark of the financial con, but there are many different cons out there, and they don't all work on the same emotion. The overriding factor though, is that the "mark" – in the case of our discussion the potential cult inductee – needs to be a willing participant in this little con; they need to *want* something. Our con man (i.e. cult leadership) is just going to give them what they want, and by degrees, little by little, they are drawn in until "the water is boiling".

So, what are the emotions that make this cult con, specifically this MA cult con work? Well I guess the best way is to tell you some of my experiences.

First you need to know something about my nineteen year old outlook and feelings.

It's the late seventies and the U.S. has, for about a decade now, been introduced to the MA via such things as Bruce Lee movies and TV series like "*Kung Fu,*" and Chuck Norris in "*A Force of One*". Sure, there are those in the know who have been into the MA for many years before this, but until the seventies it was pretty much unknown in the mainstream U.S. culture.

Because of these Hollywood influences, the public is usually under the impression (or at least everyone I knew was), that the MA was something practiced by Shaolin monks who wandered the countryside searching for meaning and doing good. In fact the MA as characterized by these accounts, was a lifestyle where everyone could "know themselves" and live in peace and harmony with their fellow man and indeed, the universe.

When you are what Eric Hoffer in "*The True Believer: Thoughts On The Nature Of Mass Movements*" calls "the discontent," of which he gives many definitions, you are looking for change. A nineteen year old whose parents were just recently divorced and who is struggling to understand what he even wants to do with his life, sees many discrepancies between how he's been taught that people should treat each other and how they actually do—1979 was a record-breaking year for murders in Chicago, topping 1000 that year—and sees duplicity everywhere. He is just such a "discontent" who is looking for change.

What better way than to embrace the MA lifestyle? A lifestyle where everybody can learn to live in peace and harmony as a warrior monk! Hey, I didn't say I was a *smart* nineteen year old! Not stupid either. I was a nineteen year old who *wanted* something though.

January 1, 1980, enter the MA school. Yes, they were open on New Year's day, the only school in a ten mile radius (hell, probably more) that was. The ad looked soooo much better than the others. It had the look of, umm, well, like it was an honest to goodness Zen Buddhist temple or something. Like I knew what one looked like or what, or even if, there was a connection between that and the MA. But in the ad it looked like the place I had been searching for. Not one of these other cheesy dojos that you might find the Jim Carey character of "You Attacked Me Wrong" in*.   There were many of those around to be sure. When I went in I was *not* disappointed!

I went in and they quickly got me talking. I wasn't much of a challenge as I proudly proclaimed why I was there in no uncertain terms. I'm sure they were just wringing their hands in anticipation. They put on quite a show, what a demonstration, what a beating I took, *I was hooked*! They gave me exactly what I was asking for, just like any good con man would. I wanted something, and they provided it; it was a con built just for me.

Let me say something right now though, before I go on any further. I wouldn't trade the MA training I got from this group. I know of only one person personally that I would train with who can hold a candle to them. You know who you are Bro. I know many excellent martial artists, people much more advanced than me in many ways, but truth be told, from my point of view, the folks I learned from would turn us all upside down and inside out. That's just my opinion. Let's just say that I received *very* good training. I'm about to paint them as the vermin that they are, but they were some great martial artists. *Sigh*, if only they had gone about things on the legit, it could have all been different for them,

* http://www.youtube.com/watch?v=XAWFBbQa_84

and me for that fact. The same ends would have been achieved as that which was sought through nefarious means: what a pity.

One thing that they did teach me, Oom/Yung, or Yin/Yang or whatever you want to call it, the principle remains the same, nothing is either all good, or all bad, there is a little of both in everything. I am what I am today because of my time there, and a lot of things I see every day in other people I'm glad they beat out of me. They did it for reasons that were not so noble, but the result has served me, so I guess it wasn't all bad.

OK, back to the cult-bashing!

So anyway, they've seen what motivates you, they've given you what *you* want, you've signed up, now they have to do two things; they have to keep you signed up and they have to "test" you to see if you're "cult material."

You see, just because you are a student in the school, it doesn't mean that you are a member, or could be a member, of the cult. Not everyone makes the grade, after all. Some folks will simply be students for a while, some folks will just be fodder for their coffers and some will be chosen to be in the inner group, the select few, the "elite". You have to be "tested" first to see if you're a fit. This is where the immersion by degrees comes in. Where the weird shit starts at situation A and progresses to as far as you can take. If you make it through to the monumentally weird shit, then like our frog you are in the boiling water and are cooked.

Kind of a wild ass thing about the first couple of groups I mentioned, they populate the forums and spout all kinds of shit about being taken advantage of by the big bad cult, but they weren't even *in* the cult. They just happen to be a student at the school and figured that they were in the cult. Some of these silly sons of bitches even spout off like it's a badge of honor that they "were in the cult and escaped". Shit! They don't even know what they don't know. I guess it's just their fifteen minutes of fame after the FBI/IRS/ATF raid (more on that latter)!

Anyway, now the tests begin (and I don't mean belt tests).

It all starts with something small, such as going somewhere to get some lunch for the instructor. You see, he's in a MA uniform, and he'd get weird looks if he went out in that and got his own lunch, so could you just do this for him. Now this is not to say that *every* instructor who asks a student to run next door is a cult leader testing you, so don't get me wrong, but that's just it. It's something that *anybody* might ask, so it's not too far on the wired-shit-O-meter, but it tells them if you'd do a little something for them.

Side note, I just mentioned an instructor being a cult leader, but in the real deal, the "Master," the top of the group, the grand high poobah is not going to be the guy sitting behind the desk in front of you. He/she's going to be some deity figure that is up on the wall in a photo. The guy might not even be alive any longer and you might have a band of crooks cashing in on his legacy, but if he is alive, he'll make *very* limited, few and far between visits when your particular dojo is "worthy" of such a visit. After all, the familiar cannot be as mystical as the exotic!

Back to our immersion by degrees. The things that will be asked will start to go further on down the scale. Could be an odd errand, could be passing flyers for the school, could be "special" sessions called at odd times, could be washing or fixing the instructor's car, but whatever it is, it will get further and further out there as time goes by. What they are looking for is the point where your weird-shit-O-meter goes off.

If you keep on going along with things, they'll keep on giving you the next level to see if this is where you jump out of the pot.

All along you will be given the doctrine of the group in small doses. As you digest these more will be added. It's a total immersion. Physically you will be pushed, mentally you will be pushed, and spiritually you will be pushed. The idea is to see how far you are willing to go in all areas.

All along they will make sure to keep giving you what it is that you initially sought them out for. If they do not, then you will be lost for sure. Of course you can be lost at any point in time during this whole procedure, but then that's the point, to see who is willing and who is not.

Oh, let's not forget the most important part of all of this: you will be pushed financially. In fact all of the rest of this is really just warm ups for this portion. Well, not really, a lot of that depends on the mentality of the leader. That is to say, just how much of a megalomaniac (s)he/they can be. Money is not always the key, sometimes it's power, as in power over people (to what extent can I control their lives) – most often it's both. This is a financial thing after all though, so you're going to be asked to part with money and lots of it.

It starts with small steps like getting on the advanced course. Pretty soon you find out that the advanced course is not really *that* advanced because there is another after that, and so on. This will progress until you are on the most advanced course that's offered, or so you think, but we'll get back to that later.

To sum up the experience so far you will be pushed to spend more and more time. This time will be split among several areas like more and more intense physical training (on the order of four hours a day for six days a week for starters and even more later on). The whole time you will be indoctrinated with the groupthink – a lot of "this is a us/them"- based spiel that is meant to slowly start to get you thinking that 'only the group has The Truth™' and that 'only the group cares about you' and 'only the group…' etc.; it depends on the group's agenda. You will be asked to do things that are farther and farther out there to see what it is you will do for the group, and you will be asked for larger and larger amounts of money because after all, you can't put a price tag on your mind and body and what you are learning you can't get anywhere else. The sad thing is you're not even in the cult yet. I say it's sad because things are going to get even weirder and wilder when you *are* in the cult, but for right now, they're just weeding out those who aren't so serious.

At this point you might ask, "Why are you going along with this?" Well, remember the part about wanting something from them? Remember that a good con man is just seemingly giving you whatever it is that *you* want? Well, they've not forgotten. All along they'll make sure that you are getting the fantasy dream that you're there for in the first place, because after all, if it was obtainable anyplace else (hint, hint, there's a reason I said fantasy) why would you do all of this? No, they'll make sure that you keep getting the dose of alternate reality that you crave.

For some folks it's the killer commando Kung Fu fantasy. For some it's peace and happiness for all. For some it's a sense of belonging to a group when no group has wanted them before. It could be any one of a million things. That's a hallmark, really, the fact that this group can be all things to all people at the same time. They simply shape reality to custom fit the individual.

One of the techniques, if not *the* technique, is through the training. After a couple of hours of grueling training, when you're beat and dead tired, that's when the indoctrination sessions usually begin. Always physical, then mental, that's the key. Yin then yang, hard then soft, action then words. They know the subject well and *that* is why so many go along with this. Not everyone however, which is why this is a weeding out process.

After you've gotten to a certain point it's time to join the group in earnest. If this was the mob they would say that you are now a soldier. For the MA cult this is your first degree black belt test. Up until now it's all been playtime folks, now comes the real deal. You are either going to be in or out at this point. You will decide that this is the life for you, or you will be pushed to the side. If the latter happens, then it's only a matter of time before you leave for good. Usually if you've gotten this far they will do everything in their power to get you in because you've shown that you have been willing to go along up until now and they've invested an awful lot of time, but hey, even at this point it's not going to be for everybody: it mainly depends on how much you are still pursuing that "thing" you wanted and if in your eyes they've delivered. In my case they did, or of course I should say it *seemed* as if they did. If so, you're in!

Now is when *all* of the fun begins. The weird-shit-O-meter would be going off on just about anybody else you know, except other group members of course, because the stuff you're about to see is so wild that it'd make the average person's head spin. You, however, have been exposed to so much by now that it's just another day to you.

At about this point it'll be suggested that you move in with some other members of the group. Remember you're in, but you're still the lowest member of the group, so if it gets too weird even for you, they run the risk that you'll bolt. So for now, it's a suggestion. Part of the reason is financial, and part of the reason is control.

Control because you can now be monitored when you're not "on duty," that is at the MA school. I say on duty because you are now an assistant instructor. They need free labor after all, and teaching is part of your training. You are expected to do a certain amount in and around the school. This will not be limited to helping teach; there will be other errands and chores. Of course you will also have to keep up your practice – how are you ever going to pass for your next belt and become an instructor if you don't?

The financial part is because if you recall you thought you were on the highest course there was. Well surprise, that was the highest course for "civilians" my friend: for those in the *real* group (cult) there is the *real* training, and it's not cheap. That's why they make the friendly suggestion that you live with other assistants. If they can get four, or five, or six of you living in the same apartment, the rent can be spread out and you'll have that much more money available to pay for that "Certificate" course you are now on. You are going to need it after all, when the day comes that you are qualified and can open your own school.

No dufus, it won't really be *your* school, they're just calling it that for now to keep you going. It's really the carrot and stick approach that they use. Most of the time you are chasing the carrot, but at this point, they just might not hesitate to use the stick if the situation calls for it.

Living with other members lets them also keep tabs on you when you're not in the school. They'll know when you're coming and going because the other members will have to report if asked. It *is* for your own good, however, because "the path has many pitfalls and we need to keep watch on each other lest we fall in."

Your time will be so taken up, what with a full time job (how else are you going to get money to give to them, silly), your time at the school and your own lessons and practice. At this point a sixteen hour or more day is normal and it could go higher. In fact pretty soon it *will* go higher; for me it got as high as a twenty two hour day, I shit you not. With all this time you'll start to see less and less of your friends and family until it dwindles down to just about none. Your family will start to get concerned, your old friends will just give up on you and stop calling.

The group leaders, what Marc likes to call the "Bitch Squad," will not forget to point out that "See, we told you they were only fair weather friends, they've left you." Of course it is *you* who have left *them*, but this fact will escape you because they've been telling you it would be coming all along and now it's happened – "See? They were right". Marc's description (see link below)of them is right on, by the way – with the exception that if the supreme leader is always on premises and they just keep the peasants at bay, I tend to think it's more of a cult-like group as opposed to a full cult. In our real deal the leader will almost *never* be there. He will be worshiped from afar like a real deity and make a once a year appearance to the masses. The Bitch Squad will have much more frequent contact with him, though, and that access is the promise that you're working towards now: being one of the lucky few. http://www. nononsenseselfdefense.com/cultauthority.htm

You will get some time to spend on your own, but it will be vanishingly small. Saturday nights, Sundays, holidays and precious few other times will be yours. You will now be spending just about all of your time with the group or at work, and there will be little time aside from that. Just about all of your money will be going to them as well. The weird stuff will keep coming too. It will get to the point where you might start to feel like you're a slave to whatever a higher up asks of you and in fact, you are. Oh sure, you can give it all up, but remember that "thing" you wanted? Well that'll all be gone (of course reality is that they never had it in the first place, and even if they did, *you* wouldn't be getting it). Yes, you keep *yourself* there. It's almost complete

The day will come however when you've finally arrived. You will pass your second-degree black belt test and you will hold your breath. If they are so inclined you will be made an *instructor*. You are now a full-fledged member, my friend. In the mob you'd be a "made guy".

All pretense will be dropped at this point. You are so far in that they can pull out all the stops now. Your indoctrination is so complete that they'd have to do something heinous in order for you to consider leaving now.

It will not be suggested as to where you live, you will be *told* where, and with whom, you will live. You will see these as great opportunities because of the arrangements. They will always have a senior (read: 'higher belt') instructor in every house, with a bunch of more junior instructors. This way they can keep good tabs on what you say and do and eat and drink and how much you sleep and just about every aspect of your life. You will still be expected to hold a full time job to keep money coming in. Yes, they get money from all of the students being "tested" for membership in the group, but you need to keep "earning" too. This is a pyramid after all. *All* of your money will now go to them. They will give each house an envelope to pay the bills every month, and each instructor will get an allowance. Of course quite a bit of it will be spent on the higher belts whenever they want something. You ever see the "Sopranos" when the more junior members have to pay for the dinners for the senior members? It's the same idea.

All of your time will now be spent either working at a job, in the school, or with the group doing some kind of activity. Most times you'll have Saturday night off, and sometimes you'll have Sunday off; most of the time there'll be something to do on Sundays though. After all, it's the only day that the schools are closed and there's always something that needs to be fixed at the compound.

That's right, there is a compound. That's where all the higher belts (read 'Bitch Squad') live. It takes a *lot* of maintenance to keep up. After all, it's every instructor's hope to get high enough up the ladder to live on the compound. Every once in a while somebody gets that high up. The more instructors that do, the more the lower members have to take care of: *they* aren't going to do it, after all!

For the meantime though, this is your existence. You can still spend holidays with your family.

There might be a day, the day you've been waiting for, when you can "sit down" in a school. What this means is that you are the head instructor in that school. The term is used because in every school there is a desk in the office. The office is where a lot of the conversations about "higher knowledge" take place, but more importantly where all of the contracts are signed and all of the payments are made. This is where the millions – yes, you read that correctly, millions – of dollars are taken in. You think I'm kidding, but I could do a little math for you that would make your head spin.

Of course nobody but the big man sees *any* of it. The Bitch Squad gets taken care of, but that mostly comes from the fact that they have to pay for nothing – the lower level instructors buy it all for them.

Only the most senior instructor at any given school gets to sit behind the desk. So if you are the most senior instructor, in charge of running one of the schools, you "sit down" at that school. If we are following our mob analogy still, you are now a captain. You have a crew, and your school will be expected to "earn" a certain amount. This will go up the pyramid of course; you just get your allowance and the house bills paid. Sure, you'll be a senior guy, you'll get a higher allowance and you'll be placed in a house with a group of juniors for you to watch over. Of course you'll have your crew that you must teach (those soldiers that are coming up under you). Ah, respect!

You've been in the group somewhere between five and ten years at this point. The time frame depends on how hard you've worked and if you've learned all of the lessons well. That's both physically and mentally. You'll need to be very good at MA after all, but you'll also need to be able to take the folks coming in off the street, find out what motivates them, and set up their version of utopia for them. In short you need to be able to be a good recruiter. This will be measured both in bodies and in dollars. After all, if you can't get bodies in you can't do squat, but if you also can't separate them from their money, then you can't "lead" them: a person will put their money where their heart is! Get their heart in first and their money will follow.

I'm skipping a lot of stuff, paraphrasing all of this if you will, for the sake of brevity. Yes I know it's insane to speak of brevity in an article this long, but if I gave all of the in-depth explanations and "talk tracks" behind all of these things, the psychobabble that makes all of this work, this thing would be tens of times, if not a hundred times, loner. Shit, maybe I have a book going here. If you want, and I've had enough to drink, ask me in person and I can do some impressions for you that will give you an idea.

At this point the weird shit is so far out there that I won't even begin to tell you about most of it: you wouldn't believe me if I did anyway. We are at situation Z and beyond. Shit, we're beyond ZZ! I'll just stick with the stuff that caused the raid. Remember the FBI/IRS/ATF raid I talked about way back when? Well here it comes.

Just like any other bunch of crooks these guys don't like to report all of their income. In fact, they reported almost none of the income. I, on the other hand, had almost no income to report, so I was cool.

I won't go into just how they did all of this. Accessory after the fact and all of that.

I will say that just like the depictions of the mob that you see on the "Sopranos," there is a *lot* of infighting, backbiting and jockeying for position going on amongst the Bitch Squad. You see, there is a Bitch Squad in every major city that the group had operations in. This was an international group and only a precious few made it to the ultimate Bitch Squad. These were the guys that shared in the wealth with the big guy. These were the guys that everybody in the organization wanted to be, and these were the guys that other members of the lesser Bitch Squads would every once in a while try to make a "hit" on. One of these betrayals led to the raid.

It was a classic case of the betrayed getting snatched up by the feds, who had been watching and waiting for their chance, and got it. They did the classic: here is the evidence that your "friend" provided. You have a choice, we can send you up the river alone based on the tip your "friend" gave us, or you can give us all of the information we need to take them all down and you go free. Guess what happened!

So there we were one night, having an after-hours lesson. I was a "captain" the guy who was "sitting down" in the school having a lesson with my "crew". It was the same at scores of schools in a dozen states; it was s.o.p. (Standard Operating Procedure). That's when the raid hit. They hit at all of the schools and both of the compounds (there was more than one in the country) all at the same time. Many agents with lots of guns poured through the doors.

Because of an investigative reporter's five-day report during sweeps week (actually because of the footage she shot for them that didn't air on the nightly news) they had given an order to shoot to kill anybody who tried to move. They figured they would hit us with such overwhelming force that it would be foolish to try and resist. When the odds are three to one against you and they have assault rifles and you have a sword, you just lie down when they say to lie down.

They took all of the records, they took a lot of statements, and they took just about everything they could cart off. Looked in all of the picture frames for secret documents. Looked for the keys to the codes that everything was written in. Hell, they didn't need to look very hard; they knew where everything was already.

The aftermath, well, the big guy and the top eighteen went to jail. Funny how that was the exact group that all of the Bitch Squads wanted to be in, the "top eighteen". They were the guys who got all of the money, the top of the pyramid. The rest of everybody else was small potatoes to the feds. They wanted the ringleaders.

Thing is, you would expect that this would end it, but no. A lot of gangs, and a lot of crime "families" are run from prison. Such was the case here. You'd be amazed at how many people stayed with the group.

I'm very happy to report that the whole of my group left en-masse. I guess we had our limit and got while the getting was good.

In the eighteen years since we left there's been a lot of thinking going on. As I said before, I don't want to throw the baby out with the bath water. The martial arts training was excellent, despite what you hear from schmucks on the internet. A lot of folks who were peons in the system back then have inflated their rank and have gone on to things that make us look like "children at play". It's pretty funny to think that the same guys who couldn't cut it are dissin' the guys who could wipe the floor with them but are safely behind bars. Pretty pathetic if you ask me, but if it gets them off then hey, what the hell, let 'em yak. I thought the training was good. In fact, if they stuck to that and did it legit, they could have been very successful at it. I guess greed does things to people.

I can also honestly say that because of what I went through, I'm a much stronger person. I didn't regale you with all of the tales of the mental and physical pressure. The sleep deprivation, the pressure to "earn" a certain amount, and all of the rest (I'll just stop right there because I already said I was paraphrasing the whole experience). I will say though, that after having gone through all of that, what a lot of folks look at as a big "problem" ain't nothin' but a thang. I often get asked how I can let stuff roll off me like water off a duck's back. I just tell them that they don't even know pressure (try getting yelled at for eight hours straight like the ref on the Bud commercial).

It's the sum total of my life experiences that have made me what and who I am today. That was one of them, so it is a part of who I am. I happen to like who I am, so I don't necessarily look at it as a bad thing. Sure, I would have liked to get the same benefit without having to go through the same fire, but it is what it is. I'm out now, have been for eighteen years, and it's all water under the bridge.

In fact, if my having been through it and telling about it can help others avoid it, then that's my part to give. I'm glad I can help.

Like I said, I've paraphrased my experience. I've left a lot out. I just wanted to show those who asked that there is much more than a possibility that the Martial Arts can be a fit for a cult, it's a one hundred percent certainty that these beasts exist. Not just the cult-like groups, who in my opinion are really just benign bunches of yahoos stroking their esteemed leader's dick, but the real deal. Virulent groups that will chew you up and spit you out when they are done with you, if that day ever comes.

Antarctic Martial Traditions

by Jesse J. Alcorta

Most stories that involve some questionable claim or actions usually start out with "No shit, there I was…". Everything here is true though.

In October of 1992, I got on a C-141 Starlifter and left Christchurch, New Zealand for McMurdo Station Antarctica. I was recently hired by Antarctic Support Associates to work in the Crary Science and Engineering Center at McMurdo. The C-141, also known as the "Tube of Pain" is noisy, vibration-inducing and a very cramped space when you cram 140 other people dressed similarly in Extreme Cold Weather (ECW) gear. Every FNG (that's Fucking New Guy) has a camera and wants to take a picture either outside the plane before they get on, while they're in the plane and once they get off the damn thing. My first thought when I got off the plane at McMurdo Station was "…damn my cold weather pants don't work and man does that cold make my knees ache…" We say it's a harsh continent.

In the course of twenty years I have come across a lot of people that were either practicing the martial arts, claimed they knew martial arts or at least wanted to learn something like that. I have met and worked with at least the following styles – Goju Ryu, Tae Kwon Do, Tai Chi, Hapkido, Shotokan, Hwa-Rang Do, Kempo, Jeet Kune Do, MMA and a few others that escape me.

Well, no shit, there I was on a ¾ sized racquet ball court that wasn't lit to half the standards of a dark room and I was practicing the Tae Know Do form Won-Hyo. The guy next to me was watching me go through the form with as much power as a person can when he is freezing off half his ass. He reciprocated by demonstrating Pyong Four. We practiced forms for about fifteen to twenty minutes. It's hard to be sure when the clock doesn't work right because it is frozen. My breath was forming fog in front of me. The floor was too cold and covered in volcanic dust to really want to take your shoes off.

We started working on some one-step sparring techniques. One-step sparring involves pre-arranged counters to a simple pre-agreed attack or sequence of attacks. In most hard styles, one-step sparring is like a prelude to self-defense or free sparring. When we exhausted our repertoire we moved on to a bit of free sparring. You don't really know how limited your joints are due to cold temperatures until you try working out at 42°F (indoors). I'm sure someone will tell me I'm whining.

It wasn't much longer when two more guys joined us and we realized we had been working out for about ninety minutes. They wanted to spar but we had enough of a workout for one day. I bowed to my new friend and we parted company. It wasn't an official class, just me and one other guy training because that was what we did back home and any semblance of normalcy was welcome. I picked up my semi-frozen water bottle and grabbed my jacket and left. Note to myself, not to place water bottles next to outside walls…

McMurdo has a weight room for the animals and gym rats to pump iron. First person in the room gets control of the stereo and then everyone else gets in the queue. I had a tape of the Doors playing and some squid (that's a Navy puke) pulled it out to play something akin to 'speeddethmetal'. Yeah I'm pretty sure that is all one word. The kind of music that gives one an eye ache and nose bleed every time the bass thumps.

I told the "gentleman" that the music in the tape deck was mine and it wasn't polite that he pull Jim Morrison out of the machine. I was told "Deal with it…" He turned and high-fived one of his squid buddies and started bench pressing something around the weight of a car. I was curling about fifty pounds on the bar when Squiddly was standing next to me. Damned if that weight didn't get heavy. The bar tilted and a twenty-pound weight slid off the bar. No collars make that happen. The weight fell right on his foot and he got plenty pissed off. I told him "Deal with it…" and left the premises.

Regular martial arts classes aren't possible despite what some people think. There are long days and lots of work to get done. The typical workday is nine hours and six-day work weeks. I have had a lot of ten to twelve hour days. People are enthusiastic at first and then the place grinds them down. If you start with thirty people, I promise the next class will only have twenty five people. By week six you might have five people left. I prefer to teach in small groups of two to four people. More material gets transmitted and we all get more out of it.

Walking down the halls of the lab doing all the hand movements from *djuru* (Silat forms) has been one of my favorite pastimes. The halls aren't that long but you might spend a lot of time walking around doing things. The two or three minutes from one end of the hall to the other add up in the course of a day if you're regular about it.

I liked to work out in the Receiving Dock occasionally. My friend Jen wanted to learn self-defense but not martial arts. I started by teaching her three simple hand movements. Jen is a slightly built girl and I figured she should have some smack to talk. It took almost three years for her to learn to say, "Don't make me bust a cap on your ass, bitch," without laughing. To this day Jen still can't say it without laughing.

I spend much of my free time in the Gerbil Gym. The Gerbil Gym is the gym with all the cardio equipment. Formerly it was called the Acey-Deucy and was a bar for people to drink themselves stupid. There isn't much room for people to work out since the room is pretty much taken up with equipment. The room in the back holds about four people comfortably if they stay in their corners.

This room has a heavy bag. I actually saw a guy break his foot on it. I kind of helped him do it, sort of. I was practicing kicks on the bag being mindful not to kick the bottom of the bag. It had a bunch of concrete in the bottom to weight it. Now I'm a 3rd degree TKD proponent and think I know how to kick correctly. This 1st degree black belt comes in with a friend to work out. He starts telling his buddy what is wrong with my form.

So I start hitting the bag a bit harder and the walls are shaking from the bag being jolted. Mr. 1st degree comes up and says he is going to show me the correct way to do it. He does a couple of jumping round-house kicks. Certainly impressive but not all that strong and I tell him so. I ask if he can do a side kick. He snaps off a couple that drives the bag. I tell him that I have a killer front snap kick that can lift a guy off the floor. I do a couple of nice front snap kicks but nothing spectacular. Joe Black Belt tells me he can do better. He proceeds to deliver a front kick to the bottom of the bag. The bag sure did rise and Joe did break the bones in his instep. I can't recall how many times I've seen MMA wanna-be guys drive their knee into the bottom of that bag only to stop after the first shot.

Back in the early days of the Gerbil Gym there was a bit more room and I could practice some weapons. I had a Bo, tonfa, nunchaku and a few other toys that you shouldn't have on a plane but I got them on and down to McMurdo anyhow. I was working a Bo kata and a couple of squid were fooling around with some bamboo poles nearby. They wanted me to teach them Bo but their manner of asking was more harassing than serious. I wasn't interested but they persisted. So I proceeded to do my kata and finished by busting the bamboo stave over one's head. I had done another good deed for the day.

My typical workout in McMurdo starts around 8:30 pm. Some nights the gym is full and other times it is deader than a funeral home. I try to get in at least four workouts a week and sometimes I can be up to six days on with one night off. I try to do forty five to sixty minutes of hard-paced cardio because the food is free and plentiful. I spend another fifteen minutes on core exercises and stretching. I may also add in light weight workouts. I used to be a big gym rat and hit the weights hard. The last several years has proven to me that the core strengthening was really what I needed.

I spend a focused ten to fifteen minutes on my Silat forms. I am limited to what I can be doing since I may end up sharing the backroom with at least one or more people and there is a lot of junk in there. My instructor tells me that ten to fifteen minutes of focused practice is better than an hour or more of general working out. In other words whatever I'm doing I need to do it with understanding.

If I'm training with a partner or two then I try to introduce a concept and then work in a few techniques to reinforce it. We don't work a long time, but I'd rather stick to one or two things and remaining focused on it. I take a similar tack at seminars. Seminars contain a ton of information. I take great notes but I can't focus on the instructor. I look at my notes later and wonder what the hell I was thinking. Some people take notes but don't look at them or fail to organize them in a manner that makes sense. The context of the notes gets lost. Instead I try to remember three things. The next time I see that instructor I have his three things and the next three that he is giving me. Information gets repeated all the time. It makes me a slow student but a very good one because I am always progressing forward.

I can honestly say I have been to the South Pole. The South Pole, in one hundred years, has seen less than 20,000 people I believe. I have made over eighty trips in twenty years. I have done my forms at the South Pole. It is a killer workout that lasts about five minutes. The South Pole sits at an altitude of 9500 feet. The atmosphere is squashed at both ends of the Earth which makes the physiological altitude closer to about 10,500 feet, on a good day.

Try working hard for any amount of time at two miles above sea level when the humidity is no more than 3%. I know you are going to be heaving shortly. It happens right after your pulse skyrockets and the headache develops and you get dizzy. It takes most people about five to ten days to acclimatize to the altitude. You have to drink a lot of water because it is so dry. I say if you ain't peeing every twenty minutes you ain't drinking enough water. Of course I can also say that I have done my forms in the middle of the desert in a hole in the ground surrounded by radioactive waste...

Kamioooka Prison

by "Douglas Hill"

I had been living in Japan for nearly ten years, serving in the U.S. military then working in a traditional Yokohama hotel when my past finally caught up with me.

Night of innocence

Mid-December 2000, I was invited to a *kikizaki kai*, this translates into a *nihonshu* (*osake*) tasting party, very much like a wine tasting.

When we arrived at the venue in Yokohama, we were presented with six 1.75-liter bottles of limited production sake. My friends and I proceeded to have a wonderful time; the sublime flavors of the presented varieties were a true joy to the palate.

When it came time for me to leave the venue and head home, I found it very difficult to differentiate left from right. This resulted in my taking various trains in opposite directions...repeatedly. All whilst emptying the contents of my stomach onto the train tracks of the local subway.

I did, in fact, make it home at 1 a.m. albeit it took three hours to complete a one-hour trip…par for the course.

Upon entering my two-bedroom apartment, totally exhausted and spiritually spent, I was looking forward to a quiet day off. I removed my clothes and crawled into my happy place, right next to my lovely wife, while my two beautiful children slept in the next room. My slumber was deep and peaceful, full of contented snoring.

That morning at 10 a.m.…

Someone was shaking my foot. Kicking out to shake off this nuisance, I returned to my warm, intoxicated bliss. Said foot was caught and held, waking me up.

I pried my eyes open, the light painfully reminding me of the previous evening. I saw three shadows and wished for at least as many aspirin. Was it really mid-morning? It was incredibly bright and way too early

189

for me to be waking up. Whoever was rousting me was about to receive an earful.

"Is your name Douglas Hill?" asked one of the shadows.

"Yes. Now leave me the fuck alone! Who are you? Get out of my house!"

"Mr. Hill, you need to wake up. We are from the Narcotics Division of the Yokohama Police Department."

"Huhh? The who? The fuck? From the what the fuck? Hang on a second, wait one moment. All I did was puke on the train tracks last night, give me a break! You can't arrest me for that!"

"Mr. Hill, you are being charged, under the Japan Controlled Substances Act, with importation of marijuana. We have a warrant for your arrest and also a warrant to search these premises."

Now the vague shadows were slowly coming into a hazy focus: one very large male, one nondescript guy of average size and a female, all Japanese and all holding badges whilst staring at me as if I were the devil incarnate.

"Huhh?? Ok, well shit...as I am buckass naked can I at least put on some clothes?"

"No, you cannot get dressed. Please read this warrant now! We are placing you under arrest." A document was shown to me, complete with numerous official stamps.

"Hey, fuck this, one of you is a woman! I need to put on some clothes. I need privacy!"

"OK, Mr. Hill, get dressed without leaving your bed and stay in plain sight."

I slowly proceeded to get dressed, putting on whatever clothes were near the bed. In hindsight, I should have dressed warmer … I struggled into a pair of shorts and a t-shirt.

My wife of eight years, crying, along with my two year old daughter and seven year old son watched me leave the house under the escort of three narcotics detectives. Two other officers remained to search our house.

I was not handcuffed; I was told this was to save "face" in regard to my neighbors and family. I was placed in the backseat of an unmarked Nissan. My next stop, Port Authority Retention Facility, Yokohama Bay.

I eventually ended up in an interview room. Left to my own devices for what seemed like three hours, I slept in my chair.

At one point, I requested to speak to someone from the American embassy. The gentlemen "attending to me" laughingly obliged my request.

About two hours later, an embassy representative arrived.

"Mr. Hill, I have been informed of your charges and am here to help you in any way possible."

"Thank god! I didn't do it, please help me!"

"I am sorry, Mr. Hill, but at this point all I can do is provide you with advice."

"Advice? Well, OK, that is better than nothing. What are the chances of getting a lawyer? How have you seen these cases develop in the past?"

"Well, I have here with me a document listing available lawyers. However, as we are not in the United States, I cannot recommend any legal advice.

"Most of these lawyers are not English-speaking and may not be of any assistance to you.

"My recommendation is for you to sign this document, [he pushed a sheet of paper under the glass partition] allowing us to go public with your current situation, contact your next of kin and allow justice to take it's course under the scrutiny of the U.S. judicial system."

"Huh? Let me see if I have this straight, you want to put this in the news and tell my family in the States? You come here with your little bag of rubber stamps and tell me to go public? Please do not charge my family for the gasoline and have a very nice day."

I asked to be escorted back to my holding cell.

A detective came in and offered me smokes and green tea. I gratefully accepted. I took another nap. I later learned that the guilty tend to sleep during this time, whereas the innocent are in a constant mode of panic.

I was photographed and printed. My fingerprints were too large for their forms, and this caused a bit of a problem.

I was then driven a short distance to my "accommodations" for the evening.

My cellmates were two Japanese homeless men, who were very happy to have a place to stay. With a foreigner to talk to their lives were complete. Comic books, porno mags and smokes were hidden under the tatami mats. What more could you ask for? Green tea was even provided upon request. These guys thought they were staying at the Hilton; I thought I was completely and totally fucked.

Evening of my first night

The guard asked me if I played sports. I told him, "Yeah, I was a line-backer in high school." I was immediately and ceremoniously awarded two packs of smokes ... "yeah".

Day 2: In-processing

I woke at 6 a.m. and was given *shokupan* and *ocha* (bread and green tea). After breakfast, I put the porno mags I'd borrowed back under the tatami mat and left my cell. I did not know if I would be returning or what would happen next.

Driven to the city courthouse for my arraignment, I was unceremoniously dumped in a three by three meter cell with an open toilet and ten other men. The only available spot was right next to the shitter. Upon entering the cell, everyone just kinda looked at me and grinned.

This cell held the best of the worst, a cornucopia of *boryokudan* (violent criminals), *chinpira* (punks), *bososoku* (biker punks), *dorobo* (thieves), *burakumin* (2nd generation Korean) *himo* (pimps) and one *ko-bun* (Yakuza underling) – the Yakuza being Japan's tattooed counterparts to the American mafia.

I took my seat next to the shitter, knowing I had the worst seat in the room, and there was not a damn thing I could do about it. We all were dressed in "three-piece suits" (handcuffs, leg irons and a belt around the waist with a chain connecting our feet to our hands).

I seemed to be the hot topic. Being the only *gaijin* (foreigner) in the cell, everyone was very interested in my exploits. It appeared that not many westerners made it to this level of Japanese incarceration! I learned a few things, told a few things and basically just waited for my name to be called.

Lunchtime!

The guards threw a bunch of *shokupan* (prepackaged bread) and packs of *ocha* (green tea) into the cell. I lunged forward, grabbed and hoarded a fair amount. This resulted in instant bargaining power, so I could get the hell away from that toilet.

Shortly after lunch, my name was called. I was escorted to another floor for the next step of my in-processing

I was placed alone in large room with twenty empty folding chairs, all of which faced a wall plaque that was the width and height of the encompassing white wall. The plaque was inscribed with the current confinement laws. But, since the words were written in *kanji*, I had not a clue as to what it said.

After thirty minutes of totally mindless staring, and wishing I had studied Japanese harder, I was picked up by a police officer. He explained that the information on the plaque (confinement law): *Japan's laws allow you to be held up to ten days for no reason. This can be extended for any reason up to twenty days before charges are filed for any crime.*

Now I started to worry.

I was escorted to the prosecutor's office of Mr. Yamamoto (a middle-aged, well-presented individual). He greeted me and told me to be seated. I was then introduced to my translator, Mr. Suzuki (a lazy, belligerent older gentleman).

I was informed I was being officially charged with the illegal importation into Japan of sixty grams of marijuana with an estimated street value of 500,000 yen. The prosecutor (Yamamoto san) added he would do everything within his power to see that I was charged and sentenced to a minimum of ten years in prison. I would then be deported from Japan, never to see my children again.

My jaw dropped, and my eyes began to cloud with tears.

Prior to leaving my interview, I politely told Mr. Yamamoto that I felt his interpreter's English sucked!

Late evening of my second day

My new home—Kamioooka Prison, Yokohama, Japan.

The rest of my jail in-processing was the same as in most other developed countries, full strip, cavity search, "verbal dressing down," full body x-ray, etc.

It was at this point I lost my Rainbow brand flipflops and was given the Japanese universally Size 8 shower shoes. (I wear a Size 13).

My original clothes were returned to me, along with a paper bag containing "extra belongings." I didn't look into this bag until later.

I was escorted down a corridor, past a few "community cells" and entered the solitary confinement ward. It seemed the prosecutor felt I was a violent flight risk and deemed it necessary for me to be separated from all staff and other inmates.

I was escorted past one cell that had a huge Japanese fellow occupying it. He was surrounded by magazines, had a TV and seemed quite content.

My room, a two by two meter cell on the third floor, was made of concrete blocks. Against the back wall was a traditional Japanese floor toilet. At the top of the rear wall was a barred window with no glass. One tatami mat was at the entrance of the cell. I was provided with a foul futon that had not seen sunlight in a decade, a soba shell pillow and a World War II wool blanket in the same condition.

My issued items were: 1 aluminum teapot with 1 lid, 1 tea cup and 1 stack of paper for the toilet.

There was a speaker built into the ceiling for the endless motivational speeches and occasional announcements.

Please remember that upon leaving my home, I was wearing shorts and a t-shirt, and it was December. I was cold, bone-deep, teeth-chattering cold.

I looked into my bag of "extra belongings" and found a t-shirt and two pairs of white cotton socks. I became colder just looking at these items. It appears that after I was arrested, the remaining officers had asked my wife to provide me with extra clothes. This amounted to the extra t-shirt and socks.

9 p.m.—Lights out announced.

I made my bed and now was the time to lie in it. Lying there shivering, fearing, wishing, wondering, contemplating as only a Westerner in a foreign prison can.

6 a.m.—Lights on! However, the lights had never actually been turned off. I folded and stacked my futon, blanket and pillow.

6:15 a.m.—The overhead speaker started in with "happy daily calisthenics" and a woman commenced singing exercise songs as if we were in day care. I politely declined to participate. A passing guard shouted through the bars of my cell door, "I am your teacher, you must learn! Do exercise now, or later you will remember with regret!"

"Yeah, yeah, yeah, fuck you."

A prison guard in Japan is lower than a cop. And that is pretty bad considering cops are considered lower than the mafia...fucking inbred prick. I think I now understand why the prosecutor put me in solitary confinement. It was so I would not hurt anyone...and I now realized I have the infinite potential to inflict pain on others.

I asked "teacher" what the schedule was.

From 6 a.m. to 9 p.m.

- No lying down allowed.

- No touching your bedding.
- No standing unless during the twice daily exercise pre-programmed muzac.
- Following the exact exercise program: unnecessary, can exercise as desired.
- One bath per week.
- One hour outdoor time every two days.
- Legal visits allowed; family and friends prohibited.
- Family allowed to send money for lifestyle increase, but no contact options provided.

Twice a day at 07:00 and 19:00 an inmate delivered hot green tea. It was poured directly into our pre-issued kettles.

Yeah, I was cold. It was about 7°C, (45°F) in my cell. I wore two pairs of socks, one pair of shorts and two t-shirts. My hands seemed to be spending most of their time in my shorts, which made for difficult book reading, as turning the pages was a numbing experience.

I quickly learned to use the hot teapot as a *yutanpo*, (old-fashioned hot water heater). Sitting cross-legged with the teapot resting on my inner thighs, I would cherish the warmth. This was when I was happiest: a book written in English, warm legs, fingers just under numb. But my pleasure was always short lived. Once the tea was room temperature, (about forty five minutes) I would proceed to drink it and recommence shivering.

I was cold, so very cold. I wore everything I had, which was almost nothing, except for the one extra pair of socks. I would stare at those extra socks for hours on end thinking, "I am not cold enough. I do not need them yet." I never once put on that extra pair of socks; I used them as a symbol of strength.

We were also issued books. When the library cart came by, I borrowed one of the three English books available. It was a love romance crap novel, but it was long, five hundred plus pages, so I was content. My prisoner ID number was entered on the back page at the bottom for issue, and then I was reading.

It was shortly thereafter I noticed on the back page a prisoner ID number entered three different times over a period of three years ... *Holy shit*! A foreigner had been in this place for over three years and is probably still here, he may very well plan on reading this book for a fourth time. But, I was told the maximum sentence was twenty days.

At that moment, my entire way of thinking changed.

Negative thoughts

- How long would I be here?
- What would happen to me?
- What could I do to improve myself?
- What would happen to my family?
- What could I do in order to assure integration into general population?

Positive thoughts

- I would become a native-level speaker of Japanese.
- My martial arts would improve.
- I would get some really cool full-body tattoos.
- I would leave Japan at ground zero and disappear.
- I would make contacts that would help me disappear.

Day 3, bath time

Once a week, we were allowed to bathe. In Japan, bathing is essential. The saying "cleanliness is next to holiness" is an integral part of society.

I found myself with twenty men. No speaking allowed, not one word.

We were escorted to a large changing and bathing area with six faucets and buckets, as many stools and a large two by two meter *ofuro* (hot bath).

Everything was strictly monitored and regulated. We were informed that talking or fighting would result in disciplinary action. We were issued short towels and instructed to place our clothes in the cubby holes on the wall. We then were lined up, "nut to butt," for entry into the bathing area, a hot and steaming utopia of scrubbing and cleaning bliss. I was utterly amazed at the body art displayed, work that many westerners claimed to have seen or others try to copy. Tattoos from the ankles to the wrists. Days could be spent inventorying the art displayed. This art was present on perhaps eighty percent of the men there. Moreover, out of twenty, I would say almost half were missing at least some or most of their left pinkie finger – a common sign of loyalty to their boss and a method of atoning for mistakes. I was the only *gaijin*.

Three-quarters of the men lunged straight toward the bath. Holy shit, this is so very taboo in Japan. We all must wash first before entering the bath. I soon learned on the "inside" this rule does not apply.

Unfortunately, I was one of the remaining five guys who did not jump straight into the *ofuro*. Instead, I went to one of the faucets with my bucket and rag and proceeded to properly bathe myself. I noticed the remaining four guys bathing alongside me were fairly foul in both appearance and smell.

Looking over my shoulder, I thought to myself, "There is no way that I will be able to have enough time to soak in the tub, especially considering all of the guys who are already there."

Oh well, I proceeded to bathe myself with the bucket and faucet. I looked over my shoulder one last time toward the pool. To my great surprise, there was an older Japanese man, obviously *oyabun no kyodai* relaxing in the warm water and looking straight at me.

I was very surprised since an *oyabun no kyodai* is a Japanese Mafia ringleader, who reports directly to the Yakuza "God Father".

I politely returned the stare. The ringleader then slowly raised his arm and pointed in a downward motion toward the bath in an inviting manner with his index finger. I nodded my head in acknowledgement.

He then placed the same hand half way into the water and made a wavelike motion. All but four men left the pool. I proudly walked over and entered the *ofuro*, sitting next to the *oyabun no kyodai*.

As I luxuriated in my few moments of warm bliss, soaking in a wonderfully comfortable haven of water, watching various flakes of skins dance glamorously in the *ofuro*, my lips even with the water, he quietly mumbled to me, "*Nani o shita no* [what did you do]?"

As I replied, "*Taima no hanbai* [sold marijuana]," I was instantly hit on the back of my head with a *bo* [a wooden staff] by one of the guards, who was wearing silly red rubber boots.

"*O-hanashi damei iiteru daro*! [I said no talking!]."

Oh well, I got to soak for a few minutes anyway, it was worth the bump and bruise.

Day 4 onward

My daily interrogations …

Five days out of the week, I had the unique pleasure of experiencing interrogations by the narcotic detectives and/or the prosecuting attorney.

On the days of my detective interrogation, I would be met at my cell by two guards, strip-searched and escorted to a four by two meter room with a chair and table bolted to the floor. My cuffs would be attached to a bolt in the floor, and, for the next six to eight hours, I would have the joyous experience of being interrogated by two detectives.

They were the same detectives every day. One guy was a sixth dan *Kyokushin* master weighing 100 kilograms, he was the quiet one. The other was a little guy, and he was the one who did all of the talking, yeah, the same guys who woke me up a number of days ago in my apartment.

I would be questioned relentlessly and repeatedly. The detectives always thought they were one step ahead. And I always thought how warm the room was.

For days, they tore my life apart. At one point, a customs officer interrogated me for three hours. He finally grabbed my arm, pointed to an old IV needle scar and informed me that he knew I had injected drugs, and that he was currently investigating a one-ton meth seizure in Yokohama, he therefore did not have time for my bullshit.

I politely informed him that, at that time, I was in the hospital for a hernia operation, which resulted in the IV scar, and that I was not currently in the possession of one ton of meth.

During a further interrogation, the detectives had me write down all the places in the world I had been while stationed in the US Military, drawing pictures of the ocean track of the aircraft carrier I had been stationed on, etc.

Instead I wrote: "The quick brown fox jumps over the lazy dog's back."

The detectives looked at each other and then the little guy asked me what the hell it meant, I politely informed them, "It has every letter from A to Z in my own handwriting. If you are trying to build a case based upon handwritten letters, then this is all you need. Now send me back to my fucking cell 'cuz I am going to miss yard time!"

The following day, the detectives informed me that my New Year's holiday, (the most important Japanese holiday of the year) would be spent in solitary confinement. "But they will be serving you *o-mochi*, (a traditional rice paste dish that all Japanese enjoy at year's end)."

I became semi-violent, lurching out of my seat, the only thing holding me back was the rope tying me to the floor through my handcuffs.

I yelled to the detectives, "Fuck your *o-mochi*, Americans celebrate Christmas!"

On the days of my prosecutor's interrogations, these outings were a bit more formal and occurred four times. We were transported by bus to the prosecutor's office, since it was about a twenty minute ride. This was a great event and much anticipated!

My own personal joy came during the "line up and march" process prior to leaving the prison compound. The guards, "teachers" would line us up "nut to butt" with our cuffs. A rope lead would be strung through all the inmate's cuffs. The prisoner in the back would be the "anchor" while the front prisoner would be the lead with a length of rope remaining on both ends for the guards.

I took serious joy in fucking this up.

I had become used to the mini slippers that did not even come close to accommodating the width of my foot. I was a proficient shuffling walker. As I am a 2m tall, 120 kg, (6ft 6in 260lb) champion tug-o-war anchorman, I would plant myself, dig in, lean back and puulllll, resulting in sore crotches all the way up the line and one spectacular face plant in the front! This resulted in the splitting of my mini sandals.

The bus rides were uneventful, drapes on the windows, no legroom…however, the most painful aspect of this bus ride was the fact that we were driving through my "stomping grounds" and that I was now a passenger on the *boryokudan* bus; I had never called in sick, I just disappeared, now I was a passenger on the "dirty level/no social recognition" bus that all Japanese shun. To add to the scorn, our bus driver made a point of driving by the hotel I had worked at. I have always felt this was done intentionally.

Once at the prosecutor's office, the day became incredibly long. Solitary cell, hard bench, and, by this point, the guards did not like me much. I was usually given a book to read that was written in Arabic.

Mr. Yamamoto would review the newest information in my case. He also offhandedly informed me that my wife had also been arrested and my children were in foster care. Of everything that happened to me, this was the most difficult thing for me to absorb, do whatever you want to me, but to involve my children? I was devastated. I again began to seriously consider my pluses and minuses in regard to my current life and future potential.

I was informed that if I admitted my guilt, my wife would be set free and my children would be returned to her. All Mr. Yamamoto needed was the name of the person who sent me the drugs.

I lied and gave a fake name. He knew it was a fake name, but this is how you do things…right?

Day 4 onward, my daily life

Yard time, we were escorted onto the roof and placed in individual concrete cells.

I proceeded to practice basic *Okinawa Shorinji kata* (forms, a series of martial arts moves in a specific pattern). When I shouted a *kiai* (martial arts yell), a guard came in and thumped me with his cane.

I was quiet after that.

During my yard time, I could stand on my tiptoes and barely see over our wall (the wall height was designed with Asian height standards), into the general population of the actual Kamioooka prison. It looked to me to be about seventy percent Japanese, twenty percent African and ten percent mutts.

This motivated me to work harder and faster in the off chance my next destination would be gen. pop.

When we returned to our cells, I was always disgusted at the bugs I could see crawling through the hair of the person in front of me. I began to appreciate solitary confinement.

Once a week, (Friday) during my yard time, I could smell *karage* (deep fried chicken nuggets) being cooked in the main prison kitchen. This was one of my small happy times. I fucking hate chunk veggies and that was ninety percent of the food served. I pretty much drank broth and ate rotten rice. My second favorite meal was a loaf of bread with a packet of honey.

Sometime around Day 10, I was sitting in my cell while staring at my extra pair of socks and practicing *seizan* (meditation) when an entire package of *choco* pies (Japanese ding dongs) were tossed through the bars into my cell by a passing inmate; no words were spoken.

Holy shit what is this?? Is this a bribe? What was or would be expected of me?

Should I eat them? If I did, what would be expected of me? Was a note going to be dropped off later if I ate the chocolate delicacies? For three days, I stared, in the seizan position, freezing, at a pair of socks and a package of *choco* pies.

In the end, I was very lucky.

The *choco* pies were simply expired surplus goods given to us, instead of being thrown away by staff.

I was released at the end of my twenty days of solitary confinement.

My interrogators told me that doing drugs was wrong, but in Japan drinking was fine and to please change my life because they were watching.

It seemed a family member in the States tried to send me two ounces of high-grade marijuana through the mail via a friend of mine on active duty in the U.S. Navy and stationed in Japan. That ruined his career.

The Japanese are socially-oriented in that they prefer to release you, broken, humbled and humiliated, back to your family. From this, you are expected to rebuild your life and make amends to all you have affected.

My wife, also having been arrested and interned due to my mistakes, was released at the same time.

When I returned home, my boss and father-in-law were waiting for me. My kids also, were there.

I spent Christmas in jail but made it home in time to enjoy *o-mochi* with my wife & kids.

It may have been easier to do the time and get kicked out of the country.

Having to make amends for your wrongs is a truly humbling, life-changing experience.

I am humbled for the rest of my life.

To this day, I am still repaying my debt.

My family has forgiven me.

I still live and work in Japan. I have since built a two-story house and work at a very reputable company.

I have become a Japanese salary-man.

Checklist for Leaving an Abusive Relationship

by "Jael"

Even in the dusk, spotting the light before it fails is enough to awaken the desire for life, light, freedom and health. When the possibility is sparked, knowing how, when, where, and why to leave a violent marriage brings rumbling from the depths as the harbingers of change. It's observing what is, seeing the patterns. It's giving permission to yourself not to be able to save another or the image others accept as the truth. Knowing that your observations, decisions, words, and actions can lead to a place of safety is a huge step on the path of a new life.

Questions to ask

- Have you been hurt? Or are you living with the threat of bodily harm or death?
- Do you have a place or bag that is truly private where you can keep a small notebook?
- Do you have any time to yourself when you can plan and later prepare?
- Is there a place, sport locker, friend, family where you can leave a set of clothes, keys?
- Can you find a way to make copies of legal, medical and financial records to give to a lawyer?
- How can you build a routine of having short periods of time to yourself with a vehicle or using public transport?
- Can you leave an overnight bag in the trunk of a car for yourself and other family members, for "emergency use"?
- Do you have a circle of a few people you can trust and depend upon for support?

- What objective family, friends, or professionals know you well enough and you trust enough to ask for "barometer readings" to check one's perspective?
- Is a restraining order realistic in gaining the space and security you need?

Practical considerations

- Keep information and plan in notebook so you don't have to remember or panic.
- Overnight bag, spare set of clothes, keys, legal, medical and financial records
- Make a copy of all the cards and info stored in your wallet and put with your stuff so if separated from purse you have access to information.
- Slowly set aside money, as much as you can manage. It may not be much.
- Emergency monies not only in wallet, so if you are separated from purse you still have monies.
- Have a tiny radio, or mp3/radio and flashlight so if are moving about you will not feel as isolated and be safer at night.
- If you have a car try to always have a minimum of three quarters of a tank of gas, so travel and distance aren't issues.
- Use of Time:
- Building a varied routine of leaving environment so it is accepted and it isn't as stressful leaving, giving less signals.
- Collecting the items above and find a place to store them, whether trunk, locker, storage, friend, family.
- Identify your support circle where you can feel secure.
- Seek a smaller circle who can read what's happening, how you are and you trust their judgment enough to listen and act.

Losses often encountered

- You'll never be able to take enough with you.

- Take the few practical and irreplaceable items.

- You'll have to make decisions on your own and take responsibility for them, losing the victim attitude.

- Home, the sense of place, is important. Figure out one or two things, or rituals that mean 'home' to you that you can do, or bring.

- Your daily role and relationship will change, but not the value of who you are. This is a circumstance where loss brings gain as you come home to yourself.

- Seek to be aware of something outside yourself that has beauty, or strength that inspires you.

- If you have a religious or spiritual practice lean into it instead of backing away out of a sense of sorrow.

Waking up

- Just to come this far in thinking and planning is a huge step in regaining your own life.

- Remember to listen to music, read, pray, exercise, eat well as you are waking up and coming home to yourself.

- Lean on your spirituality and community if it is a safe place. Learn to act thoughtfully, not reactively.

Place

- Consider and plan for two or three temporary places as a landing pad. It may be short- or long-term dependent upon circumstances.

- Consider whether you need to contact a women's shelter as a first step. Not as a point of failure, but as one of safety, education and support.

Support

- Friends and places you feel welcome and safe.

- People who know you and you trust to objectively tell you what you may not want to hear and help you do what you need to do.

- Professionals who understand the issues and whom you trust and can be frank with, without fear or shame, so you can grow stronger in the weak places.

Benefit

- Learning to leave is a huge point of awakening. It may take decades, or seconds.

- Trusting your own judgment and gaining trust in others' and learning to accept their perspective as a counter-point to learn from is crucial.

- Others' perspectives or examples may become a model of action, which can be helpful.

- Recognizing the cycle of power and abuse is eye-opening.

- It can help you reclaim your voice and power.

- Use the cycle as a way of objectively observing and monitoring when it is prudent to leave.

- Gaining objectivity brings energy and stamina when you need extra reserves.

Learning to leave is the bridge between what is and what can be in your own life. The bridge can be strong if you take the time to build it. If it is one you can barely scramble across, it still has served its purpose.

Awakening, organizing, accepting others, and forgiving oneself all are part of this process. It is a metamorphosis that is not for the faint-hearted. If you have survived to the point of awaking you have the candle of hope to lead you to a new sense of who you are. Give yourself a breather from relationships and develop solid friendships for a period of time you find acceptable.

Utilize the support you have for balance, strength, and learning to see yourself through someone else's eye. This isn't a step-by-step flight plan, but a flexible outline –meet your own needs. Don't be discouraged if you find yourself needing to leave more than once. Use it as a stepping-stone to cross further the next time.

Coming to acceptance of your own weaknesses, strengths, and capabilities will leave you in good stead as time passes. It takes time for the false guilt to leave for abandoning the relationship. My life took years to fully turn around after I made the early decisions and took steps of leaving the home I'd known as an adult. It was good and hard work learning to strike out on my own when I already was exhausted. Time, determination and perseverance on my part were the healers. Don't let go of your faith in God as you understand him. Faith can sustain when days are very dark. Ten years from now you may not recognize the woman you have become as you kept working on who God wants you to become.

Death, the Teacher

by E. Rushton Gilbert
(but my friends call me Eddie…)

Death? What's so scary about Death? It's going to happen to all of us sooner or later. So why get all worked up about it?

That's the way I always thought about Death. I've spent some time in the Marine Corps. I've spent some time as a Police Officer in the inner city. As a matter of fact, I'm still on the job as a cop.

I've faced Death on quite a few occasions. Big deal, right? The adrenaline pumps, the heart goes "pitty-pat" a little stronger and faster. The body shakes a little bit if you're not careful.

But those encounters are usually over in a heartbeat. The situation is corrected. You're still alive. Time to move on.

"Nothing to see here, folks. Move along…move along…"

Do you remember the old TV police series where the Sergeant always looked out at the Police Officers at the end of roll call and said, "Be careful out there!"?

Not a problem, Sarge.

Cover…Concealment…Tactical advantage…

It's all covered in the Academy. And, more importantly, you learn it on-the-job when you hit the streets. You learn to think ahead. You learn to always have the advantage. You learn to adapt to the situation.

Somebody's pointing a gun at you? They start shooting at you? You settle down into that quiet place way deep down inside and *live in the moment*. You don't allow anything to distract you from survival. You take care of business. You're still alive. Hey, it's over in a heartbeat.

Not a problem, Sarge.

You're searching for a-man-with-a-gun in an old, dark, abandoned warehouse? You take it slow. You remember your training. You find him. Or you don't. Either way, it's over. You're still alive. Hey, it's over in a heartbeat.

Not a problem, Sarge.

But…

What about when it's *not* over in a heartbeat? What about when it keeps on going for a *long* time? What about when you have to face Death *every day*, for a long time?

Well...*now* we've got a problem, Sarge.

Let me tell you a little story...

I've always been a stubborn little prick. It's just part of my genetic makeup. When I got to Marine Corps boot camp at Parris Island, way back in 1970, I was seventeen years old. I was five feet, four inches tall. I weighed in at a whopping 102 pounds (had to get a waiver to even get in as a "Skinny-Body").

The first words that my Senior Drill Instructor said to me were, "You ain't got enough *meat* to stay in *my* platoon, boy!" But, being the stubborn little prick that I am, I made it through and served just shy of nine years active duty in the Corps.

When I went through the Police Academy, I was a forty-four year old grandfather, with a hernia. I had to do the physical training just like all the young recruits. I had to baby that hernia so that it didn't tear open completely before I passed the final tests. But, being the stubborn little prick that I am, I made it through and am still a cop in a major metropolitan police department.

I said all that to say this...

Back in 2000, I started feeling *really* tired, *all* the time. I don't mean just the "*I need a little break*" kind of tired. I mean the "*I can't even get in and out of the patrol car without having to lean on something or sit down and rest*" kind of tired.

Those six-foot-high chain link fences that I used to get over easily started feeling like they were twenty feet high. Those ten-block-long foot pursuits that I used to breeze through started feeling like six-mile runs. I was in big trouble, but didn't want to admit it to myself.

My wife finally convinced me to go to the doctors to get checked out. They ran some blood tests. They called me back in about a week later. They asked, "Just how long have you felt like this?" I said, "A couple of years since it started. It finally got bad enough to make me get it checked out."

"Well," they said, "You've let Hepatitis C pretty much kill you. You should have come in right after you noticed it. You've only got about a 25% chance to make it, *if* you take the treatments for a year. And you may be too far gone for the treatments to work anyway." Being the stubborn little prick that I am, I had allowed Hep C the time it needed to get the tactical advantage over me.

Needless to say, I was stunned. After all the years of *"being careful out there"* something that I never even suspected could hurt me was *killing* me. I couldn't believe it. All the guns, all the knives, all the bad guys trying to do me in by whatever means necessary, hadn't worked. All it took was a little drop of blood from some turd that I had arrested.

You see, being a cop isn't like on TV. They don't show you the broken glass, the gravel, and the holes in the sidewalks that are the reality of the inner-city streets. All it takes is to wrestle around on the concrete with some turd, and blood is everywhere. Your blood…his blood… blood that's all mixed up together, and all over both of you. I found out, the hard way, that it can be a much more dangerous situation than you thought it was.

So, that's where I stood. The Docs prescribed an Interferon/Ribavirin combination to treat me for the Hep C. Side effects: flu-like symptoms and fatigue, depression, irritability, sleep disturbances, and anxiety.

Also, they make sure that it has to be refrigerated, so it'll really hurt like hell when you inject yourself in the side with it. It's hard to believe that something that cold can *burn like hell* when you stick yourself with the needle and jam it in.

Just freakin' great.

Something else about me you need to know:

I'm diagnosed with Asperger's Syndrome. That's on the high-functioning end of the autism spectrum. It's not like classic autism, though. I don't sit and rock back-and-forth and stare off into space. I just analyze the hell out of everything.

Whatever rudimentary emotions I have aren't like what most other people seem to have. For example, I really can't grasp the concept of *"romantic or emotional love"*. If I love someone, it means that I'd take a bullet for them.

I tend to take life as it comes. It *is* what it *is*. When I've faced Death in dangerous situations that were quickly over, I felt *nothing*.

No fear. No hate. No anger. Just *calm*.

I analyze the situation, determine the best course of action, and then execute it. It's over in a heartbeat. No need to dwell on it. It *is* what it *is*. I might get a fleeting glimpse of Death out of the corner of my eye, but it's nothing to get all worked up about.

But I found something out when I had to stand toe-to-toe with Death for a year. It's *not* the same. It's *not* over in a heartbeat. It gives you time to examine Death. It gives you time to examine yourself. It gives Death time to teach you about yourself.

So, I started doing what I do best. I started *analyzing* myself and Death. I started analyzing what Death really meant to me. I started to take Death (and myself) apart, to see what made us tick. There were some things I needed to know.

How would I handle the spiritual aspect of the whole thing?

Would I start feeling sorry for myself and just give up and die?

Was my whole philosophy of life flawed?

Does society really give a rat's ass that I might be dying because I was trying to serve and protect them?

Do I really give a rat's ass about society any more?

Am I a coward, or a hero?

What if I *don't* die? What then?

I'm going to try to work my way through those questions above while you watch.

"Get the popcorn, Frannie... This oughta be good!"

How would I handle the spiritual aspect of the whole thing?

First off, I needed to deal with the spiritual aspect of the situation. You know, that whole "eternity" thing? What was I going to do about that? Well, here's how I dealt with it: I prayed. Yep, I prayed.

Now, before I continue with this part, I know that I'm probably going to offend some people reading this. Oh well. It won't be the first time.

So, if you think you've got all your little religious ducks lined up, and don't want to be bothered with the truth, skip on past this part. If you get offended easily, or don't really want to hear about this sort of thing, skip on past this part. I won't mind, and we can stay friends. Don't say I didn't warn you.

For those who are interested in how I dealt with the spiritual aspect, read on.

Like I said, I prayed. Facing Death on a daily basis will make you do that, unless you're a fool, or an atheist (sorry to be redundant there). I happen to be a Christian. Why? Because it's the only faith that makes sense to me.

Remember? I analyze the hell out of *everything*. I've examined other faiths. I've tried my best to make some kind of logical sense out of them. They just don't make any sense. They don't work.

True Christianity is a one-on-one, personal relationship with Jesus. I don't have to be perfect, because Jesus already is. It doesn't depend on what I do, or don't do. It doesn't matter how I act, or don't act. It doesn't matter whether I smoke, or don't smoke. It doesn't matter whether I cuss, or don't cuss. Yeah, I probably ought to do better but, if I don't, He's still got me covered.

He paid the debt for my ugly, nasty, sinful nature when He died on that cross, then rose to life again. I don't have to wonder, "**W**hat **W**ould **J**esus **D**o?" He already did it. He's still doing it right now.

If your theology doesn't work on the street, it doesn't work at all. I'm a firm believer in street theology. If it's not practical, I can't use it in my business.

Do you want some really *deep* theology?

Here it is: "Jesus wept."

Jesus, the Creator of the Universe, *cried* when his friend Lazarus died. He *cried* for the man's family in their time of grief.

Then, He brought him back to life!

That's how *Jesus* rolls. I'm good with that.

I also noted where Scripture promises, *"The last enemy to be destroyed is death."*

I now know that I (through Jesus) have the tactical advantage over Death. We have the high ground. Death might take me down now but, in the end, Death loses. I'm good with that too.

Just so we understand each other, when I talk about my Christian faith, I don't mean that watered-down, namby-pamby version of the Christian faith that "Churchianity" tries to pass off as true faith.

I've never been one to follow someone's man-made rules and regulations of how I'm supposed to act, dress, talk, and behave. If you're a Christian, and find yourself on that kind of religious "hamster wheel" you have my sympathy. I'd advise you to step off of it and never look back. I don't really care what "the Right Reverend Doctor" whoever says. I care what Jesus says.

Now, if you're one of those folks who buy into that whole "Circle of Life" kind of crap from the kids' movie, just try asking "The Universe" to help you out the next time you get in a jam. By the time "The Universe" gets through laughing at your silly ass, you'll be toast!

Hey, I'm not preaching at you. I'm just trying to introduce you to the right Person. I've done my job.

I'm just trying to tell you what I know to be the truth. If you decide to make other choices, that's on you.

Are we still friends?

Yes? Good.

No? Get over yourself.

Moving right along…

Would I start feeling sorry for myself and just give up and die?

The Docs suggested that I attend the "group therapy" sessions for Hep C patients. I went to *one*, and only one. Everyone there was basically having a "pity party" for themselves.

"No can do, Doc. I'm outta here!"

So I guess that answered the question about whether or not I'd start to feel sorry for myself and just give up and die. Not for me. It made me want to puke just listening to them.

To those who whine about how "Life's not *fair*…"?

You're absolutely right. Life's *not* fair. Life is *excellent*, if you make up your mind to live it that way.

The proper attitude, and a good sense of humor, will get you through any situation.

Was my whole philosophy of life flawed?

I guess the hardest part of the whole experience was trying to figure out whether or not I had just thrown my life away for no reason. I'm not afraid to die, but I don't want to die for "*stupid*".

I've always felt the need to serve society in some capacity. I've always been willing to die for what I believe in. I just found myself questioning whether or not I had believed in the right things.

I found myself, more and more, examining *why* I'd always wanted to serve society. I came to the conclusion that I'd been doing it for the wrong reasons.

Before, my philosophy had always been:

"God is great, beer is good, and people are crazy."

No, wait a minute. That's not it. That's a country music song that I happen to like.

My flawed philosophy (metaphorically speaking) had always been:

Sheep need to be protected from the wolves. Why? Because it's a difficult and messy job to clean up sheep guts. It's much easier just to keep the wolves from ripping the sheep open in the first place.

The sheep don't really have a clue, but somebody's got to keep the sidewalk clear of sheep guts. The sheep don't *really* care whether I live or die. They just don't want to get their guts ripped out.

And, with all due respect to Colonel Grossman, I was *not* a damn sheepdog. I was a wolf hunter. I was a wolf stopper.

The sheep were, at best, a secondary consideration. They didn't usually even enter into the equation, except maybe as "wolf bait" every once in a while.

I was happy just to hunt wolves, and stop them, *before* they got the chance to mess up my sidewalks with sheep guts. Did I mention that cleaning up sheep guts was a difficult and messy job?

My time in Death's classroom taught me that my old philosophy was wrong. I learned something about myself, and I learned something about people in general.

What did I learn?

Read on...

Does society really give a rat's ass that I might be dying because I was trying to serve them?

Do you know what changed my mind about that flawed philosophy? I started watching people. I mean really *watching* people. I don't mean just watching them as being part of a bad situation, and whether they'd distract my focus from doing my job. I mean watching them to try to find out how they interacted with other people.

I watched my wife, Ada Gilbert. I watched her as she showed true compassion for others. I watched her as she put others peoples' needs before her own. I watched her as she put up with my stubborn, autistic little ass, and supported me through the whole ordeal.

She's my soulmate, my lover, and my best friend. She's the kind of person that I wish I could be.

(This is me, with a silly grin on my face, waving at the camera... *"Hi Ada!...Love you, Babydoll!...I guess this writing thing is working out after all, huh?"*)

I watched my former partner, Anne-Marie Ziska. I watched her as she took the time to *really* talk to victims and offer them comfort. I watched her as she went out of her way to make sure that victims, and their families, were taken care of through the whole mess they'd been drawn into. I watched her as she went around, on her off-duty time, and volunteered to help out with organizations that met the needs of abused and neglected children, battered wives, and senior citizens.

(*"Rest in peace, Annie...You earned it...You were a better cop and a better person than I'll ever be..."*)

As a side note, I've gotten to know two more people that have made me realize that humanity isn't just a complete waste of perfectly good carbon compounds. I didn't get to know them until after my year-long Death class, but I've got to tell you about them. As a matter of fact, they're the reason that I'm writing all this down.

The first one is Marc MacYoung. Although he too is a Brother in the "Stubborn Little Prick Brotherhood" he's one of the best men I've ever known. I've seen him help people that most folks wouldn't give the time of day to, just because he's that kind of a nice guy. He's a *for real* bad-ass, with a heart of gold. Plus, he's madly in love with the next person I'm going to tell you about. *That* fact, in and of itself, makes him okay in my book.

(*"Hi Marc...Uhh...You know I was just kidding about the 'prick' part, right?...Right?...You know that, don't you?...Don't hurt me, Bro..."*)

The second one is Dianna Gordon. She faces Death each and every day, and continues to march. She goes through pain and situations that would have most of us curled up in a corner, sobbing. She takes care of business no matter what. She's one of those rare individuals who just say to Death, "Talk to the hand!" In my book, she's a *real* hero.

(*"Hi Dianna... Ma'am, you have my complete and unmitigated respect. It takes guts to do what you do. I want to be just like you when I grow up. Nah...who am I kidding? I'm never gonna grow up..."*)

Do you know what else changed my mind about people?

Police funerals. Yep, Police funerals. I starting noticing that a lot of people, who didn't even *know* the Cops, would line the streets when the funeral processions went by. They were just regular people who didn't have to be there, but came anyway. And they were *crying*. Now, I might be autistic, but even *I* know that crying means that people care. It changed my whole outlook about people and society.

Do I really give a rat's ass about society any more?

All of that "people watching" I did made the "*Do I really give a rat's ass about society?*" question easy to answer. If Ada and Annie could be the kind of people that they were, and if people cared enough to show up at a Cop's funeral, and show that they *really* cared about them dying to protect them, then I *did* give a rat's ass about them. *I* could care deeply because *they* cared deeply.

I needed to know if I was a coward, or a hero.

Sometimes, a hero is just a coward that didn't have time to think it through. Well, I had plenty of time to think it through *this* time.

Am I a coward?

No, I'm not.

Am I a hero?

No, I'm not.

It *is* what it *is*.

What if I *don't* die. What then?

I'll tell you something. Facing Death day in and day out for a year, not knowing whether you're going to be worm food shortly, can teach you a lot about yourself. It can give you the time you need to really think about what's important to you, and what's not.

After a year, the Docs ran the final Hep C tests. They were negative. I'm still alive.

I am, much to the astonishment of the bad guys and "wolves" throughout the City, still a cop.

I'm also, much to the dismay of the literary world, a freelance writer.

I've learned a lot about myself, and about other people. Being autistic, I still believe that there are only two kinds of people in the world:

Me and everyone else.

But I found out that there are two divisions of "everyone else".

There are good people, who need to be protected and served

And there are bad people, who need to be hunted and stopped.

And I'm just the man for the job.

Why?

Because I'm a stubborn little prick.

Hope Your Fantasy Stays One

by "D. Weeks"

Come on. Admit it. I know you've got that secret fantasy. It's not socially acceptable, but damn it. You've put in your time at the dojo and the firing range, adrenal stress training and combatives. Awareness is your middle name and your tactical flashlight and folding knife are merely basic preparation.

If you could admit it, if no one would ever know, if you were being truthful and honest, you would admit that there is a part of you that craves the accolades and acclaim that you think will come from having successfully defended your family from evil men.

Hell no. I wouldn't admit that to anyone.

The crackhead and self-described bad man gets out of jail tomorrow. What the hell are you going to do? Your wife put him there with a phone call. He has no job, no money, no place to live, and his few personal belongings were stolen from the F-150 when it was repossessed. His Harley is gone too, back to the bank. All the result of a phone call.

It doesn't matter that she created and exacerbated the situation, she's still your wife and you can't leave her hanging in the breeze, and besides, you have kids. What if he comes to the house looking for some payback?

Things didn't start out that way. Janice met him out at the local bar. Dave was just a normal guy from Chicago, divorced with a couple of kids. A construction carpenter having a spot of bad luck in a bad economy, struggling to find work. Our marriage was struggling. She insisted her new friend was just someone to shoot pool or go bowling with once in a while. A guy friend just like she had when we met. I wasn't ready to issue an ultimatum, and she hadn't crossed any lines.

Activity partner, sort of a friend of the family... he was over for Thanksgiving dinner and seemed like a pretty nice guy overall.

It wasn't long before the stories about Dave got interesting.

219

First, it was the attempted suicide at the ex-girlfriend's house. Janice told him if he got suicidal again she would call the police. He made mildly threatening noises about that remark.

The holidays passed relatively uneventfully until the start of the New Year. He'd been staying with his cousin a couple of miles away from our house, and had always insisted to my wife that she not relay his stories to his cousin or ex-girlfriend. One day, while visiting, incongruities between what she'd been told previously and what he was telling his cousin precipitated a comparison of stories while Dave was out of the room.

At last, the truth started to emerge. For some years, Dave had been a low-level crack user. That is what led to the break up with his ex-girlfriend. And the cousin was about fed up with his shit as well. Not long after that conversation, Janice found out that Dave had been stealing some of his cousin's things and pawning them to support his addiction.

Eventually it got back to Dave that the three (Janice, the ex-girlfriend and the cousin) had been comparing notes and had a pretty good idea of what Dave had been up to and Dave got to talking in fatalistic terms and making veiled references to killing himself, so Janice called the police. She was on one line talking to the police while Dave was elsewhere on the phone talking to the police telling them she and his cousin are crazy. What a stupid mess. I counseled her to just forget the money she'd loaned him and walk away. Told her to stop answering the damned phone, too, but between proximity bias and the state of our marriage, she wasn't going to listen to me.

The cops picked him up and took him into custody for evaluation. After determining he was no threat to himself, he was released some hours later at which point he started blowing up Janice's phone with angry messages. I loaded up the only firearm I had at the time, my M-14. I sure as shit had no idea what to do except that I was afraid of Dave coming by the house and figured I'd rather have the gun available than not.

That crisis passed. The next one followed in short order.

Dave insisted that he needed to talk to Janice in person and if she wouldn't meet him out, he would have to come by the house. She was still unwilling to see any threat and given an apology for the things said on the phone the night before, she went to the cousin's house to talk to Dave and perhaps get some of the money back. Does any part of this sound wise, or like a smart move? I didn't think so even then, but she wasn't listening to me.

At the cousin's, he took Janice's phone and wouldn't give it back. That was the spark that sets things off between Dave and his cousin and pretty soon, they were trading blows and grappling in the living room in front of Janice. A moment later, she ran out of the house, and called the police, then returned after the police arrived. Dave barricaded himself into the back bedroom and when asked if he was suicidal, quipped that yes, he wanted to suicide by cop. At this point the local SWAT team as well as police officers from a neighboring jurisdiction came to the scene. Eventually, Dave was taken into custody again for evaluation.

Janice returned home, and I kept my rifle loaded and handy.

The next day passed uneventfully.

On Monday, I stopped by a friend's house to get his 9mm handgun for something more handy that a battle rifle. When I get home, Janice told me that the cousin had gotten a temporary restraining order (TRO) against Dave and he was no longer living in his house. Then, she heard from Dave that he had packed his truck and was moving back to Chicago, but was broke and needed money for gas. So, a couple hundred dollars later and things could get back to normal. Right?

Wrong.

As the days passed, Janice, still in contact with the cousin, found out that Dave had in fact not left for Chicago. The next Friday morning, after dropping the kids off at school, she got a call from Dave inviting her to meet him next door to his cousin's house where he was breaking the restraining order getting his Harley. She called the police and he was arrested for violating the TRO.

The ex-girlfriend arrived and as cosigner on the notes for the F-150 and the Harley, she returned the motorcycle to the dealership and left the truck sitting (full of Dave's stuff) awaiting repossession.

I went and bought a shotgun (Mossberg 590A1) and ammo.

At this point, we had no idea what would happen or how long Dave would be in jail. Given that it was pretty damned obvious who got the cops involved, I sent Janice off to a hotel so as to divert any attention away from the kids. She stayed a couple of days and then came home because Dave was still in jail.

Instead of the expected two days, Dave spent six days in jail and finally got out by negotiating a deal with the state for a one-year suspended sentence for violating the cousin's restraining order. Simultaneously he was served with the ex-girlfriend and Janice's restraining orders.

Because Dave was getting out of jail, Janice went off to the hotel again, and I began preparing in earnest. Well, perhaps that's not really the right word to use. I felt completely unprepared despite my training and planning. I was finding out that there is a big damned difference between training and reality, that the simplest things while highly adrenalized is more difficult, and that there are decisions and details and other things that are glossed over when it's only a fantasy.

The kids asleep, Janice at the hotel, the shotgun loaded and on top of the dresser in a known and constant and easily accessible place... now came the part that affected me the most.

My oldest daughter slept downstairs and the stairs go down right inside the front door. My youngest daughter's bedroom to the right creates the alcove where the front door is located. As I stood facing the front door, I had to soberly and calmly as I could, calculate where I could not shoot because if I did I'd risk killing my daughter. I had to decide right then, what are the hard limits? When will I shoot? Those decisions made and defined with no ambiguity, I did one last thing. I leaned the 6' aluminum stepladder against the door so that if anyone came through the door, the ladder would fall, making a racket and working as something of an alarm as well as presenting an obstacle for the intruder. Then, I went to bed.

I woke in the morning and everything was the same as the night before. I got the kids ready and off to school, and then headed to work.

Once home from work, I tried to maintain things in as normal a state as possible. The kids met Dave and liked him. I couldn't very well tell them that at this point, he was the bad guy. Once the kids were off to bed, I once again took a trip around the house, listening for anything unusual. Then, I went to bed.

Sometime in the night, I woke up to a strange noise. I lay there as still as possible straining my ears, trying to hear any unusual noises. Was it Dave come to take his revenge? One minute. Two minutes. Nothing. I got out of bed and retrieved my shotgun and with my finger on the safety, crept out into the foyer. The ladder was still balanced against the door. I stood and listened with all of my senses extended to maximum sensitivity. Nothing.

I put the shotgun back on the dresser and went back to bed, but sleep didn't come easily.

When morning came, I was in no way well rested, but it was the weekend and at least I didn't need to get the kids off to school. We spent the day away from the house and had dinner with mom at the hotel.

Before bed on the third evening, I felt like I was ready to have a meltdown. The stress of maintaining myself in a high state of alertness was beginning to take a toll on me. I've spent years working on being aware, but having never had to be at a peak level of awareness, I had no experience there. I didn't know how to avoid burnout.

On the fourth day Janice came back from the hotel, sure that I was being paranoid. Shrug. Who can say? I didn't change the routine because of her disdain.

With Janice home, I left it in her hands to get the kids off to school, and later that day we heard from Dave that family from Chicago came out and got him. The end? Not quite. If I learned one thing, it's that just because it seems over doesn't mean that it is in fact over. I maintained my vigilance for another week, sleeping with the loaded shotgun.

Nothing happened. There was no attack against my family, no vandalism of our things. The monetary cost was low, a few hundred dollars I didn't really have. The emotional and psychic cost was huge.

Maybe your training is better. Maybe you are ready. You've thought through things, made the hard decisions. Maybe you are ready. I wasn't, though I believed I was. .

I truly don't know if anyone else can take away the same lessons I did. You can live a clean upstanding life and still end up rubbing up against the criminal element. Whether Dave was truly a bad man or not is immaterial. He could have been, but he didn't live thirty miles away in the ghetto. He lived four miles away.

I used to have a fantasy about being the conquering hero, the manly man who stood in the gap between my loved ones and the bad people of the world, and perhaps because I'm willing, in some ways I do stand in that gap. The difference now is that this one miniscule little taste of the reality of having to step up has disabused me of the fantasy I held before, and makes me exceedingly glad that nothing happened.

Section 5: Advice

A little fatherly advice from a cop, a bouncer, and a former cult member. Enjoy.

Things I know now That I wish I knew then

by Kasey Keckeisen

I've been training in martial arts for twenty years, and I've been a cop for twelve. It has been a long educational process. Looking back, there are some things that I've learned along the way, that had I'd known then would have saved me a lot of headaches. I wish someone would have taught me these things before I needed them. So if I had a DeLorean with a flux capacitor, these are the things I would go back in time and teach myself. The things I know now that I wish I knew back then.

De-escalation starts with you

Screaming "calm the fuck down!" rarely ever calms anyone down. If you don't believe me next time you are arguing with your wife tell her to calm down. Or better yet tell her she is being irrational and that she needs to calm down. See how well that works for you.

You have to be calm (or at least appear calm) first, before you can even attempt to de-escalate someone else. This is going to be very hard for men in general, and specifically young men eighteen to twenty five.

Young men are wired to play social dominance games, and emotions are contagious. When someone gets in your face and starts shouting at you, you will feel compelled to show them who is the boss by shouting back. The more irate they are, the more their emotions will affect you.

So, how do you avoid this game? First recognize that you are getting pissed. Then adapt. Recognizing the game allows you to play it. A strategy that worked for me was when I felt myself getting angry and I felt the need to shout or insult I would take on the persona of Eddie Haskle from "Leave it to Beaver". You are still going to want to win the dominance game but instead of me shouting back I would win by killing him / her with kindness.

Him – *You fat fuck, instead of giving me this bullshit ticket why don't you go arrest some real criminals!*

Me – *Sir* (my mouth said sir but my brain said cock sucker), *I'm ever so sorry for any inconvenience I may have caused by stopping you today. Routine traffic stops account for clearing over 80% of all major unsolved crimes. If you feel I have made an error in pulling you over for travelling 56 miles an hour in a 35 mile per hour zone there is information on the back of your citation you can use to appeal you ticket in court. Thank you for your cooperation. Please drive safe, and you have a great day* (my mouth said have a great day but my brain said go fuck yourself).

I wasn't great at calming myself just yet but I could play the role of someone who was calm, and polite while still "winning" my perceived social dominance challenge. What is he going to do? Complain that I was too polite?

Also, contagious emotions work both ways. If you are calm and speak progressively slower and quieter they will mirror your behavior.

This will become easier as you get older. You will get better at it with experience. As you gain more experience you will feel you have less to prove. The less you have to prove the easier it is to avoid social dominance games. The easier you avoid these games the calmer you become.

An example of this you will see is the experienced Sergeant. When you watch him operate he just seems to know what is about to happen and squash it before it does. He may not be able to put it into words but over a career on the street he has developed a system of recognizing his behavior and the behavior of those people around him

So all you twenty one to twenty five year old cops need to develop your own system of recognizing that you're becoming agitated, and strategies to implement when you recognize it.

Do not insult them

Do not insult them. That is one of Peyton Quinn's rules of conflict. Past me (all you twenty one to twenty five year old cops) read Peyton Quinn.

If you didn't calm yourself down and you allowed things to escalate you probably ended up insulting them. This may have made you feel good, but it never ends well and gets in the way of getting the job done.

Do not:

Imply someone lacks parenting skills by naming them "The mother of the year." Even total shitbags that are routinely arrested will take that personally and generate a complaint. Plus you lose credit with them next time you have to deal with them. And you will be dealing with them again, and again.

Do not:

Question someone's sexual preferences. When someone tells you they fucked your mother last night it will feel good to respond with something like, "That surprises me, I didn't think you were into chicks". However, that response will not get you any closer to accomplishing your job. This guy will feel the need to regain face somehow. If not by attacking you he may attack your partner, the Corrections Officer when he gets to jail, or his wife or kids when he gets back home. Don't make someone else cash a check your mouth wrote.

Also even if you are substituting these phrases in place of more overt insults (mother fucker, cock sucker, etc…) avoid the phrases cutie pie, Gilligan, or sweat heart – any phrase that implies he is effeminate or homosexual. Guys take any assault on their manhood personally. If you take their manhood away they feel the need to regain it one way or another.

If you can stay cool, de-escalate yourself, you are less likely to insult them.

If you do not insult them, you are less likely to get into a physical confrontation.

Even so, professionals will be faced with situations where they need to take physical control of violent subjects. When this happens end the confrontation quickly.

End it quickly

It is far better to start with high levels of force and ease up as you gain control than start with low levels of force and take damage while you attempt ineffective tactics.

The longer a confrontation continues the greater the chances for injury for all parties involved.

The hardest fight I was ever in was against a five foot nothing, one hundred and nothing pound drunk female, because I hadn't learned that lesson yet.

She was verbally confrontational, and passively resisted being removed from the car (both pre-attack indicators). Then she actively resisted being handcuffed after she was put on the ground. My partner looked at me like – dude?, you're a 250lb Jujutsu stud, why can't you cuff her?

Here is why:

I didn't take her seriously as a threat (arrogant)

I was working harder on not hurting her than controlling her (also arrogant)

She was playing to the crowd, trying to generate an excessive force complaint.

My partner and I worked together and got her into cuffs without further incident, or the crowd intervening. But things could have gone very bad very fast.

I would have been better off bouncing her the second she resisted being removed from the car, pinning and cuffing her before she even knew what had happened.

If you are going to use force on someone you better be able to justify your actions.

Articulation

The word articulation is used over and over again in school and at the academy. An officer must articulate his actions were reasonable under the circumstances. It is used over and over but never actively practiced.

The first part of articulation is knowing your state statutes on the use of force and knowing your department's use of force policy well.

The second part is being able to translate those statutes and policies into common ideas that anyone can understand.

You need to describe the totality of the circumstances – the details that influence your use of force decisions.

They can be divided into Influential Circumstances and Officer/Threat Factors.

Influential Circumstances

- Inability to disengage
- Proximity to weapon
- Injury or exhaustion
- Hazardous environment
- Special knowledge
- Surprise
- Ground level

Officer Threat Factors
(Except for gender, all OTFs work both ways)

- Skill
- Size
- Strength
- Numbers
- Mental state
- Gender
- Sometimes age
- Disability

So using the example of the drunk female from above, even though I was larger, stronger and more skilled than her I could articulate using higher levels of force because of inability to disengage, and a hazardous environment.

Inability to disengage – as a Police officer I have a duty to act. If I let her go she would have driven off and could have seriously injured herself or others.

Hazardous environment – a large group of her friends had come out of their trailer homes to watch the arrest. The more she resisted and yelled, "Ouch, help!" the more the crowd was becoming agitated. I was severely outnumbered. The longer it took me to end the confrontation, the more opportunity the crowd of her friends had to interfere.

How do you actively practice articulation?

Debrief

Remember, good articulation is translating complex concepts from statutes and policies into common ideas that anyone can understand. The way you practice this is storytelling.

Remember that experienced Sergeant I mentioned earlier? On the last day of our shift (if call load allowed) after bar close when every thing slowed down we would smoke a cigar in the garage and solve the world's problems. This included swapping "war" stories.

The description of the incident with the drunk female you've read so far is fairly dry and clinical, like you might find in a rookie report.

That's not the way you tell the story over cigars. Over cigars it might sound like this:

The call came in that a drunk woman was driving a big red pickup and nearly hit the complainant. The complainant had been drinking with her in the trailer park and was pissed that she was driving to go get smokes. The complainant was so pissed that that when the truck nearly hit her she chucked a doughnut at the truck. While I was talking to the complainant the truck came back. The complainant said, "Here she comes." So I got in my squad car and pulled the truck over. As I approached the truck on foot I could see the doughnut the complainant threw in back of the truck. The driver refused to get out of the truck. I pulled her out and put her on the ground. She started yelling ouch, ouch quit hurting me. This brought out all the party-goers to see what was going on. Like a live episode of "Cops." The driver started really fighting back now, locking her arms and actively resisting my attempts to put her hands behind her back. She keeps yelling "Ow ow somebody help me he is hurting me." Now all her friends that have been drinking with her at the party are getting mad and start yelling, "Get off her, leave her alone!" Steve looks at me like, 'dude what the fuck? You're some sort of 250lb Jujutsu stud. Cuff this broad before the crowd kicks our ass.' So Steve grabs one arm and starts pushing. I yell, "Put your hands behind your back, stop resisting." She won't budge for Steve. I look at him like it's not that easy, dick, if I push any harder she is going to dislocate her own arm. So Steve pushes his arm, I push mine, we meet in middle and finally get her cuffed. We get her in a squad and get out of there before the crowd can turn on us.

If you were sitting in a jury, which version of the story would you understand the clearest?

The more practice you have storytelling the easier articulation becomes and the better your reports become.

Another part of storytelling is playing – what if?

Reactive – What if you could do that call over again; what would you do different? What would you do the same? Why?

Proactive – If an alarm at the bank came in right now what would you do? What if there were people still inside?

Law Enforcement is minutes of heart attack excitement split up by hours of mind-dulling boredom. You are going to have to kill time. Might as well kill time with things that will make you better during those minutes of heart attack excitement.

Who do you debrief with? What do you do until you become skilled at articulation?

Surround yourself with good people

When I first started at my current department, the schedule was divided so there was an "A" side and a "B" side. My first few months I worked a split schedule. A few days with one side and a few days with the other. The two sides couldn't have been more different. The "A" side liked their jobs, worked hard, played hard, and enjoyed putting bad guys in jail. The "B" side hated their jobs, did the least amount possible, just enough not to get fired, and enjoyed bitching about the "A" side. When the Officer hired after me was off of FTO (Field Training Officer) I got first choice as to which side I would work with. I was very fortunate that I got work with the "A" side. I modeled myself after them and became a very successful Police Officer. If I was hired second I would have got stuck on the "B" side. I fear what kind of cop/person I would have become if I was surrounded by that influence early in my career.

So, past me (all you twenty one to twenty five year old cops) seek out and surround yourself with good people, the type of people you want to become.

Dealing with Administration

Anyone in Administration has been off the street for a long time. You have to understand they have become an entirely different animal and treat them as such. You can't work with them the same way you do with other Operators, they speak a different language. Once you understand that you can use that. Here are some concepts I learned the hard way that will help.

1. How does it benefit them or the organization?

If you are trying to get your Administration to approve something you have to ask yourself – how does it benefit them or the organization?

Generate a list of benefits your boss or the organization will receive if he approves your proposal.

2. Ask for their help/input

Admin knows you are very different from them. If they perceive you are doing your job and their job (better than them) they become agitated. When they become agitated you will find yourself in similar social dominance games as we discussed in de-escalation. If you recognize the game you can play the game.

Try this:

• This is my rough idea.

- This is how this idea will benefit the department and you
- You have a lot of experience with things like this. What do you think is the best way to do something like this?

Wow, this meat eater knows I'm a good administrator and sought out my expertise in administration. He is smart, this must be a good idea.

3. The purple rose

After they give you advice and you refine the proposal put things in there that don't cost you anything if they get cut.

Which brings us to…..

4. Allow them to make it their idea.

So after you refine the proposal, bring it back full of purple roses and the stuff you want. Seek out further advice from Admin. They will cut out a bunch of stuff. If you don't give them fluff to cut, they will cut what you need. After they have left their mark on your proposal it becomes their proposal.

Wow, this meat eater knows I'm a good administrator and sought out my expertise in administration. He is smart, this must be a good idea. Changes into – *Of course it is a good idea, it's my idea.*

You both win.

I learned these lessons the hard way and paid a price for them. Even if I could go back I don't know if the past version of me would have been able to learn those lessons with out paying that price.

But maybe someone reading this is smarter and more mature than I was then. If so I hope this can save you some headaches.

So, past me (all you twenty one to twenty five year old cops) remember:

- De-escalation starts with you
- Do not insult them
- End it quickly
- Practice articulation
- Debrief
- Surround yourself with good people
- When dealing with Administration:

  1. How does it benefit them or the organization?

2. Ask for their help/input

3. The purple rose

4. Allow them to make it their idea.

I didn't learn those lessons by myself. Good people guided me and took me under their wings. I'm proud to pass what they taught me on. If you read this and it helps you, be sure to take what you learned and pass it on to the dumb ass rookie you're working with. Because that was all of us, once.

Be Nice

by Alain Burrese

I was wet. I was cold. And I wasn't happy that the band wasn't playing. The big differences between me and the angry crowd were 1) I was sober, and 2) I was being paid to be there. I liked the band, and had been looking forward to hearing them, but the main reason I wasn't happy that they weren't playing was that it just made my job more difficult.

It was an outdoor Black Crowes concert in Montana. I was working security when an unexpected wind and rain storm blew in. While the roof over the stage would protect from a straight downpour, the open sides did nothing to protect the sound equipment from the horizontal rain blowing in with the severe winds. While some people were busy trying to keep fences, tables, and portable outhouses from blowing away, I was assigned to keep people from hurting each other and to keep them away from the stage. Besides not wanting any of the angry mob to damage the stage or equipment, we had a legitimate concern with lightning being attracted by the metal structure and wanted to keep people safe from the additional potential danger. I was sure the show was not going to go on, but they hadn't made any kind of official announcement to the crowd. This lack of communication from the band and producers was only making the situation worse. Did I mention I wasn't happy?

I noticed an individual who was both large and loud. The way he was yelling and behaving had the potential to incite the already angry crowd toward a situation where people would get hurt. I thought, "Shit" to myself, as I started through the crowd toward him. It was my job to keep people and property from being hurt or damaged. As I neared him, I noticed the tattoos on his rather large guns bulging under the tight t-shirt. "Great, a former Marine," I thought. Alcohol must have been keeping him warm.

As I approached, I tried to keep Patrick Swayze's lessons from the movie *Road House* in mind. I've always liked tough guy movies, and that one had it all. Cinema masterpiece? No. But it sure was a fun tough guy movie, and it actually had a few tidbits of good advice. Swayze's character Dalton provided some in the speech he gave to the Double Deuce employees when he took over as cooler, "All you have to do is follow three simple rules. One, never underestimate your opponent. Expect the unexpected. Two, take it outside. Never start anything inside the bar unless it's absolutely necessary. And three, be nice." It was the third rule, be nice, that I was especially trying to remember. This is actually a very good rule when bouncing or working security. Your demeanor, especially being nice, can prevent an awful lot of trouble and violence. Swayze continued his lesson in the movie by saying, "I want you to be nice, until it's time not to be nice." This too is an important consideration, and those who work in security need to understand when each is appropriate.

The former Marine noticed me approaching as the crowd around him started to part when they recognized I was moving toward the largest and loudest of them. He squared himself and puffed out his chest a bit. "The boy knows a weight room," I thought to myself. Arrogantly, he said, "You're gonna need a lot more friends, and that flashlight ain't gonna help you." I was on my own at the moment, and I silently commended him for noticing the D-cell Maglight in my cargo pocket. It was at this very moment that I had a choice. And I had to make the choice instantly. I could puff up my own chest and come back with something to the effect of, "It's not me that needs more friends." Selecting this choice would almost certainly guarantee that things went physical. Not really the best alternative when you are being paid to prevent such occurrences. Or, I could choose to be nice. I choose the latter.

I continued toward him in a non-threatening manner. I think this surprised him a bit, because he was really expecting me to respond aggressively as in choice number one. I walked up to him, placed my left hand on his shoulder in a friendly gesture, and said, "You're my friend, aren't you buddy?" He didn't really know what to say. I continued, "See all these people; I'm just trying to make sure no one gets hurt. I'm as pissed about the rain and band as you are. Also, I see you were a Marine. I was 82nd Airborne and a sniper instructor with the 2nd Infantry Division. Thank you for your service." I held out my hand. He accepted it, and as we shook hands he said, "Thank you for your service too." We talked a few minutes more, everything was cool, and I left to deal with others. He wasn't a problem the rest of the night. Fortunately, the night wasn't much longer, because shortly after I spoke with him they made the official announcement that the concert was cancelled due to the water-damaged equipment, and people would be able to get a refund the following week from whatever venue they purchased them from. The crowd then dispersed.

Far too many physical altercations could be prevented if instead of being aggressive, people would simply be nice. And while natural for some, it really is a learned response for others. Learning to be nice, even when you sometimes don't want to, is a valuable skill when dealing with aggressive behavior and wanting to prevent physical violence. Does it work one hundred percent of the time? Of course not. But then, nothing does. However, being nice first does allow you to defuse and prevent many situations before things get out of hand. And you can always go from being nice, to not being nice, if you have to. But you can't go the other way. If you start out not being nice, you can't back up and change to being nice. It's too late, and you've already blown that opportunity. So if you don't want to take it from me, take it from Patrick Swayze as Dalton, "I want you to be nice, until it's time not to be nice."

Choosing to Leave a Cult

by "Chop Ki"

In a previous article we discussed what a cult looks like, how it operates, how they will try and test you to see if you are the right sort of person for inclusion and how to get you to commit. We were specifically speaking of martial arts cults, but the specific aim of the cult doesn't have to be martial arts; the basis is a con, and a con can run in many areas.

What if you have suspicions, or it has been flat-out pointed out to you, you've examined your situation and decide that you are in a cult, or even a cult-like group? (Please see the previous article for the distinction between the two.) How do you get yourself out? It would be very easy, and very flip to simply say, "Well then, just quit and move on," but that doesn't really do the situation justice. Yes, just like being an alcoholic, the first step is admitting it. You have to admit to yourself that you are in a cult. That is no small task and just might take an overwhelming preponderance of evidence from several sources before you would even begin to give the idea credence. Just like our little frog from the last article, you might just be sitting in your pot of heating water, slowly being cooked and you don't even realize it.

It just might be that your indoctrination into the group, and your willingness to be complicit have you in so deep that you can no longer see the light. It might take something monumental to get you to realize that something is amiss. I'll tell you what it took for me and several hundred of my compatriots; it took a week-long exposé by an investigative reporter airing a half hour segment in prime time on a major network news program. *And we still didn't believe it!!!*

No, no and no I say! They are wrong!! They don't know what they are talking about!!! They are taking everything out of context!!!! We are not in a cult!!!!! Oh how wrong we were, and after the preponderance of evidence was just too overwhelming, we were forced to consider the fact that maybe, just maybe, we were deluding ourselves. If it looks like a duck, walks like a duck, quacks like a duck…etc.

Hopefully one does come to see it sooner rather than later, and that it doesn't take a drastic and monumental occurrence to let the truth come to the fore, but once it does, where do you go from there?

Well, if you recall from the previous article, a con has two sides. Yes they are painting a false picture for you in the hopes of getting you to commit, but you must remember that it is the picture that you requested them to paint. Yes Virginia, you have set this situation in motion, these folks are just giving you what you want. You walked in the door with perhaps some unrealistic expectations. Maybe had a vision of a situation that is even pure fantasy. The con is just giving you that fantasy. In essence, you hold yourself in the cult; therefore, you also hold the keys to your release.

Admittedly, there are probably some situations where this is not the case, but unless there is an instance of duress, there is nothing really holding you to the cult. If there is physical, mental, financial, or legal duress, that is a different matter. In a lot of cases, perhaps even the vast majority of cases, there is no such duress and you are really and truly quite free to leave at any time. So why don't you?

The reason, though not "simple" as in easy, is not complicated. You are complicit in your bondage to the group. Remember that thing you wanted? Well you still want it. You are afraid to lose it. It is still being promised to you and you are afraid, deep down inside, that your opportunity will vanish if you make a hasty choice to leave. You have deluded yourself into thinking that your dream is still possible. Sure you might have to put up with a lot of bullshit, but if you can still attain your dream, well then, isn't it all worth it? In your mind you have convinced yourself that staying means eventually reaching your dream, goal, whatever you choose to call it.

Trouble with that is you will never attain your dream unless it was something that could have been attained by you, all along, without their help. That is not to say that you wouldn't have needed *someone's* help, that depends on the goal, just that you don't specifically need *their* help; as in the leadership of the specific cult you are in. In fact, they most likely are not capable of it in the first place.

This fact, however, is what makes leaving difficult. You have to re-examine your dream. The reason you joined in the first place. Is it realistic? In my case it was not. The world living in peace and harmony, all getting along in a Zen Buddhist nirvana, is not so realistic, but try telling my nineteen year old self that. Over time though, you even lose sight of the initial reason. You start to focus on other things, like how much time and effort you have put into this thing. How much money you have given over to reach this dream of yours. How much sweat and pain you have gone through. Then there is an insidious fact that is specific to the martial arts cult.

Learning a martial art, you are learning a multitude of things. Yes, you are learning how to handle yourself physically. You are getting strong, you are getting fit. Coordination and control are increasing, as well as many other physical attributes. You are also learning, at the same time, many mental attributes. How to push through pain, how to concentrate better, how to focus, how to remain calm in the midst of a storm and many others, including *to never give up*. That is a double-edged sword, my friends. You learn to do or die, to keep on going, to keep striving to reach your goal. Well, what if your goal can't be reached and your learned response to keep on striving, no matter what, is working against you instead of for you?

These are the things you must overcome. You must first see the reality of the situation you are in. You must re-examine your reasons for being in the situation in the first place. You must decide if your goals are realistic and if so, whether they can be obtained elsewhere. You must overcome the tendency to not want to throw away all of the time, and effort, and money, and whatever else you think shouldn't have been wasted. You must know when it is time to stop striving for something that is holding you in a situation that is against your best interests.

When you look at it realistically, a lot of these things were not wasted. You have put in time and effort, but if you have been trying you should be in better physical condition than when you started. Learning things like patience and determination, confidence and self-control, you should be mentally better off as well. Being in a martial arts cult, and this one depends on how qualified, or not, the instruction was/is, you should be able to better defend yourself. These things are not wasted; you will be taking them with you, so all is not lost. So what really do you have to lose? The chance to achieve an unrealistic dream? I'd say you have nothing to lose.

Oh, there is the money, but quite honestly, besides the power trip that the cult leader(s) get from the adoration of the membership, your money is what they were after all along. So by staying you are just throwing more money down the rabbit hole. It's not like this were a casino where you could say to yourself, "well, if I keep playing I can win it back," which even if it were a casino that almost never works because the game is rigged in favor of the house. This isn't a casino game however, so there is *zero* chance of you getting your money back, so forget about that right now. This fact makes the money that is gone irrelevant and the longer you stay it just gets worse.

So what to do? Well, after examination it is your unwillingness to give up on your dream that is the sole tie. Understandably, giving up on this isn't all that easy. After all, aren't our dreams for the future what make us who we are? I'm not talking about something superficial and unspecific, "I want to be rich," is not a dream that makes us who we are, unless of course it becomes obsessive. No, something more on the lines of, "I want to become a great martial artist so that I can teach others how to be safe and therefore give them peace of mind." That speaks more to who we want to be, but is that something we can only get in this one specific place? I think not, so a dream like that isn't an anchor to this group. Maybe something more along the lines of my 'world peace and can't we all just get along' dream. Now that one we have to examine.

Something like that made me who I was, and in some small measure who I still am. But was it attainable? They told me it was. I even had a nice pretty picture painted for me of how it was not just possible, but how it would be done: with this group and this group only. Well, after closer examination, I had to revise my vision. In essence, I had to kill my old dream. With that old dream being so much of who I was, I had to figuratively kill my old self and become someone new and *that* was the anchor that was holding me there.

It's not an easy thing, even if just figuratively, to kill your old self and become someone new. Oh, you don't have to do it all of the way, but a substantial part of the way is necessary. It is getting to this point, being able to change your inner vision and thereby change who you are that is the key to being able to walk away. This does not mean you need to abandon your core beliefs. You don't have to go from being a "good" person to being an "evil" person, but you do need to re-evaluate just what it is that makes you tick and alter it enough to become, figuratively, someone new. It is a new but hopefully improved you however. Perhaps a bit older, wiser, more realistic you.

Once you realize that this is something you can and will survive, then it's just a matter of giving notice: "notice I'm not there!" All joking aside, it's really just better to fade away and let them wonder what became of you.

Now take that first step.

Section 6: Philosophy

It's not all busting bones and war stories. Sometimes the way you see something is just as important as what you see.

Gambling With Your Life

by Marc MacYoung

When it comes to poker, I might as well just hand you my money and save myself the time.

Yet, I routinely gambled. I wagered not just my life, but chances of being crippled or maimed for the rest of it. Getting a tire iron upside your head can leave you with the blunt force trauma version of Alzheimer's. Getting shot in the guts can mean shitting in a colostomy bag for the rest of your life. I was gambling on those stakes.

When I talk about this kind of stuff, people often think I'm setting them up for the sales pitch about my ultimate fighting system. First, there ain't no such critter.

Second, there ain't anything to sell. You can't sell a mindset, a mastery of violence or reality…you only can claim you do.

Third, what I'm talking about is not a macho fantasy vis-à-vis the 'warrior mindset' or posturing about what a big dick you need to 'make it out in the streets.' Injuries and death are the potential results of engaging in violence. Ain't nuthin' sexy or cool about it. And while we're at it, attending friends' funerals sucks. There's a hard truth about this subject: If you do manage to develop what it takes, it'll turn you into a grim, fucked-up asshole, who believes all life is cheap, including your own.

If you're smart, you'll take this attitude into a job where you have a better chance to keep it from eating you alive. Having the goals and purpose of a job should help keep you from sliding into drugs, booze or eating a bullet. That's because the job gives you a bigger purpose for gambling like this.

But, even then, it isn't sexy. When it's your job to tell nasty people no, gambling for those stakes is just another Tuesday night. Nothing special, just another shift.

During that shift, you're trying to attain the twin goals of not bleeding and not having to hospitalize some idjit. And usually that's a drunken, pissed-off idjit, who thinks making you bleed is a grand idea. A bad night at work is when the guy (and his buddies) aren't drunk, but armed.

They come looking to rob the place or kill you for some transgression against their little ducky feelings. Problems like that don't just end with a body hitting the floor — there's usually a lot of paperwork and people who don't believe you were the good guy. That's because, most of the time, the person who 'wins' at violence is the one who crossed the line. It makes it a hard sell to convince the authorities you didn't do that.

That's why I want to talk to you about gambling and odds — because violence makes a whole lot more sense when you think about it in terms of controlling the odds.

When I say that, a lot of people think I'm talking about stacking the deck. While that *is* part of it, you have to realize something important— it's a two-way street. The other side is trying to stack the deck, too. It's easy to win at cards when you're the only one cheating. But it's a whole different game when everyone sitting at the table cheats, too.

When it comes to violence, everyone is going to be cheatin.' And that's where things get complicated. You may think you have an ace up your sleeve. Hell, you might even have one. But recognize that other guy has three or four. If he didn't think he had something that'd let him win, he wouldn't play.

That's the game you've joined. Or you're working your ass off so as not to have to play it. The stakes aren't just pride and emotion. They can get real serious, real quick – even if you thought you were playing for such penny-ante shit as your pride.

Now let's talk about a really bad attitude that has popped up lately regarding violence and self-defense. And that is the search for the 'magic pill.'

I'm borrowing this idea from the health and fitness world where people often are willing to do *anything* to lose weight — except eat right and exercise. They are looking for the pill that will give them the results they want *without* having to change a thing about their lifestyles. There's an entire industry based on producing these magic pills.

When this same idea creeps into the subject of dealing with violence, you have some problems. There ain't no such thing as a magic pill, but it goes even deeper than that.

The idea of 'not changing anything, but still getting guaranteed results' is something a part of us knows is a pipe dream. Yet without smoking opium, it is something many people still seek. They want that one thing that is going to do everything for them and is guaranteed *never* to fail.

It's bad enough when we're talking weight loss aids, but 'magic pills' for self-defense? Now, we have a problem. I'm talking about people who want some way to walk out of Ragnarök without a scratch.

Ain't going to happen. It especially ain't going to happen, not because of their 'fighting' prowess, but with their current level of people skills, knowledge and awareness. The magic pill they're looking for is to use when the shit hits the fan. Their interest in keeping the shit from hitting the fan in the first place is functionally nil. That's neither a survivor's attitude nor a gambler's.

I recently had someone ask about stun guns. He started by telling me what he thought he already knew. And that was they were less reliable than the shooting-type of tasers. He knew all sorts of stories about stun guns failing and just 'pissing attackers off.' Despite this presumed failure rate, he asked if I still recommended them.

I get these kinds of questions a lot. *Sigh.*

Let's take a look at this question from the magic pill perspective. First off, there's a difference between inflicting lethal damage and stopping power. Someone can be fatally wounded and still functional enough to take you with them. Mostly it depends on how dedicated they are to taking you out. Pain alone won't stop someone hellbent on killing you. (So if you've pissed off someone that much, it's on you.)

Handguns are notorious for lack of stopping power. With that in mind, you might want to consider how likely a punch is to stop someone. What this guy wanted was something that had the immediate stopping power of a rocket propelled grenade (RPG), but was nonlethal.

Second, I can walk up behind someone, sucker punch him, and there's a good chance the guy will stagger, if not fall. But let's change the scenario. That same punch in the guy's face — when he is enraged, slightly drunk and charging me — will bounce off like a thrown ping pong ball. Both when and under what circumstances you use something has a major effect on whether or not it works. Another huge factor is who you use it on. Using a stun gun on an eighty year old woman from behind tends to have more stopping power than using it on a 250lb enraged dude, who is barreling down on you.

What this guy was looking for was something that worked immediately under *any* condition. Again, a magic pill that did all the work for him anywhere along the process — but especially out on the extremes.

Third, what he was looking for was something he could just pull out and use to poke someone. *Zap!* That was it, nothing else. Pull it, stick out your arm and push a button. That was all the effort needed. (Inserting a snide side comment, this also allowed him to focus on his obviously much more important emotional state.) Talk about wanting a weight loss solution while refusing to 'eat less, move more.'

Stop and think about what he was really looking for. A simplistic, no brainer, ultimate stopping power, works-under-any-circumstances 'magic pill' with which he didn't have to do anything else. Oh yeah, it also was nonlethal. Those were reasonable expectations, right?

Going back to the gambling analogy, this guy was looking for an ace to put up his sleeve. The *one and only* thing he'd need to *always* win. Sound silly? Sitting in the comfort of a chair and reading this, it's obvious.

But it's not obvious if you're the one looking for the magic pill.

Think about the inherent blind spot in this approach. If you have a magic pill, why would you need anything else? More importantly, why would you need to do anything else? Just pull and zap. All your fears are soothed if you can find such a simplistic solution and don't have to think about the situation.

Unfortunately, while the magic pill approach does wonders for your fears, it does nothing to actually reduce the danger. In fact, it just might increase it.

I'm talking about actual danger that is wildly different than what your imagination cooks up. Because violence doesn't happen the way most people think it does. The way it really goes down is what you need to prepare for to be physically safe. But getting that information can be hard with all the macho posturing, fantasy and agenda groups out there trying to sell you their so-called 'truths' about the subject.

My response to the guy was to tell him that technology alone wasn't going to do the trick. There were things he'd have to do over and above using his 'magic pill.' Things like jumping off the tracks when a train was barreling down on his ass. Of course, sticking his spark box out and pushing the button as he dodged increased the odds of both the dodge and 'sparky' working. If he didn't get off the tracks, an attacker would either plow into him (giving him a shock, too) or blast the stun gun out of contact.

Wow, isn't it amazing how just standing there and expecting the stun gun to do all the work increases the chance of failure?

And that brings us back to what a professional 'gambler' does to increase the odds. Oh wait, before we talk about that, there's something else I need to mention. I've talked about the magic pill in terms of an item (Also known as 'talisman thinking.' Think about holding a cross up to scare off a vampire. Now change it to a self-defense item to scare off a bad guy.)

The biggest version of magic pill thinking is slightly harder to spot if you haven't first seen it in the form of a self-defense talisman. Where you'll see this thought process the most is in the form of some ultimate fighting system. That is to say, an art (or system) that promises to teach you to handle any kind of 'self-defense' situation. I'm especially talking about systems that promise to turn you into some kind of martial art stud, urban commando or master of reality-based self-defense. All you need to do is learn this killer commando system (take this magic pill), and you'll be the ultimate bad ass.

And you'll believe it. Right up until some street weasel says, "Hey, it's cool man." And when you turn to swagger off, thinking it's done, he shoots you in the back of your head.

Welcome to what you *don't* learn about violence in your search for a magic pill.

Oh yeah, we had a name for someone trying to shoot you this way. We called it Saturday night. That's when things got real exciting. Yeee-ha! It's what you have to expect when you tell violent people no.

Now let's tie this back to gambling and what you need to do to increase your odds. Pretty much everyone knows the lines from the Kenny Roger's song "The Gambler:" *You got to know when to hold 'em, know when to fold 'em, know when to walk away and know when to run.* Good advice that, but those aren't my favorite lines from that song.

The lines that always got to me are: *If you're going to play the game boy, you gotta learn to play it right.* The gambler then proceeds to list the number of things to take into consideration if you want to make it – including holdin' and foldin'.

That's a really good approach because it widens the subject past the focus on the unrealistic goal of always having a winning hand. Or in this case, past some magic pill or talisman that allows you to beat anyone up.

When you start looking at the subject beyond the limits of seeking a magic pill, you start seeing little things you can do that will up the odds in your favor. What are the five or six things that you can do to bump your odds up to eighty percent, instead of relying on only one thing?

Each element contributes to the collective sum of the odds. The more little things you add and can control, the more your odds creep up, bit by bit. While you'll never be able to get the odds to one hundred percent, bumping them up to ninety percent or ninety five percent is a pretty good thing when the stakes are you bleeding out on the sidewalk.

Now the weird thing about this is a lot of stuff that can increase your odds doesn't have an obvious connection with 'self defense.' For example, what do people skills have to do with winning a fight? Well, people skills go a long way toward avoiding punching someone in the first place. Or someone wanting to punch you.

Hell, some of the best books I ever read about avoiding a fight were etiquette books. Turns out if you're polite, sincere and don't screw people over, they have a lot less reason to try to cave in your skull.

Equally important is — when you've been polite and social and yet someone is still coming at you — it becomes real obvious it ain't social violence. Odd thing is someone, who is relying on your being social so he can commit asocial violence, tends to change his plans when he sees you've shifted gears because you know what he's up to. Funny how recognizing your willingness to shoot him in the face if he attacks tends to change folk's minds.

Another benefit about this approach is you start looking at your personal safety for the long term. You realize your odds of not getting hurt really go up when you start paying attention to when to hold 'em and when to fold 'em. For example, there are some people you just don't want to go up against. There is no shame or loss of face for not playing for the table stakes some folks play for.

I'll also throw in this freebie, the guys who are the most dangerous are usually the ones who – to use a poker term – have the smallest 'tells.' It's not the wild-eyed, drooling-in-your-face mad dawg who's the most dangerous. (Although odds are good such a person will beat you bloody if you give him an excuse.)

Be more far concerned about the guy who doesn't seem concerned about your 'message' of what a big bad ass you are. Take for example, the guy who, calmly, leans back in his chair and keeps his voice level — as his hand floats out of sight under the table. If someone isn't getting uptight about your threat displays, odds are you dun tree'd yourself a bad 'un.

I gotta tell you, one of the best things about looking at this subject from a bigger perspective is you learn how to prevent the other guy from increasing *his* odds. That's a life-saver.

Little things that didn't mean too much before become *really* important once you look at it as a matter of keeping the odds in your favor. For example, his moving his empty hand toward a position where people normally carry a weapon is something — if you let him complete the move — that significantly screws your odds. He might just have a magic pill under his shirt.

If he moves slow and tries to act casual, then a snarled, "Keep your hands where I can see them" can keep the odds in your favor. More than that, if he has a lick of survival sense, he'll recognize you know what he is trying to do – and you will react appropriately to the danger of the increased stakes. If he goes for it fast, busting a bottle over his head or shooting him might be the only chance you have of staying out of the hospital or the morgue.

That's how you stack the odds in your favor. You start collecting little skills. Little things that add up.

More than that, you'll begin to understand the best way to 'win' in a rigged game is to not play at all. There are lots of ways and reasons not to get suckered into a violent confrontation. Going back to the odds game, there are ways to bump up your chances of avoiding a physical conflict to ninety nine percent. I know the idea will make a lot of folks, who have never been there (and are insecure about it), say, 'Yeah, yeah, but sometimes you have to ..."

Yeah, I'll be the first to admit you gotta do what you gotta do. But just make sure you really have to do it.

Staying out of it is one of the best ways to keep the odds from catching up with you. Giving in to the urge to tell someone to fuck off can have lifetime results. Odds are good this guy will be out of your face and life in a few moments. But if you give in to the impulse, well, remember every time you 'play,' you're taking a chance.

The stories in this book will help you begin to understand the stakes you're playing for. But more than that, they talk about all the other things you need to understand about the game. That's how you keep the odds in your favor. After all, "If you're going to play the game boy, you gotta learn to play it right."

The stakes are too high not to.

There is no Magic

by Fred Ross

There is no magic. Most people say that they agree. They no longer believe in Santa Claus or the Tooth Fairy. Look closer, though, and you'll find minds rife with magical thinking.

What is magical thinking? The best example I know of is from Richard Feynman's essay 'Cargo Cult Science'. It's available online, and everyone should read it, but here's the relevant passage:

> *"In the South Seas there is a cargo cult of people. During the war they saw airplanes land with lots of good materials, and they want the same thing to happen now. So they've arranged to imitate things like runways, to put fires along the sides of the runways, to make a wooden hut for a man to sit in, with two wooden pieces on his like headphones and bars of bamboo sticking out like antennas—-he's the controller—-and they wait for the airplanes to land. They're doing everything right. The form is perfect. It looks exactly the way it looked before. But it doesn't work. No airplanes land."*

This is magical thinking, a ritual or incantation that is supposed to work despite the laws of reality. Everyone in the developed world looks at the cargo cults and says, "How stupid can you be?" We have our own brands of magical thinking, though. Have you ever bought a lottery ticket, hoping to win? If you buy one every week for the whole of your life—-that's about four thousand tickets—-your odds of winning are between one in ten thousand and one in a hundred thousand. For a single ticket, it's between one in ten million and one in a hundred million. For comparison, the chance of that the average American will be killed by lightning is about one in eighty thousand. How about car accidents? That's one in eighty four. People don't understand these numbers, so let's put it into perspective: if you think buying a lottery ticket is worth it because you might win, you should also plan your life around you and your two best friends all dying in separate car crashes. Do you? If not, then buying a lottery ticket is a magical ritual that you do, and no more.

I know of three kinds of magical thinking. The first, appeasing spirits, has fallen out of fashion in our society. We don't regularly pour a libation to the gods before drinking wine, or leave milk out for the fairies. There are cults that do it, but you probably don't have to worry about it.

Playing the lottery is a perfect example of the second kind: suspending the laws of probability. The events of your life are random. Just play what-if for a little while. What if your parents got run over by a train? What if your mother married that bartender from New Jersey instead? What if you had gotten the umbilical cord wrapped around your neck in the womb and came out mentally retarded? Most of us don't play what-if because it's too impossible to see what little turning point might have made a difference. Even in works of art based on it, such as the film *Run, Lola, Run*, no one plays very far. If they do it tends to be disturbing, as in the opening chapters of Bulgakov's *Master and Margarita*. Your future will be as random as your past. Will you trip and break your arm tomorrow? Will you find a dollar on the street? Will you be struck by lightning?

Breaking your arm and getting hit by lightning aren't equally likely, though. You're probably more likely to die in a car crash than by lightning, unless you live at the top of a mountain in storm country with no roads and no cars. There is some probability of events. You can affect that probability with your actions. If you never buy stocks, for example, you can never lose money on them. If you never go near the ocean, you'll have a hard time drowning in it. If you stay out of areas with high crime rates, you're less likely to be victimized. Not all attempts to alter the probability of events in your life are magical thinking. It is only magical thinking when some ritual or incantation, such as buying a lottery ticket, is supposed to change the odds for you just this once.

This is important: magical thinking is all about intent. I have a friend who plays the lottery as a form of voluntary taxation. She buys tickets with no expectation whatsoever of winning. This isn't magical thinking. She is certainly putting more of her money into the state budget. An old lady who puts out a saucer of milk to feed a stray cat is doing the same physical act as another putting out a saucer of milk for the fairies, but one is magical thinking and the other is not.

The third kind of magical thinking tries to change the essence of a thing. I know someone who got rid of sugar from her diet to lose weight, but replaced it with honey on the basis that honey was "natural." "Natural" here is an incantation, but will the honey suddenly have zero calories just because of your naming? Other people takes antibiotics for any illness, whether it is a bacterial infection or not, expecting the drugs to cure them. But why would such a ritual cure a viral infection or a case of malnutrition?

Magical thinking to change essences comes from mentally sweeping a mess under the rug. The details of which antibiotics affect which classes of bacteria, and which diseases are bacterial and which aren't, are complicated. The biochemistry of sugar metabolism is worse. Most people want right answers, until they find that they're difficult. Then they want simple answers.

How do the two kinds of magical thinking in our society manifest in the martial arts? Here are some examples.

Get on most martial arts forums and you'll find an argument over which style is best. Saying, "X is best" is an incantation said in hopes that it will magically turn its sayer into an invulnerable warrior. It's pure changing essence. The next level of sophistication assumes that you'll have to do some work, and asks what is the best martial art to study? That is, if I put in my time, what will magically make me into an invulnerable warrior? This is no different. It's still a ritual.

We can continue. What's the best style for you to work on? Now we've left changing essence and entered suspending probability. Say you got an answer. What are the chances of a master of that system teaching within an easy distance of your home? Be honest. How many of you have any kind of martial arts master living next door, let alone one of a particular style? All you can hope to ask is, "Given my situation and interests, what is the best instruction within reach?" That's a really sensible question, and usually has a clear answer.

Let's take another example: "qi" (or "ki" if you prefer Japanese). I remember my instructor telling a class, "Drill your strikes left arm first, then right." One of the students asked why. One of the under instructors started to say something about qi flow. The instructor told him that most people are right handed, so their left hand usually needs a little extra attention. Do the left first. That's all. I'm left handed, so I've started my drills with my right hand ever since, which has worked well for me.

Qi carries the burden for all kinds of things. Ill health? Your qi's out of balance. An old man capable of hitting really hard? Must be projecting qi. It's an all-purpose incantation for whatever ails you.

So what difficult answer is lurking under the surface of this incantation? Well, do you know when your stomach's upset? Do you know when your muscles are sore or overextended? How about when your joints are well aligned? You have a huge range of internal senses of your body's state, most of which you don't consciously feel or have learned to ignore. That mass of sensation is qi, and it's the work of years or decades to track down all the tendrils and learn to interpret them. All the other stuff like being able to stand unperturbed while someone pushes as hard as they can on you? That's learning how to use the muscles and bones and nerves of your body, and that's not simple either.

My next victim is kata, which is typically buried in layers of magical thinking. Do you have any motions in your forms that you slide through, not fully sure what they are? Those are rituals you do in hopes of becoming a great martial artist. It could be even more basic, though: most karate systems teach a first form that begins with a step to the left with a low block, and followed by a step with a punch, but do you know how to actually use those motions on an opponent? Do you fight the way that you move in your forms? If not, then, though you may know that this is a punch, that is a kick to the knee, it's still a ritual.

Now say you know exactly what that motion is for, and you can flow through it effortlessly and effectively. What are the odds of you being in a situation where it's useful? Consider the hurricane kick from tae kwon do. It's fun to do. It's impressive to see. If you try it against someone who really wants to hurt you, you may as well bare your breast for their knife. Devoting your finite practice time to it is a ritual meant to suspend probability and make the world yield situations where your flying kick will save the day.

How do you rid yourself of magical thinking?

For changing essences, look at the thing itself. Can you concretely demonstrate it? A foot is very concrete. I'll show you mine if no other is available, and then we have a clear, shared understanding of the word "foot." A front kick is a little harder, but not much: thigh lifted with knee bent, knee straightened to push against something with the foot, then retract the leg and put it down. We demonstrate body parts and motions and quickly arrive at a shared understanding.

What about something abstract like a kata? Break it into pieces: here's the first couple motions, and a demonstration of them. Here's the next few. Here's the link between the pieces. As the concepts become more abstract, the amount of detail required grows and grows. A demonstration of "karate" is essentially training in the art plus a knowledge of its history and development. It's complicated and requires a lot of work.

Once you've figured out the mess behind the word, are you trying to suspend probability? There is no substitute for numbers here. What is the probability of being grabbed in a bear hug from behind by someone who really means you harm? What are the probabilities of other events, like dying in a car crash, being hit by lightning, or getting stabbed? If someone who means you ill is much more likely to stab you than to grab you from behind, then perhaps you should train for stabbing much more than for bear hugs. It may seem obvious, but do you actually know the relative likelihood of the disasters you're preparing for? A lot of us are more likely to be in a bad earthquake than to be assaulted by ninjas.

Getting the probabilities to compare isn't always easy. One of your best sources is the government. The FBI and other federal law enforcement bodies publish crime statistics[*] The National Safety Council provides probabilities of various kinds of death[†]. The National Weather Service will give you numbers on storms and natural disasters[‡]. There are organizations tasked with nothing other than producing usable probabilities. If you're truly stuck, try asking your local research librarian, a public servant tasked with helping you find such things.

An invaluable tool for figuring out relative likelihoods of getting in situations where you can use a particular move is Rory Miller's one step drill: very slowly one person makes a single move. The other person makes a move in return, equally slowly. They go back and forth, continuing from where the last move got them. The slowness of the drill provides time to investigate, and prevents the players from getting hurt. One move is a step and a punch or a step and a block, not a step with a block followed by a punch. Playing with this drill bare handed and with props like water bottles playing the role of knives, bricks, and other weapons will reveal many of your misconceptions about what happens commonly and what is rare.

All this is fine if you know where your thinking is magical, but how do you find those places? The worst way is life experience. Getting stabbed because you threw a fancy kick instead of running will probably end your magical thinking about fancy kicks, but may also kill you. I suggest a more sedate method.

---

[*] http://bjs.gov

[†] http://www.nsc.org/news_resources/injury_and_death_statistics/Pages/InjuryDeathStatistics.aspx

[‡] http://weather.gov/

Look for a passage of text about some aspect of your art. If you don't have one to hand, write a few paragraphs yourself. Describe a kata you're working on, a punch you've drilled, why you do something in a certain way in your art. Now go over it carefully. Look at every noun. Look at every statement saying, "do this" or "do that." Can you concretely demonstrate what it is and why it is done? Do you know the probabilities relevant to it?

Examine your kata. Do you know what every move is supposed to be and how to fight with it? Do you know how likely it is that you'll be in a situation where the move is relevant?

Go spend time with a very different martial art. Don't brag. Don't play up your strength or your other training. Go and humbly listen and study. Compare it to your own study. Where are the differences? It's not a question of who's right. Both systems may be stuck in different forms of magical thinking. All you want are the differences so that you know where to look.

Look at your ideals, your silent vision of the martial artist that you're trying to become. What is it? Is it a commando, a ninja, the old man that no one bothers? Is it a champion boxer or wrestler? What is the probability that becoming what you envision would be useful or even desirable in your life? Is your training actually going to make you into one, or is it a ritual you do in hopes of magically becoming what you envision?

Exorcising magical thinking is hard. It makes those around you uncomfortable, since social circles tend to share the same convictions. Is it worth it? Buying lottery tickets in hopes of vast wealth makes you poor. Eschewing sugar but eating honey because it's "natural" makes you fat. Magical thinking in martial arts can get you killed. Working at your magical thinking is probably time well spent. You should check that, though. It might be magical thinking on my part.

Learn the Old to Understand the New

by Don Roley

An amusing sentiment that goes through just about every activity from time to time is that there can be nothing learned from the past. As much as we may give lip service to learning from our mistakes, we sometimes do not pay attention to learning from the mistakes of others. We think we know it all and that those that went before us really did not know what was going on. Marketers for the latest system convince us that their repackaged version of things is oh so much better than the collected wisdom of our ancestors.

People have been beating and killing each other since Abel slew Cain (why do we have to say "slain" instead of "kill" when talking about people in the bible?) and yet the marketers advertising in the back of glossy martial arts magazines would have you think that people only started doing things once pay-per-view came along.

I studied more than one style of martial arts when I was living in Japan. Most of them trace back a few hundred years. At the same time, I was very interested in self-defense. Instead of thinking that there was nothing to be gained from things like sword training, I tried to keep my mind open. Soon, it was obvious that within the older styles, there are still a lot of the original principles that can be used today. Of course, I am not saying you will probably get a chance to use a sword to defend yourself. However, the applications change, but the core remains. Being able to use those core principles requires thorough knowledge of the subject and not just a shallow look.

One part of classical training is the use of kata. Kata basically just means form. It means a series of pre-arranged movements for one or more people to go through. Many folks might think of kata from the solo style of karate training that originated in the island of Okinawa. On the mainland of Japan, in systems traced back to the samurai, kata usually involves two people.

The biggest misconception is that the participants go through the motions robotically. This has led to many folks saying that "live" training is needed in the form of something like competition and they imply that training other than what they do is all "dead" and thus useless.

In reality, there are several methods and levels within kata training. In some cases, such as the beginning or when two novices work together, the moves will probably be done precisely and without variation. This is only part of the training and I think anyone who says that all kata training is like this has never proceeded past this stage.

Japan has a concept called Shu-Ha-Ri. You can find it not just in martial arts, but in almost any traditional Japanese art.

The first stage is "Shu" which means, "to preserve." At this level, the student is expected to copy exactly what is presented until it becomes habit.

Then is the "Ha" stage, which means "to break". Now the student starts to take apart and examine the material. With a strong base behind him, he has good examples of how things should be and has room to mess with things and determine the reasoning and principles behind them.

The final stage of "Ri" means, "to separate". At this point, the seeker is expected to take the core principles and make new expressions of them different from what he has been shown.

It all sounds very esoteric, so let me give an example many will be better able to follow.

When I started living in Japan I taught English while I was continuing to learn Japanese. As such, I sometimes tend to think it terms of learning or teaching languages.

At the beginning, we (the Japanese students in English class and me in my Japanese lessons) would learn a target sentence that used the grammar point we were expected to learn. It was not something we came up with on our own, it was a grammatically perfect example. We would be expected to learn it, and other examples, by heart. That would be called the "Shu" stage.

Once we had a perfect example under our belts to use as reference, we started taking apart the sentences and filling in new sections. The target sentence might have been, "Sara's dog is big." Then we might be told to talk about our dog instead and so we say/write, "My dog is big." Then, maybe, "His dog is big" and many other variations. This would be the "Ha" stage in the process.

Finally, after a lot of directed tearing down and reconstructing things under the guidance of a teacher, we would come up with our own sentences from scratch. One might be "My cat is pretty" or "His sister is crazy." As you probably guessed, this is the last part of the process called "Ri".

In martial arts, some folks look at the kata and see only the "Shu" portion. Unless you are part of the process over a period of time, it is hard to see anything else. Someone makes an attack, it is countered and it looks like that is all that is going on time after time.

But after the basic moves are gotten down, there are some changes in things in order to break them apart and make them alive. There are different methods and systems. For example, in the Kashima Shinto ryu, students first work out with each other with wooden swords called "bokken." The moves these novices are expected to perform are very precise with no deviance from the form. After a while, the students are given bamboo swords called "fukuro shinai" and perform the same kata. This time, if they see an opening in the other person they are expected to make an attack. The teacher usually watches to make sure the attacks are the same as could be done with a real sword (as opposed to the types of strikes you can make with a lighter weight simulation) and to catch all mistakes in both attacker and defender and correct them before they become a habit. Finally, steel swords are used. Today, I am told they are mainly non- sharpened, but that was (and is) not always the case.

Most systems I am familiar with usually are taught in small groups and the teacher or a senior student under his guidance serves as one half of the pair. Teachers differ in how they present things based on their personality, and some change over the course of the instruction. A teacher that is forgiving as you fumble the first few times through the motions will probably ratchet up the pressure as you progress. At the start, a teacher might gently mention that unless you move some body part you leave yourself open. Then someday, you might find out the holes in your technique by a fierce rap with a bokken.

One word about bokken: They were not introduced into training for the safety of the students. They were made to prevent damage to expensive Japanese katana. They are just about the mass of a light baseball bat and Miyamoto Musashi, the author of "The Book of Five Rings," was notorious for having killed several people with bokken. Even with the small number of students practicing in the older styles of swordsmanship, every year it seems someone dies or is crippled in Japan during practice using them. In Japan, if someone broke a bone during class the teacher would get someone to drive him to the hospital and we would all pitch in for a sympathy gift and that would end the matter. Here in America, you would probably lose your house in a lawsuit.

While going through the kata with someone senior to you, you never knew if they were going to throw in something else. As the junior, you had to conform to the movements as they are laid out. But the senior might substitute a cut from the opposite side than what the standard kata has. Of course, you learned to deal with that sort of cut in a different series of movements and if you did well, you found yourself flowing into that sequence as the senior pushed you to your limit.

I have sparred in a ring. I know what it is like to face someone who is there to fight and hurt you. But I never was so frightened as in some of the kata sessions I went through in Japan.

There is something quite unique when you are facing something that might kill you if things do not go as planned. The teacher (hopefully) should not push you past the point you are able to take, but in the back of your mind you know that mistakes happen and people have died doing the same kata.

While I also did unarmed kata that had much the same method of feedback, it was only in the lesson facing a bokken or other weapon that I was in actual fear of death or serious injury. I had to learn to face my fear and have my body function under the extreme stress and dump of various chemicals into my bloodstream and yet still do the techniques to a very high standard of precision. After one session with my teacher, I finished the kata, made a small bow and took two steps before I lost control of my stomach and threw up all over the gym floor. I found that my focus when doing the unarmed kata was far more precise than before I started my sword lessons. I went from thinking that sword training was useless to self-defense training to the opinion that it was a vital part of the path.

There is science to back this idea up. As it turns out, there is a section of the brain called the amygdala at the base of the brain. It is the oldest part of the brain, the 'lizard brain' so to speak. It takes over in times of danger and reacts before the mind has a chance to make a conscious decision. If you look down and find yourself a few feet away before you realize that there was a black widow spider about to crawl on your arm, you have your amygdala to thank. It also takes over when there is a large amount of chemicals like adrenaline in the blood stream. Things learned in this state come out when extreme fear is experienced. Thus fear during training is vital to dealing with fear in reality. Tim Bown, now deceased, was skilled in teaching this type of thing through scenario training. He would simulate things that would engage parts of the brain that took over when fear was felt. He was on the verge of taking the study into new and exciting areas when he passed away suddenly. His death was a tragedy for all of us.

At the end of some kata, in some systems, there is a formalized method of standing down. To outside eyes, they may look silly and mere ritual. Both participants of the form both back up, neither one giving the other an opening to attack. There are actually techniques taught on how to respond if you start to stand down and the other guy jumps in and attacks. The motions between the two are very deliberate and very calculated. As one moves his sword point, the other shifts his weight back, etc.

When you first learn it, of course, you stumble through the motions and the kindly teacher corrects you. Later the teacher changes his attitude and the cost for dropping your defenses goes up. You really don't know if he will hit you if you leave an opening because it sometimes happens. To those with no eyes to see it, both the novice's stumbling and the senior's moves seems the same. But to my eyes, two skilled practitioners doing the stand down portion are laser-like in their intensity and precision. There are no openings and no wavering in concentration under the most stressful of situations.

In this, kata and traditional training probably helped save me in a situation where many would say there was no violence.

Peyton Quinn, a self-defense teacher, was one of my favorite authors when I was in Japan. Indeed, it is through him and his posts on the AOL message boards that I first learned of Marc MacYoung. In his lessons I gained the insight that a fight does not start with the first punch, but is largely determined by the time it is launched. The dynamics of a fight are really not like what you see in a ring. Usually there is what could be called "the interview," "the woof" or what Rory Miller first pointed out as being, "the monkey dance."

In some sorts of social violence (as opposed to criminal violence which might start with a surprise attack from the back) there is usually screaming and posturing before someone tosses the first blow. If the fight is over losing face, then this is probably something like the monkey dance with both idiots trying to show they are the alpha male instead of walking away.

The 'woof' is a reference to how dogs have to build up their spirit by a show of bluster and put the other canine on edge. Humans too, can rarely go from conversation mode to throwing blows without a bit of wind-up. And the interview is a case where a person is seeking victims and can tell in the first few seconds based on the response to his comments and posturing, whether he has a victim he can safely pound on or has to make a face-saving retreat. These terms are all related and it is hard to pigeonhole them into certain definitions. A person doing the monkey dance might be doing an unconscious interview, or it might be a sociopath who is not a slave to his inner monkey, looking for a victim. Sometimes a monkey dance/woof/interview ends with violence, sometimes not. Danger arises when people think in only two mindsets, conversation or combat. When one side is trying to deny that they are in a dangerous situation and are trying to talk their way out of it, the other side has made a choice on some level to do violence and is merely looking for an opening.

In situations like this, you have to be able to realize you are actually in a fight but that blows have not been thrown. Legally speaking, it is difficult to justify a blow just because the person is screaming at you, but it is a good possibility. That is what some folks seem to be counting on. Either you throw a blow and then they will have an excuse to both hurt you and then get you in legal trouble, or you get set up for their surprise attack and get beaten before they flee ahead of the police.

Overt, hostile, racism in Japan is rare. But stick around long enough and you will probably hit the jackpot. Some jerks seem to like moving up next to you in places like trains to try to get in your face. A more loathsome sort seems to take pleasure in making comments in Japanese to the Japanese girl you are with about her morals at dating a barbarian. When you take umbrage at them, their surprise at your language ability turns to anger and they start what has been called the monkey dance.

This, of course, happened to me.

Based on what I had been learning from what Quinn put out, I knew what they were trying to build themselves up to. I could see them trying to get a fearful reaction and an opening. I saw them trying to maneuver to a spot where they could launch their sucker punch at me. I saw all this, and was able to function.

In my mind, it was like when I was facing my teacher at the end of the kata. I had no weapon, he had no sword. But after long hours of facing a person I knew could do serious injury to me I was in almost familiar territory. I gave them no openings, I betrayed no debilitating fear. It went on for what seemed like several minutes as they tried to figure out how best to attack me without me being able to defend effectively. They screamed and threatened and finally I decided that I had to attack first if I was to get out of the situation more or less intact. Strangely, it was almost a relief. I had done what I could to not be pulled into violence but my actions had been decided by their threats and the burden for what happened lifted from my shoulders. At that moment, it was like the guy right in front of me hit a wall. His face was not visible to the two guys backing him up, but I will never forget it. There was a complete change as his rage turned to surprise. It was like he knew that he was not facing someone that would be a good victim but instead would be someone that might be injured, but would be able to give damage back. He doubled the distance between us almost like a scalded cat. In a second, he regained his composure and started screaming and threatening me, but he was moving back. As the train pulled into the next station he hurled insults at me and laughed with his friends as they got off. Maybe it was the stop they were planning on getting off anyway, but part of me thinks otherwise.

I had faced a potential attack by three guys and walked away intact. Is that fighting? I would say no. Is it self-defense? I would boldly say it is far more so than learning to beat someone in a ring. I believe I owed it to the training with ancient wooden weapons in a method passed down for three hundred years. And as soon as they stepped out the door, I started trembling like a leaf in a strong wind. Thankfully, I didn't ralph all over the train.

There is no way I can believe that the lessons of the past have no relevance to what we do today.

Where the Journey Ends

by Rory Miller

People like certainty. It is comfortable to be sure about things. Unknowns are scary, knowns are not. People spend most of their lives working to be safe and secure. The need to be safe draws many people to the martial arts. If they have the skills, they reason, they will be safe. If they can be safe, they will be brave.

I think that's why I got into martial arts. I think the need to be capable drove a lot of my early development—so I studied martial arts and first aid and growing my own food and hunting. I worked as a ranch hand and a bouncer and joined the National Guard. It was all to learn more, to have more skills, to be able to control my world.

On September 4ᵗʰ, 1981 Lt. Ricky A. Miller, my brother, flew his Air Force trainer through a high-tension power line. It destroyed his head.

I was seventeen. I don't know how much Rick's death influenced me. He was strong, smart, skillful, and popular—all the things that I thought were out of my reach. The fact that someone that extraordinary could be killed so young might have pushed me to try to be even stronger and smarter and more skillful. Maybe. The groundwork was already set, though.

In the seventies, the world was supposed to end. The emissions that today are blamed for global warming were then expected to bring on an ice age. Probability mathematics "proved" that there was no chance that we would make it to the year 2000 without a nuclear war. There was no hope that oil would still be in the ground by 2020 and the eighties were to be the decade of famine: unless population growth could be halted or reversed mass starvation was inevitable. As was economic collapse and environmental disaster... all inevitable. My parents prepared as well as they could and so I was raised chopping wood and raising and butchering livestock and carrying water in buckets from a creek. My parents preached self-sufficiency: "To the extent that a person relies on others for food or water or shelter or health care or even reasoning, to that extent a person is not free."

271

So I was raised around ranchers and loggers, tough men and women who could take care of themselves. People who recovered from broken backs and rattlesnake bites and went to work anyway. People who could shoot and brawl and bullshit.

One of the first of the ranchers I met, I don't remember his name now but it is scratched on the side of a rimrock up Cottonwood Creek, was shot in the back. He was blown apart by a shotgun as he tried to batter down the door of his 'girlfriend's' room.

I went off to college. Raised outside of a town of two hundred and ten people with a graduating class of six, people were something of a mystery to me. For the first year I sat back and studied, my soul quiet as the desert. I had vowed to study martial arts, though I had only the vaguest idea of what it was, influenced by simply seeing the trailer to a Bruce Lee movie and an episode or two of *"Kung Fu"*. In one of the luckiest accidents of my life the first class available was judo and it was taught by a handful of extraordinary teachers. I loved it and I played hard.

As a *gokyu* in my third tournament I placed in the *nikkyu* and below division. My second opponent had just dislocated my friend's arm. He used the same technique on me and as I lay there in a *jujigatame* I heard my team and my coach yelling at me to tap. I didn't, and pushed my arm off of the leverage point. A few seconds later he tapped out to a choke and I had won. Acting against my teacher's and teammate's advice, I had won and it was lonely.

I returned to college my sophomore year. Danny, one of the most popular of my classmates, had died at his summer job. I never got the details, except that he was a choker setter at a logging operation, one of the most dangerous jobs there is.

Judo. Karate and tae kwon do in my spare time. Fencing and SCA weapons. My family was dirt poor and I didn't have the resources to do anything as much or as intensely as I would have liked. So no big tournaments, but I was getting a local reputation – and for more than martial arts. I'd asked a girl to dance at some dorm function. She agreed and halfway through the song stopped suddenly. "You're Rory Miller, aren't you?"

"Yes."

I realized that in the last six months I had not met a single person who had not already heard of me. I decided it was time to go someplace where nobody knew me and see who I was for myself. I caught a ride to Reno.

Reno. My first real brawls. Big insights. Heartbreak and romance and adventure. I don't talk much about Reno.

I'd expected to be gone for a summer and spent two years.

My father was possibly the toughest man I had ever met. Not wanting to disturb company he had sat eating and talking until mom noticed the blood dripping from his crushed steel-toed boot. A three thousand pound block of concrete had been dropped on his foot at work. The foot was crushed inside the boot. Mom cut away what she could with a kitchen knife and he drove himself to the hospital. I told you he was tough.

He was a Korean-era vet, a legendary barroom brawler, and a devastatingly intelligent man with an unbelievable appetite for hard work. One day he went to start the pump. Mom heard it start but she didn't hear him come down the hill. She went looking for him when the pump started to make the sound it does when the well is dry. She found him lying cold and dead.

Miroslav —Mike- was a phenomenon. A tremendous athlete even when I met him in his forties. His official army assignment had been to the national ski and track-and-field teams. He had three engineering degrees. He had the nerve to smuggle his family out of Czechoslovakia and the connections to get a twenty four hour warning of the Soviet invasion so that he could. When I worked up the nerve to ask him for his daughter's hand in marriage he was so far gone with brain cancer that he was bloated and could barely understand. It was a tremendous act of will for him to say, clearly, "I think that would be good." He died three days after our wedding. Our wedding cake was his last meal.

I returned from Reno and finished college and got hired as a Deputy Sheriff working the jail. The instructors at the academy tried to prepare a gaggle of what seemed like kids for the world they were about to enter.

While I was at the academy one of the big stories was of a local officer from my home county. Responding to a domestic disturbance call he chose to rely on pepper spray and his knowledge of the offender. He was beaten to death with a piece of firewood.

The job went well. It was a good match for my skills and inclinations. There were a lot of firsts – first jail fight and first really big fight. Cell extractions and drunks and PCP and weapons. Saving lives a couple of times. I became a tactical team member and then the leader. I taught and trained and designed courses. I was called when very dangerous people needed to be talked down or sometimes taken down. Once or twice

I calmed down facilities from the edge of riots. Talked and listened and learned. Once again, I started hearing stories about myself.

Charlie was a veteran of World War II. He had fought up through North Africa and Italy, all the way to the bitter end. He had some medals in a drawer, a Nazi dagger he had taken. He was officially a hero, though he might well have laughed at the label. He didn't share stories of those times. When he faced the fact that he could no longer care for himself and his only choice was a nursing home, he put a bullet in his head.

In the midst of everything else, for two years I volunteered with Search and Rescue. It was good for me. At the time I didn't know any eighteen-year-olds except for criminals. To spend time with honest-to-god heroes aged fourteen to twenty healed much of the image I was forming of people. Good skills, good teaching. I could share things that meant much to me and learn even more.

I was happy when the Search and Rescue pager went off. It was a body recovery. The guy had taken about a hundred-foot fall off the cliff and face planted. One hand was twisted under him with split skin down a finger, gray flesh. For a minute I could see into the side of his face, a jagged-edged hole, black and empty. He was lying face down with a sharp rock sticking into his face. His pants were partly down and I thought, "Plumber's crack. That's death with dignity."

Very lucky first body: fresh; not fat; rigor, but not splayed out. When he rolled, the hand that was tucked under him would have hit me but I blocked- jujutsu reflexes- and it left a brown and red slime on the outside edge of my sleeve.

We zipped him into the body bag and rappelled him down the slope. When we got to the bottom, the cut in the trees made by the road showed a cliff and swirling clouds in a gray sky at the very end of twilight. It was a beautiful day to be alive and I was alive. He wasn't.

I will never know if he jumped or fell or was pushed, if his death were an accident doing something he enjoyed or an act of desperation.

The reason I am in this book is because a guy named Kris Wilder met me at a Jon Bluming seminar. Kris noticed that I lived on the edge between martial arts and real violence. He asked me to teach at a seminar, Martial University, held in Seattle. He also is the one who sent my book, "Meditations on Violence" to a publisher. If you have heard of me, beyond a small circle of criminals, cops and martial artists, Kris is to blame.

In the next couple of years I had the opportunity to teach seminars in Seattle and Alabama and Montreal and Cape Cod. Some people opened their eyes a little. I'm sure some were offended. Most said good things, but I expect that. No one says bad things about the only instructor with a gun and a badge.

Roy B. sent a note into cyberspace to a small group to let us know that a friend of his had been killed. The friend was a good officer, a good tactician, one of the guys who stays in shape and doesn't take chances. The kind of guy you want to be there when you call for back-up. He had come around a corner and been shot in the head. He never had a chance to use his skills or avail himself of his experience. He turned a corner and he was dead. That is all.

I gave up the badge. Not the gun. I went to Iraq, and that's where I wrote this. The contract says I can't talk or write about Iraq. Let's just say that it seemed like the next step on this particular journey.

They say that it is the journey, not the destination. It's true, but the journey is important precisely because there is no variation in the destination. We know where it ends. *We all know where it ends.* I don't know if I will over-estimate myself and rely on pepper spray and wits when I need a gun. I don't know if my own cells will turn on me and eat me up from the inside. I don't know if I will meet my match and be killed by superior skill or freakish luck. Or if I will turn a corner and simply be dead without even knowing how it happened or why.

But I know absolutely, certainly, that I will die. So will everyone I love and everything I care about. Quick or slow, from my favorite pet to the most beautiful star – everything. Dust.

People spend time and effort for a safety and security that does not exist. Smarter, stronger, prettier, more popular, more skilled, more aware, more tactically sound… nothing has saved them. People who were better than me in every category are dead.

He had been a pilot in the Pacific Theater of World War II. I had read his name in books when I was a kid and couldn't quite accept that I was sitting with him on a long night shift in a jail. There wasn't much detail when he told the story: his squadron had been hit by a flight of Japanese fighters. One of his men was hit, going down in flames, screaming for his mother.

"I had to do it. The screaming was going to wreck the nerve of everyone on the mission. I got on the radio and said, 'Die like a man you son of a bitch.' He shut up." A decision made fifty years before haunts

this man, even though it probably saved lives. More than that, the other pilots were heroes, too. Sometimes even a hero dies screaming for his mommy.

There can be no safety in a world with a 100% mortality rate.

I said that unknowns were scary, but this one 'known' is the scariest of all. So much effort goes in to preventing or postponing death. I see it all around me and it makes me tired. Time spent not dying is not the same as time spent living.

There are a handful of hard truths, very real, very powerful things and it seems that most people's lives and civilization itself is often a sad and desperate attempt to make these truths less true.

The most famous? Possibly, from the Buddha: "Life is suffering." Or, my favorite paraphrase from *The Princess Bride*: "Life is pain, Highness. Anyone who says differently is selling something."

Maybe that's a big truth and maybe it's dark and maybe it's scary, but it is profoundly liberating. Getting handed a shit sandwich with life isn't that big a deal…but the idea that it's not normal, that the sandwich of life is supposed to be roast beef with bacon and cream cheese lightly toasted with brown mustard…that's the part that hurts. The suffering, if it is that, lingers in the gap between the expectation and the reality.

Most humans through most of history have had a pretty rough deal. You don't see it in America much (no matter how hard you try to convince yourself that the country is awash in poverty and homelessness and violence—the math doesn't work when the greatest health risk to the poorest Americans include complications from obesity). We are programmed, it seems, to think that our lives are hard, and they are, but only compared to an ideal that never really existed. Things, stuff, money, don't mitigate suffering, they just focus your imagination on different things to suffer about.

I'm trying not to talk out of both sides of my mouth here. There *is* real pain. Tasers hurt. Old bone breaks and medically-installed hardware hurts in your joints when things are cold and humid. You will lose friends that you love. But most of the suffering comes from elsewhere, from an expectation that joints aren't supposed to hurt or that friends are eternal. That is the difference between grieving and wallowing. Both are about you, but one is honestly about what you lost and the other is about what you thought you had a right to.

Accepting this truth and a few others allows you to live…more? Harder? Better? It allows you to love harder because you are busy loving instead of whining that things aren't perfect and love is 'supposed to be perfect'. It allows you to play and learn, to get better every day instead of wasting time and emotion trying to figure out how good you are or if you are 'good enough.'

What do those phrases even mean? What is a 'perfect love'? What would it look, feel, taste, like? It can't be both perfectly smooth and exciting. And 'good enough'? For what? To whom? If you ever perfectly achieved it, then what?

Most of the big truths are like that: the totality of the statement is bleak: "Life is suffering." "You will die." But each of them is a key. When you quit wasting energy attempting to evade the inevitable, when you quit building a structure of lies to protect yourself from the truth, you can live at the level of truth.

Caveat emptor, though. It's really not for everybody.

So, the ball is in your court: will you spend your time and pursue your training in a doomed attempt to not die? Or will you train to live harder and truer?

Author Biographies

"Chop Ki"

Chop Ki is the pen name of a martial artist who spent 14 years in a notorious national martial arts cult. It has been nearly 20 years since leaving the cult.

"D. Osborne"

D. Osborne is a happily married IT professional living in the United Kingdom. She has studied martial arts to a far lesser degree of mastery than most of the other contributors to this volume, but has found that Verbal Judo, plus the science of "STFU," as recommended by Marc MacYoung, are the most valuable skills of all. She suffers from bipolar disorder, and has had a number of hospitalizations for acute episodes of illness, but otherwise has a completely normal life. Apart from martial arts, her hobbies are knitting, kettlebells and posting lolcats on Facebook.

"D. Weeks"

D. Weeks puts food on the table by keeping the databases running. His martial background consists of a few years studying Chinese Kenpo, dabbling at boxing until he got tired of soup, enough time at the shooting range not to be a danger to anyone, and of course, reading lots of books on the subject.

"Denton Salle"

Denton Salle been involved in martial arts since 1965 and has studied shing yi chuan since 1981 as well as spending 11 years learning a little Savate. In real life, he's imaginary.

"Douglas Hill"

Prison town, [Chino, California] High School Drop out final at the age of 16 with a GPA 0.7, [F-], hooked on fun.... left home home at 16 with a wired jaw drinking scrambled eggs through a straw, [gang fight]. Always wanted to travel, always in trouble.... Never to return to the Continental United States.

"Jael"

Jael is the pen name of a thriving middle-aged woman who taught herself to leave. She is blessed with the support of a select group of others who are an objective, wise, sounding board. Aikido and tai chi are tools that helped reclaim her life while learning to live in a new manner over a couple of decades.

Happily living with her service dog in a rural area she shares her blessings by doing therapy visits with her mini Australian Shepherd. To simplify life and reduce stressors those in need now are referred to local agencies for assistance rather than do individual coaching for those considering leaving destructive relationships. The statements and questions came out of my own life and experience of working with individuals for over 20 years assisting them with tools for making a decision safely for themselves.

"MG, FAM"

As a twenty-year law enforcement veteran, he has no marketable job skills in modern society, but has to be competent in everything from medical training to therapy. He has spent time working gangs, patrolling the border, and flying the unfriendly skies as an Air Marshal. He has just enough martial arts training to get himself seriously hurt if he tried to use it in a critical incident.

Jesse J. Alcorta

Jesse Alcorta started his martial arts in 1985 practicing Tae Kwon Do, an art he still teaches today as part of the Dango-Jiro curriculum. Jesse holds a 3rd Dan in TKD and a Shodan in Matayoshi Kobudo from Sensei Kimo Wall. He currently trains in Pukalan Pentjak Silat Sera with Guru Stevan Plinck. One day he would like to be a guru but doesn't see the light at the end of the tunnel yet. In addition he has trained in Yang Style Tai Chi, Combat Hapkido, European Fencing and a few things he would rather not mention.

Dr. Drew Anderson

Drew Anderson, Ph.D., grew up along the Gulf Coast, where he worked as a lifeguard, pizza maker, juggler and street performer, and bouncer, among other things. These days he is a psychology professor and clinical psychologist in upstate New York. For fun he volunteers as a firefighter/EMT and runs the occasional ultramarathon.

Bert Bruijnen

Bert Bruijnen teaches Historical European Martial Arts in the Netherlands. He has also trained in different Asian Martial Arts: Jiu Jitsu, Wing Chun Kung Fu, Pencak Silat. Most of his writing includes translations of 14th century Medieval Manuscripts.

He can be reached at: http://www.kdfnederland.nl

Alain Burrese

Alain B. Burrese, J.D. is an author, speaker and mediator. His books include *Hard-Won Wisdom from the School of Hard Knocks*, *Lost Conscience*, and the *Tough Guy Wisdom* series. His instructional DVDs include *Hapkido Cane*, *Streetfighting Essentials*, and the *Lock On: Joint Locking Essentials* series. He can be reached at http://www.burrese.com

D.J. Dasko

He's just a middle-aged divorced father of three who, when the kids are with their mother, likes to drink whiskey, dance, and chase pretty girls.

Wim Demeere

Wim Demeere has practiced a variety of martial arts for over 25 years, studying mainly Chinese systems and several full-contact fighting styles. He won four national titles and a bronze medal at the 1995 World Wushu Championships. He works full-time as a teacher of martial arts, self-defense and conditioning. He authored numerous books and instructional videos on these topics. You can reach him at his blog www.wimsblog.com and his website http://www.wimdemeere.com.

Barry Eisler

Barry Eisler spent three years in a covert position with the CIA's Directorate of Operations, then worked as a technology lawyer and start-up executive in Silicon Valley and Japan, earning his black belt at the Kodokan International Judo Center along the way. Eisler's bestselling thrillers have won the Barry Award and the Gumshoe Award for Best Thriller of the Year, have been included in numerous "Best Of" lists, and have been translated into nearly twenty languages. Eisler lives in the San Francisco Bay Area and, when he's not writing novels, blogs about torture, civil liberties, and the rule of law. http://www.barryeisler.com

Eric Gaden

Eric Gaden is a registered nurse who sold his house, packed everything up in an RV and travels the country working in various emergency rooms. If you want to know more please visit http://www.adventurenickel.com

Dan Gilardi

Dan Gilardi writes about fitness development, martial arts, and combat sports at his website, http://marblefitness.com.

E. Rushton Gilbert

E. Rushton Gilbert (Eddie) is a former United States Marine and is currently serving as a Police Officer in a major metropolitan police department in Northeast Ohio. His combined military and law enforcement service now spans over four decades.

He was diagnosed with Asperger's Syndrome (part of the Autism spectrum) when he was fifty-five years old. This diagnosis freed him from the self-doubts that he had lived with from his early childhood. He has since gone on to become an author and a freelance writer.

Eddie resides in Cleveland, Ohio with his lovely wife, Ada, and his four foster children. He can be reached at his website: http://www.E-Rushton-Gilbert.com

Michael Johnson

Michael Johnson has trained in some form of martial arts since 1970, starting in Tae Kwon Do. Since 1985 his two major arts have been Jeet Kune Do and the Filipino Martial Arts. Michael held the ranks of Certified Teacher and Fight Director with the Society of American Fight Directors for fifteen and thirteen years, respectively – creating their knife discipline during those years – before retiring as Fight Director Emeritus in 2010. He also holds the ranks of Master Teacher and Senior Fight Director with Dueling Arts, International. Michael incorporates his real-world experiences into his stage combat and martial arts work.

Lawrence Kane

Lawrence Kane is the author of *Surviving Armed Assaults*, *Martial Arts Instruction*, and *Blinded by the Night*, and co-author (with Kris Wilder) of *The Way of Kata*, *The Way to Black Belt*, *How to Win a Fight*, and *The Little Black Book of Violence*, and co-author (with Rory Miller) of *Scaling Force*. A technical consultant to University of New Mexico's

Institute of Traditional Martial Arts, he also has written numerous articles on martial arts, self-defense, and related topics. Since 1970, he has studied and taught traditional Asian martial arts, medieval European combat, and modern close-quarter weapon techniques. He co-hosts a weekly podcast with Kris Wilder at http://www.martial-secrets.com.

Kasey Keckeisen

Kasey Keckeisen is a Police Officer, SWAT team leader, and SWAT training coordinator. He teaches Control Tactics and Combative Measures to Universities, Law Enforcement Agencies, and Special Operations Teams. He is the United States Midwest Regional Director for an International Taiho Jutsu organization, and the Minnesota State Director for One-On-One Control Tactics. Keckeisen has extensive experience in Jujutsu, Aikido, Judo and Taiho Jutsu. Keckeisen runs Taiho Jutsu Minnesota, an organization that provides free training to Law Enforcement and Military, and operates a training facility in Elk River Minnesota. Keckeisen also writes regularly on http://practicalbudo.blogspot.com/

Marc MacYoung

Marc "Animal" MacYoung has written a book or two, he's even done a video. He might have hurt someone's feelings once. Basically, if you know who he is, 'nuff said. If you don't, it would take too long to explain.

Rory Miller

Rory Miller is the author of *"Meditations on Violence,"* *"Facing Violence"* and *"Force Decisions."* Once upon a time he spent almost two decades working Corrections as a deputy, sergeant, Tactical Team member and leader, instructor and investigator. Then he got bored and went to Iraq. Now he teaches and writes from his home base in the Pacific Northwest. http://chirontraining.com

Clint Overland

Clint Overland is a 25-year veteran of bouncing in some of the roughest bars and honky-tonks in the southwest.

Don Roley

Don Roley lived in Japan for about 15 years and studied many classical Japanese arts while there. He is a mammal.

Fred Ross

Fred Ross received a classical education from his parents while growing up in the wilds of Virginia, then worked as a physicist, a mathematician, a microbiologist, and a programmer in the US and Europe before writing his first novel while living on the shores of Lake Geneva in Switzerland. He now lives in Seattle, where he divides his time among writing, programming, cooking, howling at the moon, playing the violin, and walking in circles while claiming that it's a martial art called pa kua zhang.

Terry Trahan

Terry Trahan is happily married and lives in Colorado. He teaches Aneh Palu Kali-Silat and Applied Self Defense and is co-director of the Kapatiran Suntukan Martial Arts group. After living in several different levels of street culture, being a nomad and bouncer and working security for many subculture-oriented events he has now settled down and lives with the most wonderful woman in the world and a rescued cat. He works for a major cutlery company.

Made in the USA
Lexington, KY
12 January 2015